Marked by the Wild

Seven. A Canada to Call Forth Love: Wilderness as Cultural Influence

INTRODUCTION   *215*
From *Sacred Legends of the Sandy Lake Cree* / James R. Stevens   *217*
From *Canada North* / Farley Mowat   *219*
Canada / Walter Bauer   *221*
From *The Canadian Identity* / W. L. Morton   *222*
I Am the Dwindled Son / Alfred Des Rochers   *224*
From *The Quest for the Peaceable Kingdom* / William Kilbourn   *226*
Hail to Thee / Gilles Hénault   *228*
Island Summers / A. R. M. Lower   *230*
From *Western Windows* / Bruce Hutchison   *236*
Laurentian Shield / F. R. Scott   *238*
From *The Search for Identity* / Blair Fraser   *239*

Eight. Farewell to Saganaga: Wilderness Lost

INTRODUCTION   *241*
The Predator / Irving Layton   *244*
Railroads / Dan Kennedy   *246*
What Is Grizzly Country? / Andy Russell   *248*
Wild Horses / Patrick Lane   *252*
The Bull Moose / Alden Nowlan   *253*
From *The Great Bear Lake Meditations* / J. Michael Yates   *255*
Rare and Vanishing Wildlife / Yorke Edwards   *256*
The Boom / William O. Pruitt, Jr.   *258*
Very Short Poem / Raymond Souster   *261*
Farewell to Saganaga / Sigurd F. Olson   *262*
Héritage de la Tristesse / Gaston Miron   *267*
Transcontinental / Earle Birney   *269*
Pioneer / Dorothy Livesay   *270*
From *Western Windows* / Bruce Hutchison   *271*
Can We Not At Last Say Yes To This Land? / Hugh MacLennan   *272*
CONTRIBUTORS   *273*
ACKNOWLEDGEMENTS   *285*

INTRODUCTION

We began *Marked by the Wild* with the belief that the Canadian wilderness has been the single most important presence in our literature. Even where wild nature does not directly provide the controlling images of our literary works, allusions to the wilderness continue to subtly colour our writing. We knew of nothing in print which emphasized this characteristic. We believe that the anthology which follows offers a fresh and meaningful approach to the understanding of Canadian literature and of our culture in general.

Our feelings as to the impact of the wilderness on Canadians and their writing have been supported by established critics of our cultural scene. As early as 1866 Henry David Thoreau recalled the forces he believed to have profoundly affected the Canadian imagination. In *A Yankee in Canada* he wrote of an "influence from the wilds and from nature . . . an influence which flowed from the Arctic fastness and Western forests with irresistible tide over all." More recently, W. L. Morton, one of the most astute of the historians of Canada, has written persuasively, and more precisely than Thoreau, of the wilderness influence on our life and history. He argues that an "alternate penetration of the wilderness and return to civilization is the basic rhythm of Canadian life." This rhythm, says Mr. Morton, "forms the basic elements of Canadian character whether French or English: the violence necessary to contend with the wilderness, the restraint necessary to preserve civilization from the wilderness violence, and the puritanism which is the offspring of the wedding of violence to restraint. Even in an old industrial and urban society, the old rhythm continues, for the typical Canadian holiday is a wilderness holiday, whether among the lakes of the Shield or the peaks of the Rockies." This seems to us a persuasive argument.

The powerful hold exercised by the wilderness on the Canadian imagination has been examined not only by the social critic and historian; our literary critics have reached similar conclusions. Northrop Frye has made what is perhaps the most authoritative judgement along these lines. Mr. Frye makes quite clear what most Canadian readers either have not recognized or have been only dimly aware of: the fact that "everything that is central in Canadian writing seems to be marked by the imminence of the natural world." Another observer, George Woodcock, has maintained that "the literature of direct experience of the wilderness has continued in an unbroken tradition since Cartier," and has pointed out that wild nature in Canada "has given a special shape to our literature."

We are well aware, of course, that Canadians have written and will continue to write about urban areas; indeed, some of our most important literary artists habitually look to the city and to city life for their subject matter and themes. One thinks, for example, of Irving Layton's Montreal or Raymond Souster's Toronto. Yet even the most "civilized" of our writers, attuned to the rhythms and character of urban life, are drawn toward and explore in their work the nature and meaning of the wilderness experience. As a case in point, Mr. Woodcock cites Mordecai Richler's *The Apprenticeship of Duddy Kravitz*, in which the hero is able to discover a sense of self only by possessing a remote lake in the Laurentians. Mr. Woodcock also remarks upon the way in which Hugh MacLennan uses the wilderness experience to illuminate a central meaning of *The Watch That Ends the Night*. Again, in recent conversation, one of the most urban of our novelists, Morley Callaghan, has commented on his "deliberate use of the laws of nature" in *They Shall Inherit the Earth*. We should recognize, then, that many Canadian writers are urban-oriented, but we must at the same time agree with Mr. Woodcock that some of our finest writers are "compulsively attracted to the landscapes and privations of the Canadian wilderness." For them, as for us, wild nature is close to the centre of our literature and culture.

At the same time, there is a body of Canadian literature that is not confined exclusively either to the wilderness or the city. What comes to mind now is not the geographical context of the work, but rather the images and figures used to express the themes. A poet, for example, may write about love or loneliness or alienation – in short, about something timeless and universal – without necessarily using a specific sense of place; without using either Lake Superior or St. Catherine Street. It seems, however, that when expressing themes of this kind, the Canadian writer frequently resorts to the imagery of the wild: universal theme is stated by natural metaphor. When D. G. Jones records the journey of the self, for example, he sees it gliding by "woodlands, owl-watched, clearings where deer / drink by the shore"; Miriam Waddington expresses the life of the subconscious with images of "confounding foxes" and "sudden wolves"; and Leonard Cohen begins one of his finest love poems with the line "As the mist leaves no scar / On the dark green hill." There is, then, a considerable body of Canadian writing in which wilderness and the natural world operate in a subtle and indirect way — as image and metaphor rather than content and context. On this point we return to Mr. Woodcock. Many of our writers do not use the primitive landscape directly, he says, "yet somewhere in their visions and their forms the wilderness will always lurk."

This book is therefore intended to be an anthology of writings informed and coloured by the Canadian wilderness. The urban-oriented writer and the writer who uses wild nature only in an indirect way have been largely omitted. Instead, we have included for the most part material that confronts the wilderness directly. This emphasis stems in part from spatial limitations, but more importantly from our conviction that immediate contact with wild nature is closest to the core of Canadian experience. *If there is one distinguishing element that sets Canadian literature apart from most other national literatures, it is the influence of the wild.*

We have interpreted "literature" in a very broad sense. For our purposes the term will include not only imaginative prose and poetry but also essays of ideas, history, autobiography, journalism, and nature writing. Some of the writers are permanent fixtures of the literary establishment; some are either obscure or unpublished. We have included winners of the Governor General's Award, but we have not hesitated to use the unheralded writer as well. Most of the selections have been drawn from the work of Canadian writers who have written about their native wilderness, but we have also included several non-Canadian authors whom we consider to be significant interpreters of our natural world. What follows, then, is Canadian literature, not because all of the writers are Canadians in the strict sense, but because all of the selections are marked by the imminence of this country's wild places.

The anthology is bound together by its subject matter — the Canadian wilderness as it is confronted directly by our writers. At the same time, however, we have excluded a good deal of this type of literature. For example, writers such as Grey Owl, Frederick Philip Grove, Ernest Thompson Seton, John Livingston, and Ralph Gustafson are not here. But this is an anthology, and anthologies are necessarily selective.

In addition, the book is internally unified by its themes. In each section, we have explored, through a variety of literary genres and interpretations, a particular theme or idea. The selections, that is, do not simply duplicate one another; there are similarities but there are also differences between and among the individual works in each section – differences in diction, imagery, tone, structure, and so on.

We hope, finally, that our treatment of this central motif in Canadian literature will serve some useful purpose. Perhaps it will evoke among some readers an increased interest in the literature of Canada. Perhaps it will serve to illuminate those perennially grey areas of national character and identity. This would be good. Perhaps it will foster a greater sensitivity toward the appreciation of the wild places and wild creatures which share this country with us. The realization that they have coloured and distinguished our literature and culture may lead some readers to take an active role in protecting these shrinking elements of our Canadian heritage. That would be good, too.

Bruce Litteljohn
Jon Pearce
Upper Canada College,
Toronto

One

An Elemental Song: The Non-Human World

INTRODUCTION

The Canadian wilderness has many faces, and it may be viewed from many different vantage points. In consequence, descriptions of it differ widely. Viewed broadly and from a distance, it may seem vast, timeless, elemental, and without movement. Our selection from Donald Creighton reflects something of this viewpoint in its description of the Canadian Shield. E. J. Pratt sees the same wild area as a gigantic, sleeping reptile, "so motionless, she seemed stone dead . . . too old for death, too old for life." In the same tradition, Farley Mowat describes the North as "a primordial giant . . . . wrinkled by its own unimaginable antiquity."

In all such descriptions, the scale is immense. Time is measured in geological epochs. Detail is submerged by tectonic forces. Movement is obscured by concentration on the grand design.

Other writers view the wilderness at much closer range, emphasizing the specific and the detailed interplay of plant and animal life. Time, for them, is measured in hours, days, or seasons, rather than epochs. Being so close, they see and describe the movement, complexity, and interrelationships of living things. In their writing, elemental forces may be suggested or may quite explicitly appear; nonetheless, the viewpoint is narrower and more intimate than that of a Pratt or Creighton. Roderick Haig-Brown and Theodore Goodridge Roberts, for example, describe specific birds, while Fred Bodsworth, Harold Horwood and Franklin Russell move closer to a middle ground, dealing in details but also providing a broader context both in space and time. Horwood describes the teeming, microscopic life of the pond without losing sight of the ancient forces which brought it into being. "So," he writes, "the small and the great cycles of life meet and merge and contribute to the grand design, forever changing and growing into something new."

While descriptions differ in scope and style according to the perceiver, we remain aware that the existence of wilderness depends neither on human perception nor human intervention. Self-generating and self-regulating, it has its own dynamics. Egocentric man frequently seems to find this hard to comprehend and accept. Perhaps he is too strongly conditioned by the Christian axiom that nature exists only to serve man. Perhaps he is too accustomed to thinking in terms of natural resources – trees as pulp and paper, seals as fur coats, waterfalls as hydro-electric power – to recognize the integrity and autonomy of wilderness. Nonetheless, the wild, non-human world has a life of its own. It thrives apart from us.

It follows that, in the wilderness, the rules, conventions, and conceits of man give place to the complex and dynamic rhythms of nature. The wild lily blooms, the caribou migrate, the rock endures, the mink kills, and the rivers run on. Energy flows in endless cycles, new growth burgeons on death and decay, beaches form and recede, and the seasons revolve in response to signals and forces which have nothing to do with man.

Canadians, as few others, should recognize these qualities and characteristics, for the wildernesses of Canada are many, varied, and sometimes extensive. True, the great hardwood forests that once blanketed southern Ontario have been obliterated. And the wild grasslands of the prairie with their massive bison populations are gone forever, to be discovered only in the prose of men such as William Butler. But broad areas of the Canadian Shield, the western mountains, the coasts, and the Arctic remain largely unmanipulated and wild. Space, and the freedom that comes with space, can still be enjoyed. We can know the solitude of mountain valleys, the power of rugged stretches of seacoast, the ice-hard beauty of the high Arctic, the fascinating interplay of untamed creatures. We can involve ourselves in the flow and adventure of unharnessed riverways; observe the opulent profusion of wildflowers on an alpine meadow; share the delight of otters at play; know humility as unneeded visitors in wild places; test our souls and sinews away from the coddling insulation of the totally man-centred environment.

Canadians should know the wilderness, both in terms of its values for man and its objective reality. It is the latter which concerns us in this initial exploration of the relationship between wilderness and Canadian literature. In this theme, we deliberately exclude man, except as he is present as perceiver and recorder. We deal here with literature as it reflects the wild world – its life processes, forms, and cycles. Accordingly, Franklin Russell writes of the vaulting advance of a forest fire, and Frank Scott sings an old song of fretting leaves and the deep Laurentian river. The subject is wilderness alone – vast, varied, complex, alive, moving in accord with its own ineluctable rhythms.

From

The Empire of the
St. Lawrence

DONALD CREIGHTON

The river up which Cartier ventured gave entrance to the totally different dominion of the north. It was a landscape marked off from the other geographic provinces of the new continent by the almost monotonously massive character of its design. A huge triangle of rocky upland lay bounded by a river and a string of giant lakes. It was a solemn country, with that ungainly splendour evoked by great, crude, sweeping lines and immense and clumsy masses. The marks of age and of terrific experience lay heavy upon it. It was an elemental portion of the earth, harshly shaped by the brutal catastrophes of geological history. The enormous flat bulk of the Precambrian formation was not only the core of the whole Canadian system, but it was also the ancient nucleus of the entire continent. It lay, old and sombre and ravaged, nearly two million square miles in extent. The ice masses, during the glacial period, had passed over and beyond it, and they had scarred and wrenched and altered the entire landscape in their advance and their retreat. Scouring the surface of the Shield itself, pouring boulder clay into the valleys to the south, the ice sheets had hollowed the beds of new lakes and had diverted the course of ancient rivers. There was left a drainage system, grand in its extent and in the volume of its waters, but youthful, wilful and turbulent. The wrinkled senility of the Precambrian formation was touched by a curious appearance of youth. The countless meaningless lakes and lakelets, the intricately meandering rivers and spillways, the abrupt falls and treacherous rapids, which covered the face of the Shield, seemed to express the renewal of its primitive strength. To the south, below the Shield, the ice masses had throttled the waters into new lakes and had dammed the St. Lawrence into a long southern loop, leaving Niagara, the Long Sault and Lachine as evidence of the novelty of its course. . . .

To the south lay the lowlands of the St. Lawrence. Here the intense winters of the Precambrian formation were softened and the hot, bright summers flamed more slowly out of long springtimes and faded gradually into reluctant autumns. North of the lakes, the lowlands stretched from Quebec city to Georgian Bay – a narrow but slowly broadening band of fertility, crowded a little oppressively by the sombre masses of the Shield. South and west, beyond the river and the lakes, they lapsed easily into the central lowlands of the continent and the basin of the Mississippi. In the centre of this rich region lay that immense organization of waters which issued from the continent by the river of Canada; and this drainage system, driving seaward in a great, proud arc from Lake Superior to the city of Quebec, was the fact of all facts in the history of the northern half of the continent. It commanded an imperial domain. Westward, its acquisitive fingers groped into the territory of the plains. Aggressively it entrenched upon the dominion of the Mississippi. It grasped the Shield, reached southward into the valley of the Hudson and at last rolled massively seaward between sombre approaches which curved away southward into the Maritimes and rose northeastward past Quebec and Labrador to Newfoundland.

Surfaces

F. R. SCOTT

This rock-bound river, ever flowing
Obedient to the ineluctable laws,
Brings a reminder from the barren north
Of the eternal lifeless processes.
There is an argument that will prevail
In this calm stretch of current, slowly drawn
Toward its final equilibrium.

Come, flaunt the brief prerogative of life,
Dip your small civilized foot in this cold water
And ripple, for a moment, the smooth surface of time.

The Precambrian Shield

E. J. PRATT

On the North Shore a reptile lay asleep –
A hybrid that the myths might have conceived,
But not delivered, as progenitor
Of crawling, gliding things upon the earth.
She lay snug in the folds of a huge boa
Whose tail had covered Labrador and swished
Atlantic tides, whose body coiled itself
Around the Hudson Bay, then curled up north
Through Manitoba and Saskatchewan
To Great Slave Lake. In continental reach
The neck went past the Great Bear Lake until
Its head was hidden in the Arctic Seas.
This folded reptile was asleep or dead:
So motionless, she seemed stone dead – just seemed:
She was too old for death, too old for life,
For as if jealous of all living forms
She had lain there before bivalves began
To catacomb their shells on western mountains.
Somewhere within this life-death zone she sprawled,
Torpid upon a rock-and-mineral mattress.
Ice-ages had passed by and over her,
But these, for all their motion, had but sheared
Her spotty carboniferous hair or made
Her ridges stand out like the spikes of molochs.
Her back grown stronger every million years,
She had shed water by the longer rivers
To Hudson Bay and by the shorter streams
To the great basins to the south, had filled
Them up, would keep them filled until the end
Of Time.

The Face of the North

FARLEY MOWAT

Stretching across the upper reaches of this continent lies a primordial giant; one side rough-pelted by the dark taiga forests, the other naked under the white polar skies. This Titan-land is wrinkled by its own unimaginable antiquity, furrowed by ten thousand rivers, glittering with the Cyclopean eyes of its innumerable lakes. Its bones are the bones of an elder world – cold bones into which an eternal frost strikes deep. Its thin skin of tundra, lichened forest floor and palely gleaming water feels fleeting warmth from the summer sun. In many places, the skin is ruptured by mighty wounds which are the legacy of a glacial incubus a mile thick that implacably and irresistibly gouged into the fleshless ribs. The wounds have never healed. Remnants of the ancient ice-sheet still smother the heads and shoulders of great mountain ranges that rear out of the arctic seas to east and west. This is a world uncircumscribed, for it has no limits that the eye can reach. Seeming to stretch beyond all boundaries, this brooding Titan has many faces: some harshly brutal, some fantastically grotesque, some that are infinitely lovely.

From

The Great Lone Land

WILLIAM FRANCIS BUTLER

The old, old maps which the navigators of the sixteenth century framed from the discoveries of Cabot and Cartier, of Varrazanno and Hudson, played strange pranks with the geography of the New World. The coast-line, with the estuaries of large rivers, was tolerably accurate: but the centre of America was represented as a vast inland sea whose shores stretched far into the polar north: a sea through which lay the much-coveted passage to the long-sought treasures of the old realms of Cathay.

Well, the geographers of that period erred only in the description of ocean which they placed in the central continent, for an ocean there is, and an ocean through which men seek the treasures of Cathay, even in our own times. But the ocean is one of grass, and the shores are the crests of the mountain ranges, and dark pine forests of sub-Arctic regions. The great ocean itself does not present more infinite variety than does this prairie-ocean of which we speak. In winter, a dazzling surface of purest snow: in early summer, a vast expanse of grass and pale pink roses; in autumn, too often a wild sea of raging fire. No ocean in the world can vie with its gorgeous sunsets; no solitude can equal the loneliness of a night-shadowed prairie: one feels the stillness, and hears the silence, the wail of the prowling wolf makes the voice of solitude audible, the stars look down through infinite silence upon a silence almost as intense. This ocean has no past – time has been nought to it; and men have come and gone, leaving behind them no track, no vestige, of their presence. Some French writer, speaking of these prairies, has said that the sense of this utter negation of life, this complete absence of history, has struck him with a loneliness oppressive and sometimes terrible in its intensity. Perhaps so; but, for my part, the prairies had nothing terrible in their aspect, nothing oppressive in their loneliness. One sees here the world as it had taken shape and form from the hands of the Creator. Nor did the scene look less beautiful because nature alone tilled the earth, and the unaided sun brought forth the flowers.

From

The Sparrow's Fall

FRED BODSWORTH

It is all one land, but not a land of uniform oneness. The taiga is a mosaic of many forest patterns – patterns molded by fire and glacier and by the sedimentation of prehistoric seas.

That part of it that runs northward from Lake Superior to Hudson Bay has two distinct and very different regions created by its hidden foundations – the bedrock underneath. For three hundred miles north from Lake Superior the foundation is Pre-Cambrian rock – crystalline granites two billion years old, the roots of an ancient mountain range, with a humped and rugged topography that ensures good water drainage from its overburden of soil. The remaining two hundred miles to Hudson Bay is underlain by a bed of limestone deposited by Paleozoic seas of four hundred million years ago – a low, flat country that impounds its water and releases it grudgingly into a sluggish flowage toward the Bay.

On maps that record such things, the Pre-Cambrian region is known as the Canadian Shield, and the sodden limestone-based plain beyond as the Hudson Bay Lowland. Ten thousand years ago, a brief interval in the geologist's dimensions of time, all of this rock lay depressed like a great saucer under the gigantic burden of a continent-wide glacier one to two miles thick that had crept southward across it. Under a weight of such magnitude even the earth's rock crust had to yield, and here it was warped downward eighteen hundred feet below its preglacial level.

Climate changed. The ice burden melted back northward. But for a couple of thousand years, a Hudson Bay greatly enlarged by glacial meltwaters, and by the depression of the land around it, extended some two hundred miles inland from its present shoreline. During that period of submergence, the silts of that older, larger Hudson Bay settled in a thick and compact layer onto the limestone base of the Hudson Bay Lowland. Thus, when the water receded and the coast crept northward, it left behind a capping of clay on the underlying rock which still cups the land's surface waters, letting little of it seep away – one more impediment to the languid drainage of a land too flat to keep its water on the move. . . .

In the Shield country . . . the waters of the land are always moving, for there is a good network of lakes and rivers to carry it away. Here the trees grow strongly, flowing in a green sea up and down the hills and valley slopes, because the surface water here enriches the soil without staying to drown it. The foresters call it closed-canopy forest, because the trees grow close together and their branches interlock and screen the sun from the forest floor. It is mostly spruce forest, and here and there are the white, springy mats of ground lichen on which the caribou feed, so it is good caribou range, though not the best, because the ground-matting lichens grow richest where sunlight reaches them.

Where the Shield slopes down to the Hudson Bay Lowland, however, the forest alters dramatically; in fact, over large regions it virtually disappears, because this is a drowned and sodden land too wet in most places for trees. Here, across an area eight hundred miles east to west and two hundred miles north to south, the water trapped by the land's flat clay bottom lies in a great shallow, stagnant sea clogged with sphagnum moss – that lush and irrepressible plant colonizer that thrives in the cold, acid wetlands of the sub arctic wherever nothing else can grow. Well adapted for living in a watery world, it can even grow as a floating mat on the water's surface, if there is no bottom ooze within reach of its seeking rootlets. It is the sub arctic's slow but indomitable converter of water into land, for beneath the green living surface layer, the dead growth of earlier sphagnum generations sinks and builds up and compacts itself into a constantly thickening layer of peat which fills the water basins beneath it. When the peat and sphagnum mat has become too solid for further expansion downward or laterally, it humps upward to form hummocks, aided by the heaving action of winter frosts. Thus, some thousands of years after the sphagnum filling began, mounds begin to appear above water level, to dry in the summer sun and form islands on which other plants can oust the sphagnum and pioneer a new plant community.

There has been another process here creating islands of dry land on which plants and trees can grow. As the bedrock has slowly lifted in its recoil from the weight of ice it once carried, shifting the Hudson Bay shore northward, the receding waters have left behind a striking record of the land's marine ancestry – the gravel ridges of ancient beaches abandoned by the retreating sea thousands of years ago. Each one a hundred feet or so wide, often many miles long, they parallel the shore of modern Hudson Bay like series of curving railroad embankments, linear oases of dry land in a vast and boggy sea. The oldest of them are more than a hundred miles inland today, conspicuous relics of the seacoast that once was there.

Even in the driest regions of the Hudson Bay Lowland, more than half its area is still a network of open ponds or lakes, or vast stretches of soggy, treeless sphagnum bog. But wherever the land lifts a foot or two to give drainage, the hardy spruce and that other needle-bearing tree of these northern boglands, the tamarack, will grow. They grow invariably along rivers where ice shove and flooding have pushed up levees and the streams have cut down below the surrounding water table and thus drain water from the bordering banks. They grow on the ridges of the ancient, abandoned beaches. And they grow on the frost-heaved islands of peat – sometimes just a single tree on an island a few feet across, elsewhere a forest miles in extent where major heaving and drainage have occurred.

But the bog waters underneath are never far from the spreading spruce and tamarack roots. It is cold water, for peat is a good insulator, and ice often lingers until mid-summer a foot or two below the surface, sometimes reducing the growing time to a period as brief as two months. And it is water sharp with the accumulated acids of plant decay. Because of the water's coldness and acidity, the trees of this land have to assimilate it slowly and sparingly into their fabric of growth. And during the long winters the struggle for survival takes another form, for then the dry and wind-driven snow is a harsh abrasive to buds and twigs.

So the trees that do manage to grow here are usually stunted and contorted. They may attain near-normal growth in sheltered, well-soiled spots, but mostly they are dwarfed by harsh growing conditions, and deformed by wind and the cutting snow that the wind carries for much of each year. A spruce or tamarack here may be only a few feet high after fifty years of struggling growth. And across vast expanses, trees two hundred years old and gnarled with age are no more than ten feet high.

Since each tree represents a hard-won victory over an uncompromising climate and soil, they stand apart and alone, so that it isn't dense forest even where the trees do grow. This is a boon for the ground lichens, which grow best in sun-dried clearings among spruce and tamarack trees, though not directly beneath them. No lichens grow on the treeless bogs that cover most of this land, but on the drained sites where the stunted trees stand, the lichen is thick and rich among them. So as caribou range, it is spotty, but where it occurs, it is good range – much better than in the shaded, closed-canopy forest of the Pre-Cambrian country farther south.

There is footing on the spruce islands, and a man can walk upon them dry-shod. But he cannot walk far, for they are only a sparse and twisting lacework in a mire of sphagnum bog and ponds. This land, therefore, is impassable in summer except by canoe on its rivers. But in winter, when the bogs are frozen, the land is suddenly flung open and both man and caribou travel it with ease.

From

Return to the River

RODERICK L. HAIG-BROWN

Feeding or resting, the migrant schools held well together, usually within a few feet of the surface of the water. In the Canyon Pool, Spring had always sunk down among the rocks on the bottom to rest. Now, whenever her belly was full and the strong urge to feed had briefly left her, she rested with the school in mid-water, cushioned and drifting in the gentle subsurface swell from the violent winter storms. Over them, in the quick and scattering waves, there were nearly always ducks – goldeneyes, mergansers, butterballs, mallard, teal, bluebills, harlequins and many others, driven in by the greater storms outside. High above these there were birds of prey at most times of the daylight; occasionally grey-blue darting peregrines that chased the strongest flocks to the water just for the sport of it, because their fierce, quick brains and pulsing muscles craved instant satisfaction of the urge that sight of movement stimulated in them; Cooper's hawks, less wanton in their lesser strength, but sure and deadly when a weak or crippled bird came within reach; the bald eagles, ponderously efficient in finding cripples, always ready to battle for the kill of a swifter, more successful hunter; and the ospreys, strong keen hunters of fish, whose prowess served the eagles best of all.

The ospreys ranged widely over the estuary, searching for slow-moving coarse fish but plunging down upon young salmon whenever the schools offered themselves too near the surface. The bright clear days were best for them and a spell of frosty weather in February set them working keenly over the rippled blue surface of the bay. Almost in the breaking of the brittle waves there were copepod larvae, drawn up by the sunlight. Spring fed upon them with her school, cruising easily along close under the surface. An osprey slid down from the Oregon shore, riding into the strengthening northwest breeze. He soared on it, for love of the day and his living, graceful and harmless five hundred feet above the water. He set his wings and slid away half the height, soared briefly and slid away again to within fifty feet of the water. Then he began to hunt in earnest, working over the bay on long smooth strokes of his big wings. His neat white head, with a crest of dark feathers and the sharp, curved beak, turned this way and that as he flew. His pale eyes, small-pupiled in the bright light, saw movement of many things in the water below him. He changed his flight suddenly, hovering, rising a little in the wind, then his straightly upstretched wings and long downward-straining legs converted his body from plane into plummet and he drove down. He hit the water and disappeared into the splash. A moment later he was in the air again, flying on slow wings a few feet above the water. A few yards from his dive he checked his flight briefly and with a strong tremor of wings and body shook the water from his feathers.

He rose again to a fair height above the water, still heading into the wind; he moved ahead slowly, swinging back and forth in searching. He saw the school of feeding migrants, side-slipped directly over it, hovered briefly and made his dive. Spring had seen the shadow of the osprey's coming and had darted away from it. All around her she saw the flashes of the flight of the other migrants. Behind her, under the shattered surface of the waves, she saw the long legs and pale-grey reaching talons. Fully two feet under water the bird's strong claws gripped into the back of a nine-inch chinook. The small fish struggled, but the rough underside of the osprey's feet and the curve of the claws held him firmly. The osprey beat his wings and rose from the water.

The wind had freshened strongly and he tried to rise into it, but the added surface of the flat side of the fish slowed him down. He shook the water from his wings, struggled a little farther, then dropped back to the reaching waves. He lay there for a few moments, resting on outspread wings, his head raised and his fierce eyes looking about him in every direction. He rose again more easily and made headway into the wind. His grip on the fish was changed so that he now held it along the line of his body, its head towards the wind.

He had risen to a good height before he saw the eagle. He slid away instantly, downwind and towards the shore. But the eagle was an old bird, wise in his method of hunting. His fine head and broad tail shone brilliantly white in the sunlight and his broad black wings were carrying him swiftly to intercept the osprey before the sliding turn was fully made. The eagle came up to him and drove down. The osprey dipped, tumbled away, recovered. He was down within fifty feet of the water, but the eagle came at him again. The osprey dropped his fish and half turned in the air to defend himself. The eagle was past him with a rush of wings, intent upon the fish as it shone silver in the sunlight. He caught it easily above the water and swung upward. The osprey went back to his ranging search of the bay and in a little while stooped again, killed again and kept his prey.

The Blue Heron

THEODORE GOODRIDGE ROBERTS

In a green place lanced through
With amber and gold and blue;
A place of water and weeds
And roses pinker than dawn,
And ranks of lush young reeds,
And grasses straightly withdrawn
From graven ripples of sands,
The still blue heron stands.

Smoke-blue he is, and grey
As embers of yesterday.
Still he is, as death;
Like stone, or shadow of stone
Without a pulse or breath,
Motionless and alone
There in the lily stems:
But his eyes are alive like gems.

Still as a shadow; still
Grey feather and yellow bill:
Still as an image made
Of mist and smoke half hid
By windless sunshine and shade,
Save when a yellow lid
Slides and is gone like a breath:
Death-still – and sudden as death!

The Pond

HAROLD HORWOOD

... Under the lock and key of winter, when scarcely a ray of sunshine penetrates its surface, life in the pond is near its lowest ebb, with only a few hundred fish and a few million insects, down among the very roots of life, swimming or crawling in slow motion. Under the ice the beavers come and go. A muskrat emerges briefly from his burrow in the bank to feed on the root of a pond lily. Even these hardy animals are seen but rarely. Everything else is buried in the mud, or stuck to the stems of the plants and benumbed into deep sleep by the cold. Some have died utterly, down to the last individual of the species, leaving only the tiny blueprint of their lives, coiled and recoiled like a multi-stranded cord within the nucleus of a microscopic egg, awaiting the warmth of another year to replenish the earth with their kind. Others have left larvae, rolled into balls in a death-like stupor, also awaiting the touch of the sun to revive them. Even the few creatures that move, such as the fish and the larger beetles, do so at a snail's pace, barely flexing their muscles in the near-freezing water. The little food needed for this slow-motion life comes from the bottom – dormant larvae and eggs of summer's turbulent children.

Around the end of March the ice melts, or, more rarely, cracks and "goes out" in cascading breakup under pressure from a spring flood. At the same time the first migratory birds arrive – horned larks and fox sparrows, closely followed by robins. By mid-April every suitable spruce and fir on the dry banks of the Beaver Pond has its pair of songbirds. The yellow-shafted flickers have set up house in dead trees a few yards back from the water. Then snipe and swamp sparrows begin building nests around the edges of the peat bog at the end of the pond, where the brook comes snaking in from the upper gully. Savannah sparrows lay claim to the shrubs and herbs on the bank above. Rusty blackbirds inhabit the stunted spruces along the drowned shore where the beavers have backed the water into the forest, and a little later, flocks of warblers take over the leafy woods at the lower end. Soon every scrap of territory is annexed by one bird or another, and the air is loud with their songs. The various scraps of earth which they claim fit together like the pieces of a jig-saw puzzle, each to his own peculiar tastes. The warblers do not nest on the marsh, nor the snipe in the spruces. Nor are there any blank spaces. There are always more birds than nest sites, and whenever an empty bit of real estate occurs on the banks of the pond, some creature whose needs are exactly suited by this particular vacant lot comes along and stakes a claim. . . .

Meanwhile, as if on purpose to provide food for the hordes of hungry birds and fish, there has been a great stirring and awakening in the pond itself. Green frogs and their tadpoles that were buried in the mud all winter, looking as dead as last year's leaves, wake up and wriggle to the surface. The tadpoles dine on algae, which are now burgeoning into an underwater meadow under the shock of the sunlight. Soon they begin to sprout legs and to absorb their tails. The frogs hop out among the reeds, searching for the first swarms of flies that are hatching even now in the sun-warmed corners of marsh and pond, and will soon be followed by explosive swarms of caddis flies and May flies, rising by the million out of the sun-warmed water.

Each has its own place in the pattern. As with insects, so with larger animals. Besides beavers and muskrats, the pond has mink, a pair of loons, and a rough-legged hawk. This magnificent bird, exceeded in majesty only by the eagle, lives at the very peak of the food chain, and rides the air securely, with no enemies that it need fear, traveling on slow wingbeats around the bend of the lake, or soaring through summer mornings as the pond air rises above the night-chilled land.

Each follows the pattern that has existed since its beginnings: the muskrats gather leaves and burrow for roots, the loons dive for fish, as each is taught to do by the immortal mysteries buried deep within the mortal frame. Each stays inside the narrow limits prescribed by its nature. Muskrat food could nourish the loon, perhaps even fatten it, yet it does not trespass upon the muskrat's domain. If the fishing is poor it will go hungry rather than eat leaves and roots. The mink, on the other hand, ignores the vegetable food that grows so lushly along its native bank, and competes with the loon for fish. It will wait patiently in the shadow of an alder shrub for a fish to rise near shore. Then it will dive into the water like an arrow, rising a moment later with the fat trout clamped in its sleek black jaws. It vanishes into the woods, to be seen no more until hunger or curiosity sends it back to the bank.

The mink and the muskrat live not without danger. Should it show itself too often on the surface of the pond, the mink might be struck by the rough-legged hawk. The muskrat might easily be killed by the mink, which is perfectly at home in the water and well able to pursue him through all the passages of his burrow. And both have to keep a wary eye on the young foxes, which have moved down from the brood den on the mountain, and are growing stronger and more cunning every day. . . .

The cubs slink through the kalmia bushes and thickets of Labrador tea, poking sharp black snouts and whiskers out above the water only when they feel sure there is no larger animal about, for they might be seized by a roaming dog, by the solitary lynx that patrols this patch of woods, or perhaps by the hawk that cruises the length of the Beaver Pond watching intently through its telescopic eyes for any movement of prey worthy of its attack.

Throughout the summer the shallows are filled with frogs, multiplying at a fantastic rate, consuming vast numbers of flies, and in turn falling easy victims to everything from hawks to feral cats, which constantly prowl these woods on velvet feet. The young foxes usually disdain to hunt frogs, but the smaller and weaker cats must take whatever they can get.

The frogs that came out of the mud in spring have been mostly eaten by mid-summer, but have been replaced by a new generation of frogs in much larger numbers than before. It is then that they speak tirelessly, all night long, from the thickets of cattails, in a language that has no words and only two syllables. This chanting out of the age of amphibians contrasts and competes with another sound that crackles down through the clouds from the icy regions ten miles above the earth – jet bombers on a night mission toward the North Pole. But the sound out of the remote past, full of melancholy and ageless sadness, goes on, undisturbed even by the sound of the end of the world.

Autumn comes slowly to the Beaver Pond, creeping through the blue and yellow haze of Indian summer. Already by early July the first of the butterflies have crept under the bark of trees or among leaves on the banks to hibernate until spring. Many species of insects have vanished altogether, leaving only eggs or larvae behind. Soon the first of the birds are gathering into flocks, stirred by a restlessness to travel, while the beavers are busy cutting great stacks of tender twigs to store in the pond beside the door of their lodge against the months when they will be unable to climb the banks and feed in the forest. The single, mournful notes of migrating thrushes again are heard at night, and soon, from the north, will come the wild bugle calls of Canada geese.

So the wheel of the year circles above the pond, carrying life up to its triumphant climax in August, and down to its still, small diminuendo in December. It is a cycle with much struggle and ferocity, but also with much beauty and symmetry, not only in its individual forms, but in its total pattern, as well.

Beyond this annual cycle, the pond has a life cycle of its own. Like a living creature, it is born, it grows, and it dies. It began far back in time, more than seven thousand years ago, when a part of . . . [the valley] was blocked with rocks and clay left by a melting glacier. Here the stream that followed the glacier down the valley widened into a stretch of still water. The pond reached its climacteric when the beavers backed it up into the forest, creating a vast new territory for the nurturing of countless lives. But the very life which fills the pond slowly brings it to an end. The thick growth of underwater plants, the husks of insects, the inedible parts of animals that fall to the bottom in a steady rain throughout the summer – all combine to raise it year by year toward the surface. At last the water will become too shallow for the beavers, no matter how many outlets they plug with dams, and then they will desert the pond, or lingering, will be frozen into their lodge to die of starvation. Their dam will be broken, and they will not be there to repair it. Then the water level will suddenly fall, and the pond will become a marsh, with a stream flowing through it. As the lip where the dam once stood is worn down, the bed of the stream will slowly deepen, the marsh will dry out and become a rich meadow with a thick deposit of organic soil created so many years before by the swarming of life of the pond. When that happens a new sort of life history will begin along new routes and patterns, and the meadow will be home to millions of new creatures, all vastly different from the hordes of living things that inhabit the Beaver Pond today.

So the small and the great cycles of life meet and merge and contribute to the grand design, forever changing and growing into something new. Most of the swamp sparrows lost their nests the year the vixen brought her growing cubs to the pond. The vixen herself disappeared soon after, and perhaps no more than two of the cubs lived long enough to mate. But the Platonic idea of the swamp sparrow lives on like that of the fox, forever pure and bright, as though always freshly coined from the mint of creation, weaving the life and death of the individual – and even the life and death of his world – into the great, glowing tapestry of eternity.

From

Searchers at the Gulf

FRANKLIN RUSSELL

The Gulf lay prostrated by heat. Its dry tissues crackled as marshes dried out and lakes diminished. The heat sent creatures into the earth to sleep away the drought and invited fire to invade the breathless forests. On some days the sun seemed strong enough to set the Gulf on fire spontaneously, but even the most decadent forests refused to burn. No ordinary fire would do now; it would need to be a conflagration.

The robin found refuge in the deep forest and hunted along the banks of streams which had shrunk in the drought but still possessed mud and damp earth flanks where worms gathered. The eagle became a stream and river hunter. From the shade of red spruce he watched for unwary salmon desperate to find cooling springs and threw himself into the water, eating and bathing away the heat at the same time. In the big bird bazaars, particularly in the dense colonies of nesting murres, the heat was a killer. It spread stubby wings of nestlings, prostrated them, and roasted them alive. Around them, eggs exploded and the stench of rotting bodies and putrid eggs clogged the nostrils of the surviving colony dwellers. In the gull colonies young gulls deserted their nesting territories and huddled together under trees or in the shade of rocks. They collected along rock shorelines and bathed vigorously. Only the petrel, in her deep and cool burrow and with her long, nocturnal flights to and from the island, felt little of the heat.

A small thundercloud appeared out of nowhere and grew quickly. It settled in foothills behind the western shore and stood there, bristling with suppressed activity, before it lanced down one spare finger of fire. The timing was perfect, and with the job done, the cloud dispersed. The hills became clear and hot again, and the shore continued to receive the endless warm water of the rivers flowing out to it.

The thundercloud disappeared, but as if summoned on cue the east wind, which had been quiescent for days, took up its complementary work. It riffled the shore and probed among the forest trees. Somewhere in the forest the second stage of the thundercloud's work began. The forefinger of flame had landed in the clumpy head of a balsam fir, broken twenty years before and double-branched from its leader. It was loaded with dead and dying tissue from the insect attack. It ignited in a second, blazed like a torch for minutes, then dwindled to a thick-smoked smoulder.

The wind arrived, its timing tardy but not too late, and struck the balsam fir. The tree glowed and the smoke streamed away. In the next second a tongue of flame leaped out. A touch, a caress of wind, and the fire jumped.

It jumped, and touched the next tree and that tree exploded in a red column. The fire vaulted inland and ran at sixty miles an hour. A ghastly roaring, a series of thunderclaps, explosions, hissing side excursions, and the fire was gone with the burned and burning in its wake. As an afterthought, the fire left behind some sober flames to consume what its headlong, erratic advance had not destroyed. These flames burned thoroughly and systematically, razing everything which had been spared by that first flush of flame.

The robin, standing atop a tall fir in the heat, saw the black-and-white cloud gushing upward to the northeast, but it meant nothing to him, and he fell, wings limp, back into the shade.

The Gulf wind which had energized the fire stopped; the vanguard of flame reached the peaked ridge of the first inshore mountains. The wind expired and the fire smoke plumed upright, then turned uncertainly as it responded to slow southern air coming up the farther slope of the ridge. It meandered along the ridge, moving southeast now. In places it ran back on itself and so completed the damage it had done in its first foray. An enormous long gray cloud moved out into the Gulf. It gently smothered the petrel's island and she smelled the smoke, an alarming smell, with her nestling warm under her chest and nowhere near ready to fly. The gray cloud swept east, over the southern shallows, and died eventually in a hard blue sky.

Now split a hundred ways, the fire advanced on a twenty-mile front back toward the Gulf. It thrust arms of flame up nearby valleys. It encircled and destroyed. It remained stationary for a time and burned everything to a black crisp. The robin vaulted to the tip of a fir at the smell of smoke. To every woodland creature smoke was a signal that needed no previous experience to understand. He saw the smoke now well spread. To the north it ran west into the Gulf. To the south it rose very high and menacing, and to the west mountains were shrouded in it. His impulse was flight, but the signal was not yet that imperative. He had no stimulus to fly one way or another.

A small thundercloud, perhaps a reincarnation, appeared in the hills of the big island. Darkly menacing, it rippled with suppressed energy. The crackling spruces cried out for water, and the cloud sent it down. But in the hot air the water dissolved into vapor again and the dark cloud dropped a crooked finger and blasted a trembling aspen to the ground. The tree lay dead and smouldering. The lynx started up in his den. He smelled the smoke of the explosion and ran to the entrance. He saw the thunder-cloud twist with fire; the sky growled and the cloud fled down the valley.

In a moment the big island was on fire.

The fires burned around the Gulf in a valedictory statement for much of the forest. They reached the southern shore in two pockets, hissed, and swept the debris of centuries into molten rubbish. Behind, they left a remnant of pain and countless wreaths of thin, tired smoke. On the western shore the fire struck the defenseless birches, which died to a tree. It raced through the dense balsam fir forests and wiped them out. Havoc followed the fire's work among the hardwoods. Their leaves blackened and shriveled and burned and were whisked away before the long-lasting fires of their tough trunks began.

The robin watched the smoke gathering above him, heard the crackle of flames in the distance, and then, without further hesitation, fled downstream toward the Gulf.

The fires burned with intensive variations from region to region. Along the banks of rivers they accepted the support of winds bleeding from the continental interior and burned downstream so fast they killed nothing but raced at treetop level and sucked out the air from among the trees. In places they pulled up unwilling birds and moths and flies and bees. In the valley of the lynx the fire burned with deliberation; it burned from the tops of trees down, burned the trunks, and then went into the roots. Given the chance, it burned the ground, consuming fertility that had built up over thousands of years. Behind, it left scorched rock and the smoking skeletons of incinerated victims. The lynx turned back at the ridge to look at his valley, but he could see nothing. Dense smoke lay between the valley ridges and the thick smoke rolled downhill like viscid water toward the sea. He saw another lynx, his mate, disappear down the slope behind him and after a sigh, he followed her. . . .

The refugees poured away in flight from the fire all around the Gulf. The lynx, who had started his flight from the fire in leisurely fashion, uncertain whether he should leave his familiar valley, was now running like everybody else. The wind had risen, had taken the flames out of the valley, and the sound of them seemed closer every moment. The woods around him filled with smoke and the querulous cries of confused and frightened songbirds. He saw three wolves drift through the trees ahead of him, heard the rumble of caribou feet, and saw mice moving underfoot although they lacked much knowledge of the world's extent and were not really going anywhere.

At the southern-shore fire, raccoons and skunks stepped out into the dreaded daylight and moved away from the flames. Rabbits and deer joined them, ignoring, for the moment, a cougar sniffing into the wind at the approaching smoke. The smoke rose over the Gulf and the flames rumbled on many horizons, and everywhere teeming mice and lemmings and voles and shrews of the forest floor bounded from their burrows and nests and made short, stabbing runs. But they quickly sought cover, and burrowed deeper, and were later overtaken by the fire and died already interred.

The fires burned on for weeks, and when they were done, so was the summer. The two conclusions coincided as precisely as if planned. The Gulf lay exhausted – burned, brown, black, smoking, its tissues desiccated by the pull of the drought and the draw of the fires. The robin, driven out into the Gulf by the flames and the heat around him, had panicked and turned north, mistakenly assuming he was turning toward land. He realized his mistake almost too late when the sun emerged through the thick pall of the fires. He turned back and reached the southern coast exhausted.

The forest birds flew cautiously along the fringes of the burns, their territories destroyed or rendered unrecognizable and the meaning of their northern summer made senseless. The eagle, hovering very high, witness to the extent of the fires, saw burned land stretching out of sight, but he had no way to make order of such destruction either, so he wheeled back to his northern shore patrol.

The fires done, rains falling, the autumn a breath away, the Gulf had to face the reconstruction, the regeneration of its body. The work began immediately. Unimaginable numbers of tree seeds were already in the wind, parachute-borne, traveling fine as dust, aloft in the company of spores, stuck to the feet of birds or lodged in their crops. Some seeds came into the burns from the northern shore, some from distant continental valleys, others from the south. The seeds cooperated with each other; the big island was as likely to provide seeds for the southern shore as that shore was to send its seeds north across the Gulf.

The richest area of the Gulf was the western shore and regeneration began there, not only because of its earth wealth but because it had been the most desperately needful of revolutionary change. The dead red spruces, like tall black fingers in the expiring sun, beckoned the seeds of poplar and birch which drifted in like smoke. The poplar seeds, lightest of all, came thickest because they had gathered in the air from the most distant parts. They were fast to sprout, fast to grow, and fast to discourage other trees. It would be many years before the red spruce could displace these interlopers and re-create the forest that had been destroyed.

On high ground along valley ridges and hills where the fires had been most destructive, balsam fir would create a single-tree forest by the sheer density of its invasion of the burn. Millions of seedlings would sprout, thick enough to mat the ground at the first touch of rain. Fast growers, they would thin themselves in a few years to about a hundred thousand stems to the acre, all the while fighting for a share of moisture and space, air and sunlight, and killing each other as ruthlessly as fire. Finally, about six thousand trees would survive and grow to maturity on every acre burned that disastrous summer.

The fire, however, had not carried all before it. While it had appeared to destroy in some places, it had been tricked by the trees whose habits had been changed by other fires. When the fire hit the black spruce, that tough colonizer of thin soils and soggy pits and bogs, that survivor for five thousand uninterrupted years, it did not kill. Rather, it created. The black spruce had anticipated this fire. The cones at the top of their stems had accumulated for years without opening like those lower on the trees. Came the fire; the heat struck; the cones, seeds unharmed, opened after the fire had gone, and the seeds fluttered down, first to recolonize the burn.

The jackpine forests which had smothered the river lowlands along the western shore also welcomed the fire. Their branches reached out for the flames and drew them toward their cones. Obediently the cones responded to the heat of the fire and yawned open after it had passed, and a smothering host of seeds waited for the rains.

Old Song

F. R. SCOTT

far voices
and fretting leaves
this music the
hillside gives

but in the deep
Laurentian river
an elemental song
for ever

a quiet calling
of no mind
out of long aeons
when dust was blind
and ice hid sound

only a moving
with no note
granite lips
a stone throat

Two

A Beauty of Dissonance: The Ambivalent Wilderness

INTRODUCTION

Mixed responses to the wilderness are neither surprising nor uncommon. For many writers, it is both benign and malignant; its influence is both positive and negative. Such mixed responses are frequently generated by the contrasts and complexity of nature itself. The feeding Grizzly *(Ursus horribilis),* red in tooth and claw and muzzle, is accompanied by the gentle, spindly fawn. The fragile beauty of the wild orchid contrasts starkly with the grey, wind-whipped surf of the Labrador coast. The blueberry-laden clearing, high and breezy, adjoins the mosquito-infested swamp, low and heavy with dank, dead air. For some, the singing of wolves is at once hauntingly beautiful and chillingly ominous. For Pierre Berton, the wolf's howl "seems to echo all the loneliness and the wonder of the land at the top of the continent."

Such ambivalence may be fostered by many factors, some of which have little to do with the objective reality of wild nature. Preconceived notions, sometimes rooted in folklore or propaganda, may inject dissonance into an otherwise harmonious score. Some of these notions are simple-minded, if not ludicrous. Wolves, for example, intrude a jarring note because they are thought to be dangerous, even evil. They slink about in packs trying to eat nice people like Little Red Riding Hood and simple, good-hearted peasants (not to speak of woolly lambs). Forest fires and burned-over areas are unnatural, ugly, and bad because Smokey the Bear and the timber industry have said so. Snakes are fearful, gruesome things because they lie about in slithery coils waiting to bite, drop out of trees in darkest Africa (thereby doing in numerous explorers and harmless natives), and eat live frogs whole. Grizzly bears are indeed *horribilis*: in 1970 they reduced the human population of Canada by .00001 per cent (two people), and were widely reported as the scourge of holidaying mankind (where does that leave automobile drivers?).

Ambivalence may also be more rationally explained. Changes in season and weather may lead to contrasting reactions which support a generally ambivalent attitude toward the wilderness. One day the sun-drenched strand of beach is benevolent; the next it is malevolent under a lashing of cold rain. The pink and yellow blooms of the tundra summer are countered by the dark bitterness of its winter. Local variations may also complicate the response. The swirling, rock-infested rapids of a river may seem to harbour destructive spirits, as the Indian believed, while the quiet pools downstream may seem places of infinite tranquillity. The Lake Superior shore, viewed from a passing canoe, is magnificent; it lifts the soul. A landing is made. Slavering squadrons of blackflies, seemingly intent on war to the death, attack. The soul is not lifted. The duration of one's immersion in wilderness may also be a factor. A two-week canoe trip is rejuvenating; two months in an isolated, winter-bound trapper's shack is depressing. "It's a great place to visit, but I wouldn't want to live there."

The wilderness offers infinite variety – images and experiences for every mood and purpose. While it is in fact impersonal, it may seem harsh and gentle; it may attract and repel; it may speak of terror and regeneration. Little wonder, then, that ambivalent responses to it are often reflected in Canadian literature. "It's the cussedest land that I know," writes Robert Service of the Yukon, quickly adding that its beauty fills him with wonder and its stillness with peace. Similarly, as Earle Birney approaches the Nova Scotian coast, he responds initially to the smell of "sweet spruce in the air" – then hastily reminds himself of "how boxer waves / bully these shores." Elsewhere, in a single image, René Chopin focusses on the attraction and yet potential destruction of "Polar Landscapes": he sees the "Untrodden reef emerging resplendent from the tide." Harsh and gentle, our wild landscapes may attract and repel; nevertheless, urges Douglas Le Pan, "This is the land the passionate man must travel."

The Spell of the Yukon

ROBERT SERVICE

I wanted the gold, and I sought it;
　　I scrabbled and mucked like a slave.
Was it famine or scurvy – I fought it;
　　I hurled my youth into a grave.
I wanted the gold, and I got it –
　　Came out with a fortune last fall, –
Yet somehow life's not what I thought it,
　　And somehow the gold isn't all.

No! There's the land. (Have you seen it?)
　　It's the cussedest land that I know,
From the big, dizzy mountains that screen it
　　To the deep, deathlike valleys below.
Some say God was tired when He made it;
　　Some say it's a fine land to shun;
Maybe; but there's some as would trade it
　　For no land on earth – and I'm one.

You come to get rich (damned good reason);
　　You feel like an exile at first;
You hate it like hell for a season,
　　And then you are worse than the worst.
It grips you like some kinds of sinning;
　　It twists you from foe to a friend;
It seems it's been since the beginning;
　　It seems it will be to the end.

I've stood in some mighty-mouthed hollow
　　That's plumb-full of hush to the brim;
I've watched the big, husky sun wallow
　　In crimson and gold, and grow dim,
Till the moon set the pearly peaks gleaming,
　　And the stars tumbled out, neck and crop;
And I've thought that I surely was dreaming,
　　With the peace o' the world piled on top.

The summer – no sweeter was ever;
  The sunshiny woods all athrill;
The grayling aleap in the river,
  The bighorn asleep on the hill.
The strong life that never knows harness;
  The wilds where the caribou call;
The freshness, the freedom, the farness –
  O God! how I'm stuck on it all.

The winter! the brightness that blinds you,
  The white land locked tight as a drum,
The cold fear that follows and finds you,
  The silence that bludgeons you dumb.
The snows that are older than history,
  The woods where the weird shadows slant;
The stillness, the moonlight, the mystery,
  I've bade 'em good-by – but I can't.

There's a land where the mountains are nameless,
  And the rivers all run God knows where;
There are lives that are erring and aimless,
  And deaths that just hang by a hair;
There are hardships that nobody reckons;
  There are valleys unpeopled and still;
There's a land – oh, it beckons and beckons
  And I want to go back – and I will.

They're making my money diminish;
  I'm sick of the taste of champagne.
Thank God! when I'm skinned to a finish
  I'll pike to the Yukon again.
I'll fight – and you bet it's no sham-fight;
  It's hell! – but I've been there before;
And it's better than this by a damsite –
  So me for the Yukon once more.

There's gold, and it's haunting and haunting;
  It's luring me on as of old;
Yet it isn't the gold that I'm wanting
  So much as just finding the gold.
It's the great, big, broad land 'way up yonder,
  It's the forests where silence has lease;
It's the beauty that thrills me with wonder,
  It's the stillness that fills me with peace.

The Mysterious North

PIERRE BERTON

. . . I was brought up in a small frame cottage in Dawson City, where the walls were a foot thick and filled with sawdust to keep out the cold, where a pot of dog food – rice and caribou meat – bubbled perpetually over a wood fire, and where the water was brought around to the door in icicle-draped buckets at twenty-five cents a pail.

Our home lay nestled against the low benchland that skirts the swampy flats beside the gray Yukon River. Behind us rose the black bulk of the hills, clothed in spruce and birch and poplar. Behind those hills lay other hills, and when you climbed to the top of the farthest hills, there were yet more hills stretching endlessly into the north. If a man wanted to walk in a straight line due north he could cross those hills for four hundred miles until he reached the edge of the Arctic sea, and he would come upon no trace of human life.

I have never quite been able to escape the memory of those lonely hills. In the winter nights, when the roar of the river was hushed by a mantle of ice, when the frost-racked timbers cracked like pistol-shots in the cold, when the ghostly bars of the northern lights shifted across the black sky, we would sometimes hear the chill call of the wolf, drifting down from the wilderness behind us. It is an eerie sound, plaintive, mournful, mysterious. The wolf is like the husky and the malemute: his vocal cords are so constructed that he cannot bark, but only howl across the endless hills. If the north has a theme song, it is this haunting cry, which seems to echo all the loneliness and the wonder of the land at the top of the continent.

When I was a small boy, it used to fascinate and terrify me, perhaps because in all my years in the north I never actually saw a wolf alive. To me he was only a footprint in the snow and a sound in the night, an unseen creature who lurked in the shadow of the nameless hills.

For eleven childhood winters I heard the cry of the wolf, and then I left the country with no intention of returning. But the north has dogged my footsteps and I have never quite been quit of it. Within five years I was back again on the aspen-covered slopes of the Klondike, working with a pick and shovel in a gold camp. I spent three summers at it and then, when war broke out, I left it again, believing that this was the end. It was only the beginning: since those days in the Yukon I have crisscrossed the north from the Alaska border to the tip of Baffin Island, from Churchill on Hudson Bay to Coppermine on the Arctic coast. I have eaten moose steak on the Peace River, buffalo meat in Fort Smith, Arctic grayling in Whitehorse, and reindeerburgers in Aklavik. I have driven the Alaska Highway in a Ford, landed in Headless Valley in a Junkers, crossed Great Slave Lake in a tugboat, and chugged into the heart of Labrador on an ore train. . . .

The more I see of the country, the less I feel I know about it. There is a saying that after five years in the north every man is an expert; after ten years, a novice. No man can hope or expect to absorb it all in a lifetime, and fifteen generations of explorers, whalers, fur traders, missionaries, scientists, policemen, trappers, prospectors, adventurers, and tourists have failed to solve all its riddles. To me, as to most northerners, the country is still an unknown quantity, as elusive as the wolf, howling just beyond the rim of the hills. Perhaps that is why it holds its fascination. . . .

The high Arctic, which knows no real summer, bears little relation to the Yukon Valley of my childhood, where the temperature can rise to a hundred degrees. The treeless tundra northwest of Churchill, Manitoba, where century-old trees grow no higher than three inches, has little in common with the Mackenzie farmlands, where a stem of wheat can sprout five feet in a month. The stark, Precambrian rock on which Port Radium is perched is a long way removed from the spongy delta in which Aklavik is mired.

For the north is a land of violent contrasts. It has some of the most breath-taking scenery in the world. There is the unforgettable picture of Baffin Island rearing out of the Arctic mists, with its black cliffs and its blue mountains and its long fiords and its enormous emerald glaciers. There is the sight of Kluane Lake in the Yukon as you first come upon it from the Alaska Highway, a slender finger of the purest absinthe green, lying lazily at the foot of the continent's tallest mountain range, whose peaks plunge in purple slabs straight out of the clouds to the water's edge. There is the breathless spectacle of the Nahanni Valley with its enormous waterfall locked away beyond a series of dizzy, precipitous canyons.

But the north also contains some of the most desolate and monotonous stretches in the world. Dismal Lake, "a sombre sheet of water between threatening hills" north of Great Bear, is truly named. "Anything more unspeakably dismal than the western end I never saw," the traveler George Douglas was moved to remark. Another explorer, Henry Youle Hind, stood on the tableland above the Moisie River in Labrador and wrote that "words fail to describe the appalling desolation." Hesketh Prichard wrote that the Ungava Peninsula was "sheer desolation – abysmal and chaotic."

Indeed, there is so much monotony in the north that its very vastness takes on a sort of grandeur, like the Barren Lands that stretch across the top of the continent for hundreds of miles, their starkness broken only by those geological oddities with the elfin names: the pingoes and the polygons, the drumlins and the eskers.

The Canadian north contains more lakes than all of the rest of the world put together, all the way from little green-eyed Muncho on the Alaska Highway, to Great Bear, the continent's fourth largest, so cold that it often stays frozen until July. But it also encompasses one of the world's great deserts, the Arctic tundra, where the precipitation runs between two and ten inches yearly. The fact that thousands of lakes happen to lie in this desert country makes it all the more confusing.

The north is full of such paradoxes. In fact, it is possible to prove just about any theory by the use of isolated examples and statistics.

Is it a frozen waste? There are plenty of places where Eskimos wear fur-lined parkas the year around, where planes land on skis in June and the temperature never goes higher than fifteen degrees above frost.

Is it a sunny paradise? At Fort Smith, on the Slave River, the thermometer has sometimes reached 103 degrees above zero. This is hotter than has ever been recorded in Canada's southernmost city, Windsor, Ontario. Spring comes to Norman Wells, nudging the Arctic Circle, just as soon as it does to the Gaspé Peninsula in Quebec. The average July temperatures in Dawson City are the same as those on the central prairies. And the radio station at Resolution Island, off the coast of Baffin, has an average temperature in January slightly higher than the average for Winnipeg, eight hundred miles to the south. In fact, slightly colder temperatures have been recorded in the northern prairie provinces than have ever been recorded in Arctic Canada.

The truth, of course, is that the north is neither paradise nor wasteland. It remains a frontier country, with only two important resources, fur and minerals. (A third great resource, hydroelectric power, has yet to be developed.) It is still desperately remote and costly to reach and exploit, but it is capable of supporting if necessary (but only if necessary) a much larger population than it now enjoys. . . .

There remains one serious flaw in the northern economy: almost every community is built on a single resource. When the bottom falls out of gold, Yellowknife suffers a slump. When the bottom drops out of furs, the Mackenzie River ports face a depression. John Hornby, a bizarre and mystic little Englishman who roamed the Barrens for a generation, called that stark country "the land of feast and famine." He wanted to write a book with that title, but he starved to death before he began it. The phrase remains an apt one and it could well apply to the north as a whole.

It is this boom-and-bust psychology that has given the north a certain feeling and look of impermanence. Nobody expects to stay very long in the north – or very long in one spot. There is no agriculture to tie people to a single site. Like the caribou and the lemmings and the nomadic Indians, northerners are apt to rove the land like gypsies. The Anglican missionaries, the Hudson's Bay traders, and the Mounted Policemen are switched from post to post like chessmen on a great board. The prospectors follow the big strikes, and the trappers follow the fur. This restless shifting gives the north a cohesion it otherwise would not have. Northerners know each other, even though a thousand miles separate their homes; men living in Whitehorse, Yukon, are bound to have acquaintances in Aklavik, Yellowknife, and Churchill. But it also contributes to the feeling, strong in every northern town, that everything is temporary. Many northern communities (Whitehorse is one example) are little better than shack towns for this reason. The homes are jerry-built and so are the buildings, and often enough they are sprinkled around the countryside without thought or plan as if tossed there by the passing winds.

The fact is that most people go north expecting to stay only a short while. And yet the country is populated by men and women (my parents were among them) who have stayed a lifetime. I can never forget the story of the young Scottish bride who came to Dawson City in the days before the First World War. She brought a trunk of wedding presents with her, but she didn't bother to unpack them, for she didn't expect to stay more than a few months. But the months grew into years, and the years grew into decades. She raised a family and watched it grow up. She learned to live with the north and to love it. The crisp feeling of the snow crust breaking under the moccasin in the winter, the bright tangle of kinnikinnick carpeting the forest floor in the summer, the exploding rumble of the ice breaking in the spring, the pungent odor of caribou rotting along the riverbank in the fall – all these sensations and impressions became a part of her life. Finally the time came for her to leave the north forever, and when she did, it was with that strange mixture of relief and reluctance that every northerner faces when the day of departure comes. She packed her trunks and went her way, but one trunk was already full. For here lay the still unopened wedding presents of thirty years before, the telltale symbols of her indecision about a land which, in all its mystery, both bewitches and repels – like the gossamer fog of winter clothing the dark valleys, or the chill call of the wolf drifting down from the unending hills.

Polar Landscapes

RENE CHOPIN

The arctic heaven stars its crackling dome.
The frosted night-wind's gusty exhalation
Touches each constellation
And sets its light asparkle: the Swan, the Goat,
   the Ram.

A gauzy veil across that glass-clear sky,
One distant scarf of mist floats and is gone;
The silvered crystal moon
Plunges beneath the sea her doused enormous eye.

Strange architecture, whose familiar look
Of drift and ice-block soaring stage on stage,
Sketched on a printed page,
Stared from the safe pulp of some picture-book,

Appears enormous now: minster or hall,
The cave-worn polar pack! as we have seen
Thrown on a shadowy screen
The high faint image of a castellated wall.

Its vast façade holds on the seaward side
A portal, broadly stepped with ledge on ledge
Carved by the water's edge,
Untrodden reef emerging resplendent from the tide.

Colossal courses form that toppling height
Beyond whose pillared azure cloister blaze
Deep halls and passageways,
Where countless lustres hang their blue crystalline light,

Jewels and pins, whose metals never fade,
False stones amassed in treasuries unexplored

Among whose glittering hoard
Long since by Undine hands the Thule cup was laid.

In that far region of the polar stars
Rears the cold hell of tall convulsive capes;
And I see the twilight shapes
Of fleets that sailed the world in immemorial years,

Sheer cliffs stumbling over a stagnant sea,
Lakes spreading from a silver cataract;
Rough dolmens table-capped,
Vast cromlech-scattered plains, menhirs and tumuli.

White sacrificial bears with foaming mouth
Shall yawn with lust and tedium to behold
The sun at midnight, gold
Among the promontories of the distant south.

The proud Explorers, captives of the floe,
Exiled forever in their icy tomb,
Had dreamed of deathless fame.
The Pole, a sphinx, still waits inviolate in the snow.

On a snowy isle, hope gone, provisions gone,
Owning defeat, they cut their names at last
In murderous conquest;
Disconsolate, resigned, they died as night came on.

Aurora's rich magnetic folds descend
On Chaos' awful pit; their bright fringe streams,
Shot with prismatic gleams,
And sumptuously beguiles the heroes' tragic end.

Their fires went out, their blood ran slow and cold.
And did their pale dreams show them there, remote
Beyond the bergs that float
On hushed seas, village steeples where their knell was tolled?

Or, hell-borne harvest of a useless yearning,
The sun-drenched vine against the ancestral wall?
Or summer's miracle,
The fruitful field? the ash, the grates of home burning?

Francis Sparshott   (translator)

Maritime Faces (Approaching Halifax 1945)

EARLE BIRNEY

As the waters grey   grace meets you
but only in gulls that hook on the wind
are shaken easily loose
curve to the curving wave

Not these the mark of Canada
nor yet the sentry beat of bergs
around the fading palaces
of fog your ship salutes
but here where heads of Hebridean mould
toss in crusted dories   hard Saxon fingers
sift dour living from the drowned
and drowning Banks

Smell now the landsmell   sweet spruce in the air
but note   remember   how boxer waves
bully these shores   battling and billowing
into the stone's weakness   bellowing
down the deepening caverns
smashing the slate with unappeasable fists

See at last the crouched hills
at bay with Boreas
the old laconic resourceful hills

Something of this in the maritime faces

Into the Swamp

DOUGLAS LOCHHEAD

The mad shallows
at turtle dawn:
the darting time,
the canoe slips
on the water top
and I glide it
so close underneath
to shadowy schools,
sand clouds in
underwater piles
and the shadows grow
into thin light
in the waveless place
and what the swamp
echoes bring are
heron, bittern
and the long hidden
fight prolonged
going on
just underneath.

From

Winter Studies and Summer Rambles in Canada

ANNA JAMESON

We remained in conversation till long after midnight; then the boat was moored to a tree, but kept off shore, for fear of the mosquitoes, and we addressed ourselves to sleep. I remember lying awake for some minutes, looking up at the quiet stars, and around upon the dark weltering waters, and at the faint waning moon, just suspended on the very edge of the horizon. I saw it sink – sink into the bosom of the lake, as if to rest, and then with a thought of far-off friends, and a most fervent thanksgiving, I dropped asleep. It is odd that I did not think of praying for protection, and that no sense of fear came over me; it seemed as if the eye of God himself looked down upon me; that I *was* protected. I do not say I *thought* this any more than the unweaned child in its cradle; but I had some such feeling of unconscious trust and love, now I recall those moments.

I slept, however, uneasily, not being yet accustomed to a board and a blanket; *ça viendra avec le temps*. About dawn I awoke in a sort of stupor, but after bathing my face and hands over the boat side, I felt refreshed. The voyageurs, after a good night's rest, were in better humour, and took manfully to their oars. Soon after sunrise, we passed round that very conspicuous cape, famous in the history of northwest adventurers, called the "Grand Détour," half-way between Mackinaw and the Sault. Now, if you look at the map, you will see that our course was henceforth quite altered; we had been running down the coast of the main land towards the east; we had now to turn short round the point, and steer almost due west; hence its most fitting name, the Grand Détour. The wind, hitherto favourable, was now dead against us. This part of Lake Huron is studded with little islands, which, as well as the neighbouring main land, are all uninhabited, yet clothed with the richest, loveliest, most fantastic vegetation, and no doubt swarming with animal life.

I cannot, I dare not, attempt to describe to you the strange sensation one has, thus thrown for a time beyond the bounds of civilized humanity, or indeed any humanity; nor the wild yet solemn reveries which come over one in the midst of this wilderness of woods and waters. All was so solitary, so grand in its solitude, as if nature unviolated sufficed to herself. Two days and nights the solitude was unbroken; not a trace of social life, not a human being, not a canoe, not even a deserted wigwam, met our view. Our little boat held on its way over the placid lake and among green tufted islands; and we its inmates, two women, differing in clime, nation, complexion, strangers to each other but a few days ago, might have fancied ourselves alone in a new-born world.

We landed to boil our kettle, and breakfast on a point of the island of St. Joseph's. This most beautiful island is between thirty and forty miles in length, and nearly a hundred miles in circumference, and towards the centre the land is high and picturesque. They tell me that on the other side of the island there is a settlement of whites and Indians. Another large island, Drummond's Isle, was for a short time in view. We had also a settlement here, but it was unaccountably surrendered to the Americans. If now you look at the map, you will wonder, as I did, that in retaining St. Joseph's and the Manitoolin islands, we gave up Drummond's island. Both these islands had forts and garrisons during the war.

By the time breakfast was over, the children had gathered some fine strawberries; the heat had now become almost intolerable, and unluckily we had no awning. The men rowed languidly, and we made but little way; we coasted along the south shore of St. Joseph's, through fields of rushes, miles in extent, across Lake George, and Muddy Lake; (the name, I thought, must be a libel, for it was as clear as a crystal and as blue as heaven; but they say that, like a sulky temper, the least ruffle of wind turns it as black as ditchwater, and it does not subside again in a hurry,) and then came a succession of openings spotted with lovely islands, all solitary. The sky was without a cloud, a speck – except when the great fish-eagle was descried sailing over its blue depths – the water without a wave. We were too hot and too languid to converse. Nothing disturbed the deep noon-tide stillness, but the dip of the oars, or the spring and splash of a sturgeon as he leapt from the surface of the lake, leaving a circle of little wavelets spreading around. All the islands we passed were so woody, and so infested with mosquitoes, that we could not land and light our fire, till we reached the entrance of St. Mary's River, between Nebish island and the main land.

Here was a well-known spot, a sort of little opening on a flat shore, called the *Encampment,* because a party of boatmen coming down from Lake Superior, and camping here for the night, were surprised by the frost, and obliged to remain the whole winter till the opening of the ice in the spring. After rowing all this hot day till seven o'clock against the wind, (what there was of it,) and against the current coming rapidly and strongly down from Lake Superior, we did at length reach this promised harbour of rest and refreshment. Alas! there was neither for us; the moment our boat touched the shore, we were enveloped in a cloud of mosquitoes. Fires were lighted instantly, six were burning in a circle at once; we were well nigh suffocated and smoke-dried – all in vain. At last we left the voyageurs to boil the kettle, and retreated to our boat, desiring them to make us fast to a tree by a long rope; then, each of us taking an oar – I only wish you could have seen us – we pushed off from the land, while the children were sweeping away the enemy with green boughs. This being done, we commenced supper, really half famished, and were too much engrossed to look about us. Suddenly we were again surrounded by our adversaries; they came upon us in swarms, in clouds, in myriads, entering our eyes, our noses, our mouths, stinging till the blood followed. We had, unawares, and while absorbed in our culinary operations, drifted into the shore, got entangled among the roots of trees, and were with difficulty extricated, presenting all the time a fair mark and a rich banquet for our detested tormentors. The dear children cried with agony and impatience, and but for shame I could almost have cried too.

I had suffered from these plagues in Italy; you too, by this time, may probably have known what they are in the southern countries of the old world; but 'tis a jest, believe me, to encountering a forest full of them in these wild regions. I had heard much, and much was I forewarned, but never could have conceived the torture they can inflict, nor the impossibility of escape, defence, or endurance. Some amiable person, who took an especial interest in our future welfare, in enumerating the torments prepared for hardened sinners, assures us that they will be stung by mosquitoes all made of brass, and as large as black beetles – he was an ignoramus and a bungler; you may credit me, that the brass is quite an unnecessary improvement, and the increase of size equally superfluous. Mosquitoes, as they exist in this upper world, are as pretty and perfect a plague as the most ingenious amateur sinner-tormentor ever devised. Observe, that a mosquito does not sting like a wasp, or a gad-fly; he has a long proboscis like an awl, with which he bores your veins, and pumps the life-blood out of you, leaving venom and fever behind. Enough of mosquitoes – I will never again do more than allude to them; only they are enough to make Philosophy go hang herself, and Patience swear like a Turk or a trooper.

Well, we left this most detestable and inhospitable shore as soon as possible, but the enemy followed us and we did not soon get rid of them; night came on, and we were still twenty miles below the Sault.

I offered an extra gratuity to the men, if they would keep to their oars without interruption; and then, fairly exhausted, lay down on my locker and blanket. But whenever I woke from uneasy, restless slumbers, *there* was Mrs. Schoolcraft, bending over her sleeping children, and waving off the mosquitoes, singing all the time a low, melancholy Indian song; while the northern lights were streaming and dancing in the sky, and the fitful moaning of the wind, the gathering clouds, and chilly atmosphere, foretold a change of weather. This would have been the *comble de malheur.* When daylight came, we passed Sugar Island, where immense quantities of maple sugar are made every spring, and just as the rain began to fall in earnest, we arrived at the Sault Ste. Marie. On one side of the river, Mrs. Schoolcraft was welcomed by her mother; and on the other, my friends, the MacMurrays, received me with delighted and delightful hospitality. I went to bed – oh! the luxury! – and slept for six hours.

A Country Without a Mythology

DOUGLAS LE PAN

No monuments or landmarks guide the stranger
Going among this savage people, masks
Taciturn or babbling out an alien jargon
And moody as barbaric skies are moody.

Berries must be his food. Hurriedly
He shakes the bushes, plucks pickerel from the river,
Forgetting every grace and ceremony,
Feeds like an Indian, and is on his way.

And yet, for all his haste, time is worth nothing.
The abbey clock, the dial in the garden,
Fade like saint's days and festivals.
Months, years, are here unbroken virgin forests.

There is no law – even no atmosphere
To smooth the anger of the flagrant sun,
November skies sting like icicles.
The land is open to all violent weathers.

Passion is not more quick. Lightnings in August
Stagger, rocks split, tongues in the forest hiss,
As fire drinks up the lovely sea-dream coolness.
This is the land the passionate man must travel.

Sometimes – perhaps at the tentative fall of twilight –
A belief will settle that waiting around the bend
Are sanctities of childhood, that melting birds
Will sing him into a limpid gracious Presence.

The hills will fall in folds, the wilderness
Will be a garment innocent and lustrous
To wear upon a birthday, under a light
That curls and smiles, a golden-haired Archangel.

And now the channel opens. But nothing alters.
Mile after mile of tangled struggling roots,
Wild-rice, stumps, weeds, that clutch at the canoe,
Wild birds hysterical in tangled trees.

And not a sign, no emblem in the sky
Or boughs to friend him as he goes; for who
Will stop where, clumsily constructed, daubed
With war-paint, teeters some lust-red manitou?

From

Shrouded Trails

R. D. SYMONS

The cold winter sun is almost down. The trail is drifted deep with the snow that whips its eternal, restless way over the barren's hummocky surface. Only by feeling with their padded feet for the firmer trail bottom, built up by the few toboggans which seasonally pass here, can the huskies avoid floundering.

Soon the faint glow marking the end of the sun's brief visit will disappear entirely behind the distant spruce ridge, silhouetting it for a moment and seeming to bring it close. With the light's disappearance one will feel in all its intensity the stark loneliness of the surroundings; but while that glow paints the south-west one still feels orientated, and seems not far distant from the habitation of one's kind. Looking into that last reflection, one still sees the world in the mind's eye as an open map, all places accessible.

There is the south-west, behind that ridge from the top of which one will come to the headwaters of the familiar Nitenai. To follow that stream for fifty miles is easy – one cannot get lost. Two blazed trees – how vividly remembered! – will show us the lobstick portage. To line up the two lobsticks is a matter of minutes, and then for the open lake to receive us in friendliness to its smooth, frozen surface. How the dogs will dash out into this welcome space, and how eagerly they will make for the little opening visible in the dark line of the farther shore! Two more days through the snow-burdened woods to the post, where the almost enveloping night will be pushed back on both fronts by curtained windows and the mellow glow of oil lamps. There will be warmth, firelight, laughter, and much talk.

And from the post, as everyone knows, it is but a few days' easy travel down the great river to the railroad town – and from there? Why, from there one can go to Winnipeg! The city! But why stop at Winnipeg when the whole world is within reach? There are the oceans, east and west, the great rolling blue oceans where the breakers roar and hiss; where the spray from their shaggy crests whips one's face, as does the snow in the Keewatin country.

Ah, there is no toilsome plodding up one slope and down the next in this vast liquid barren. Great ships, gold and white and red, with gaily striped funnels and noisy throats, traverse these wastes in calm serenity, their interiors warm and glowing, and savoury with spicy food.

They go to England – merry England, with its breath-taking greenness, its spires, its red-roofed villages. They go to the perfumed Orient, where you can see colour, feel warmth, rub shoulders with white and brown and black and yellow – Arab, Turk, and Parsee, hairy Sikh and plump Bengali, turbanned nomads of the hills, and befezzed ancients of the bazaars.

Life! Human life in all its fullness; richness of sight and sound and smell. The grave murmurings of the elders, the tramp of laden camels at dawn, the shouts of the street vendors; the low, full-throated laughter of the women.

They go to Brazil, Argentina, Chile! Down the grey shores of the east coast, where the fog comes in like a soundless blanket from the Caribbean; across the Gulf, where blue wavelets dance endlessly, their little feet tripping ahead of the happy company whose gay jests ring out from the snowy decks. Along the scented coast to anchor where tinkling guitars strum from white buildings, set amidst a mass of feathery greenness around and behind.

Until the last faint blush fades from the dulling northern sky this map is real and tangible, and the world wherein we move – even this far-off Keewatin – is still tied to it by the questing of the mind's eye, by which we can so safely and so easily follow the trails we know. Faint indeed they are to a stranger, but plain as ribbons of steel to us. So plain that we can take to them almost as instinctively as a dog takes to the homeward road. In our thoughts we can be already miles ahead of the slow-moving dogs. We can feel in anticipation the downward lunge of the toboggan at the river's sudden brink, and note in advance this familiar gnarled tree, that old camping-place.

But the sun has set and there is no moon. The whining wind whips the tiny snow particles into a cold hissing serpent, which writhes across our trail close to the surface of the snow. All distance is lost in a filmy shroud, and the very surface we tread seems to be not of this solid and firm earth. We float, suspended in dreadful silence.

Even the dogs feel the change – the cold pall which surrounds us, the gloom which enfolds us; the sense of drifting, lost and forsaken by all the dear solid things we knew. Above, the northern lights rush like squadrons *en echelon,* their cold silken banners faintly rustling, to do battle with the dark *weetigoes.* They stretch forth their luminous fingers only to withdraw them, ere we have been able to guess their texture. Green and palely gold and faintest rose, they slowly dance the great nightly ballet on a fathomless stage of which the backdrop is eternity, and the wings the edge of the universe.

Still we trudge on step by step, the tightly held toboggan rope the only link with the material world. The dogs move silently, phantom-like, the leaders hardly discernible in the gloom. Only the sharply pointed ears of the nearest show darkly in his own foggy breath-cloud. The toboggan moves as silently as they, seeming not so much to be pulled by them as following them, as a canoe follows the deep un-seen current of the river.

So we all – man and beasts and toboggan – float through the frost fog, straining for the sight of some object. No longer are the dogs spoken to, for the human voice sounds impious in this all-enveloping silence, and the wrath of the lonely places seems very close. The muffled swish of snowshoes, the occasional slaps of the rope, or the rare clink of harness parts, blend themselves with the hissing of the snow to form a murmur which but intensifies the silence, like the rushing sounds in one's ear when one is listening too intently for a call that does not come. It is a murmur which makes us forget every-thing except that we are drifting on, willy-nilly, scarce aware of the movement of muscles; borne on, rather, by an invisible force which has picked up man, dogs, and load.

With a jar, we stop suddenly. So suddenly that for a moment we are lost and groping; groping for a beautiful peace we cannot re-member; groping to touch again that which has lulled us, as a sleeper waking from a happy dream seeks to recall it ere he has to face real-ity again.

Now action interrupts us. A great fresh snowdrift has formed in a hollow, and the lead dogs are already whining, belly-deep. They are extricated by main force, the trail is found and broken afresh with tramping snowshoes. We seem to have been on the trail for hours. How much further to that timber ridge where we shall camp? All at once we are weary – man and dogs.

But a few moments ago we moved by some great compulsion nor felt that we had aught to do with our drifting progress. Now the dogs lie down with great sighs to regain their wind, licking and worrying their paws to remove the galling ice particles. Sitting on the loaded toboggan, we feel the bite of the sub-zero cold and hunger gnaws. Looking around at the unending horizonless nothing, we are oppressed by a great and poignant loneliness.

The mind has become too dull now to visualize the map. Winni-peg, England, China – they are but names. They belong to the unat-tainable. We are here, and there is nowhere else. We are the last liv-ing things in the world, and soon we too must be caught up by the wind and dissipated in the fog. With this thought comes a great long-ing to touch metal, to feel silk, to stand on concrete, to lie and roll and stretch on hard, solid, warm earth; to tread sturdy planking with-

in four walls, where there is form and light and shadow; to be in a
crowd and hear a strident band blare down the street; to hear hundreds of voices all around us, so that one may speak – may shout –
without fear of the mocking answer of the storm.

Something solid! That's it – something solid to reunite us once more
with our mother the earth. Even a tree now. The spruce ridge, the
beginning of our almost forgotten map. Got to get to the spruce ridge.
Eat. Sleep. We'll take the trail in the morning (will morning ever
come?) down the Nitenai, down Lobstick Lake to the post. Sell the
dogs – give them away – anything. Hit the trail for the railroad; back
to the haunts of man; back to light and laughter and life – "Outside". Away from this gloom, this hell, this tyrant we call the North,
where the lights gibber and dance and mock. The North, which
slowly, very slowly presses his cold fingers against a man's temples,
breathes his cold breath into a man's nostrils, and wraps him in the
clammy white shroud which some day will be his last.

And hurry! Hurry! Before it is too late – mush, mush on – the
whip cracks hysterically. Will that spruce never show up? Now, just
when we have decided to leave it before forgetfulness comes, while
we can throw off the spell long enough to see the least bit of our
mental-map – has the North played a last trump card against us?

To reach that ridge which was in view before the sun went down,
now seems the utmost in attainment.

Oh blessed reality – the spruce trees! Trees dark and straight and
sharply pointed as on calendar pictures, plain against the now steely
sky, for in their shelter the snow wraiths sink to earth and have no
more power. We enter their narrow aisles, stretch forth a hand to
touch their shaggy bark, and in touching seem again to feel the solid
earth in which they are rooted. A white moon slowly rises over the
forest of dark spires; and there is the trail, smooth, shiny, and un-
drifted. The dogs are seen ahead, picked out in light and shadow –
friendly Grey and Pishoo, Sport and Rough and Peigan, and patient
Boy – good faithful animals once more, not ghosts of the starved
North.

They move alertly, pressing their feet on the firm trail; and we
are no longer alone, for our shadows are moving alongside like the
disembodied things that *we* were, back in that grey haze. The whine
of the toboggan and the creak of our good hickory sound friendly
and strong and comforting.

Far enough for today, boys. We are within the edge of the map.
Camp is soon made, dry wood gathered. And now the ruddy blaze
performs its two-fold task – to drive back the cheated shadows and to
start the bannock abrowning. The dogs crunch their frozen supper.
Hot tea sends up its steaming freshness.

And now, full-fed and safe at last, we can enjoy to the full the great gift of the golden South to the silver North – tobacco – sweet as a ham in a southern oven, fragrant as magnolia.

Well, this is good-bye to the North, we think. Almost regretfully the scene is memorized; the blazing fire lighting up the base of the trees; the good dogs, each curled in his bed; the stout toboggan lying on its side with the firelight playing on the lion's head decorating its curved front – it is a good craft that bears this well-known trademark from Le Pas.

Yes, we must remember scenes like this so that we can describe them to the new friends which we are going to make Outside.

And so to sleep.

A dog rattles a chain; two Canada jays eye the camp for tidbits. Another day has come. In the south-east a red glow grows and grows, and soon the first rays of the sun set afire the tipmost branches of the tallest spruce, putting to shame the glow of last night's fire, now shrunken to grey ashes from which a faint blue wisp still curls upward. We see all the dear familiar things of the forest – the green trees, their lower limbs hung with moss like old men's beards; shoots of red-barked willow sprouting forth from the snow. A squirrel is chattering, the jays are gliding in their silent flight, while a woodpecker – an arctic three-toed – tap-taps his searching way towards the sun.

Our heart leaps with the still beauty of it all – dawn in the wilderness! Clean sweet air, the chuckling notes of the birds. No slaves of the North are we, but free as the lynx padding his hunting trails through the eternal woods. Free to eat and breathe and sleep and travel where we may. Free to go south, to the railroads, to the far Orient or the distant palm shores – free to take the trail or not.

The map is very plain now, but the post is as far as we need to go; for tobacco and tea and flour must be replenished.

Yes, we are as free as the smoke from the moss-chinked cabin to which we shall return ere the break-up wipes away the trails we love so well.

On a night in another winter I snowshoed through a world of sparkling snow. The sky was deep purple-blue, every star like gold. Overhead rode the November moon.

Before me stretched a bush road long forgotten by man, showing only as a break in the skyline of spruce and birch. The small encroaching growth of brush had been so closely browsed by moose that but a few tough twigs pierced the white covering. Across this trail the forms of flanking trees lay etched in deepest shadow.

Only the swish of snowshoes broke the crisp silence. A spruce hen, disturbed by my approach, whirred from its sleep in the snow and disappeared on stiff wings into the shadows.

Around me was the mystery of the moonlit yet shadowy forest. On either hand the evergreens stood straight and patient, content to bear on their limbs the burden of snow which weighed them down.

Behind me the patterns of my snowshoes lay like the links of a chain binding me to the world of music and lamplight. In the unmarked wilderness there is no direction; left or right, forward or back, are all the same. But the faintest trail stumbled upon while roaming the forest instantly recalls one to an orderly world and establishes a definite point from which to survey the surrounding woods; and suddenly, that which but a few moments since was a natural environment appears impenetrable and mysterious.

Here in this silent, windless place, I thought, time seems to be standing still. After all, is not time our most exacting taskmaster, the ruthless robber of our years, whose will is law? For what the hurrying and scurrying of city dwellers but to serve this monster?

In the haunts of men, clocks, railway time-tables, appointment books – a thousand things in a thousand ways – remind us of the saying that time is money. We needs must check it by our timepieces; we must strive to hasten its passing in expectation of some business fulfilment. In the race for money to buy happiness, time – which is money – robs us not only of our youth, our days, our years, but robs us also of the opportunities to attain the greater happiness we cannot buy – a contented mind in tune with nature.

In tune with nature.

Here in the forest all things are rightly ordered, contented, patient. The rotten trees of years gone by, long since fallen before the wind, lie, as they were created to lie, among their living fellows, yielding to them the richness of their woods.

The living trees – beautiful trees, thousands of them never to be seen by men – stand each in its appointed place, each fulfilling the purpose for which it sprung up; waiting patiently for spring to be followed by summer and summer by another winter.

How few of us fulfil our destiny as do these trees and the wild things of the prairies and woods!

So I thought, as I stood silently on my snowshoes in the crisp night.

I turned homeward; and the forest stood just as it had stood before I went for my walk, and would stand always; but I had received its message.

The whip of the blizzard, the creak of saddle-leather, the grating of a canoe keel, all strike a chord and bear a message. It may be a grey message of death in the wilderness. It may be a message to conquer and attain. It may be a message of love, waking the heart as a pony's hooves waken the grass birds.

But the message of the silent places is the key to a proper understanding of all the others. Listening to it, we realize that only in our own minds are things not right, well ordered, and as they should be; and if we can but absorb the atmosphere of orderliness and patience with which we are surrounded, we shall come to find that in the Creator's scheme, as nowhere else, stand the two words – Faith and Hope.

This was good-bye to the woods – but I knew I should see them again.

The war drums were throbbing again across the water; even here in the wilderness their echoes penetrated.

The campfire was cold.

The trail was before me.

Divine Image

IRVING LAYTON

Swiftly darting in the setting light,
The doomed sparrow feels the falcon's wings.
How beautiful are they both in flight.

The Lonely Land

A. J. M. SMITH

Cedar and jagged fir
uplift sharp barbs
against the grey
and cloud-piled sky;
and in the bay
blown spume and windrift
and thin, bitter spray
snap
at the whirling sky;
and the pine trees
lean one way.

A wild duck calls
to her mate,
and the ragged
and passionate tones
stagger and fall,
and recover,
and stagger and fall,
on these stones –
are lost
in the lapping of water
on smooth, flat stones.

This is a beauty
of dissonance,
this resonance
of stony strand,
this smoky cry
curled over a black pine
like a broken
and wind-battered branch
when the wind
bends the tops of the pines

and curdles the sky
from the north.

This is the beauty
of strength
broken by strength
and still strong.

Three

Beardusky Woods:
The Wilderness as Adversary

INTRODUCTION

To the pioneer, struggling to gain a tenuous foothold in northern North America, the Canadian wilderness was an enemy that had to be conquered. Immense, inscrutable, overpowering, it crowded up to the edge of every little clearing. To a sparse population of Indians, it was home. Transient, inured to hardship, they had, over the centuries, accommodated themselves of necessity to the ways of the wilderness. Fishing, hunting, gathering berries and wild rice, in most cases they moved their lodges from place to place in a constant search for food. While they sometimes starved to death in winter, their knowledge of and relationship to the wilderness was intimate. They were a part of it.

The newly-arrived European did not share this organic relationship to the environment. His standards of comfort, his static life, his economy demanded that the wilderness be pushed back, altered, subdued. Essentially, it was his enemy. A few of the wilder spirits, such as Etienne Brulé, came close to emulating the Indian's life style, but even the ordinary fur trader carried food and material from the settlements on his journeys into the *pays sauvage,* went to ground at a fixed post during the winter, and, of course, set out to virtually exterminate the fur-bearing animals – something the Indian had never done prior to European contact.

It was perhaps the pioneer farmer, however, who most clearly viewed the wilderness as enemy. So it is that Oliver Goldsmith (1794-1861) writes of the discomfort, danger, and horror experienced by those who settled amid the "deep solitudes" and "gloomy shades" of the wilderness. Charles G. D. Roberts echoes the sentiment in prose as he writes of the fearsome menace of the panther. Given such sylvan hostility, the axe and rifle became the appropriate symbols of those who stayed and fought.

The pioneer's assault on the forest, his combative stance, his fear of and antipathy toward the wild are easily understood. But such attitudes have by no means been confined to the early settler or pioneer poet. Even now, after so much of the wilderness has been subjugated, similar attitudes persist. They are implicit in the exaggerated exploitive thrust of some who would harness, tame, harvest, or "improve" everything that is free, wild, and unmanipulated. We see them in many who still equate "wilderness" with "wasteland." They are sometimes evident in the sport hunter, the fish hog, the strip-miner, the boomers of the Gross National Product, and those who insist that parks be characterized by roads, parking lots, hot and cold running water, and indoor amusements. The same compulsion to manipulate or dominate is there, and fear and distaste often seem to be just below the surface.

The pioneer, the Arctic traveller, the lonely trapper – all had justifiable grounds for fear. Even the Indian felt it, as we can see in the Windigo stories. Recently, however, fear and antipathy toward the wilderness have found fertile soil in the conditions of modern, urban, technological life. Many Canadians have grown up in large cities where they have been almost totally insulated against the non-human world. They know little of it and consequently find it alien and fearful. For them, the sky, unfragmented by buildings, may be too big; the water, outside the bathtub or swimming pool, too uncertain; animals of a non-domestic variety, too fierce and free. The harmless spider on the wall is cause for alarm, as is the nocturnal rustling of a woodland mouse. Even natural scenery, so far removed from the concrete angularity of the city, may seem alien and ugly.

It is this peculiarly modern type of alienation that informs John Newlove's "In the Forest," and prompts Ian Young to ask "Have I been too long in cities / that I have such fear / of the landscape?" It is of our time, whereas Wallace Stegner's "Carrion Spring" deals with the prairie frontier during the opening years of this century. Whatever the time and place, we see here the wilderness as adversary – challenging, oppressive, fearful, alien, and sometimes lethal.

From

The Rising Village

OLIVER GOLDSMITH

What noble courage must their hearts have fired,
How great the ardour which their souls inspired,
Who, leaving far behind their native plain,
Have sought a home beyond the western main;
And braved the terrors of the stormy seas,
In search of wealth, of freedom, and of ease!
Oh! none can tell but they who sadly share
The bosom's anguish, and its wild despair,
What dire distress awaits the hardy bands
That venture first on bleak and desert lands;
How great the pain, the danger, and the toil
Which mark the first rude culture of the soil.
When, looking round, the lonely settler sees
His home amid a wilderness of trees:
How sinks his heart in those deep solitudes,
Where not a voice upon his ear intrudes;
Where solemn silence all the waste pervades,
Heightening the horror of its gloomy shades.

Erosion

E. J. PRATT

It took the sea a thousand years,
A thousand years to trace
The granite features of this cliff,
In crag and scarp and base.

It took the sea an hour one night,
An hour of storm to place
The sculpture of these granite seams
Upon a woman's face.

Do Seek Their Meat From God

CHARLES G. D. ROBERTS

One side of the ravine was in darkness. The darkness was soft and rich, suggesting thick foliage. Along the crest of the slope tree-tops came into view – great pines and hemlocks of the ancient unviolated forest – revealed against the orange disk of a full moon just rising. The low rays slanting through the moveless tops lit strangely the upper portion of the opposite steep – the western wall of the ravine, barren, unlike its fellow, bossed with great rocky projections and harsh with stunted junipers. Out of the sluggish dark that lay along the ravine as in a trough rose the brawl of a swollen, obstructed stream.

Out of a shadowy hollow behind a long white rock, on the lower edge of that part of the steep which lay in the moonlight, came softly a great panther. In common daylight his coat would have shown a warm fulvous hue, but in the elvish decolourizing rays of that half-hidden moon he seemed to wear a sort of spectral gray. He lifted his smooth round head to gaze on the increasing flame, which presently he greeted with a shrill cry. That terrible cry, at once plaintive and menacing, with an undertone like the fierce protestations of a saw beneath the file, was a summons to his mate, telling her that the hour had come when they should seek their prey. From the lair behind the rock, where the cubs were being suckled by their dam, came no immediate answer. Only a pair of crows, that had their nest in a giant fir-tree across the gulf, woke up and croaked harshly their indignation. These three summers past they had built in the same spot, and had been nightly awakened to vent the same rasping complaints.

The panther walked restlessly up and down, half a score of paces each way, along the edge of the shadow, keeping his wide-open green eyes upon the rising light. His short, muscular tail twitched impatiently, but he made no sound. Soon the breadth of confused brightness had spread itself farther down the steep, disclosing the foot of the white rock, and the bones and antlers of a deer which had been dragged thither and devoured.

By this time the cubs had made their meal, and their dam was ready for such enterprise as must be accomplished ere her own hunger, now grown savage, could hope to be assuaged. She glided supply forth into the glimmer, raised her head, and screamed at the moon in a voice as terrible as her mate's. Again the crows stirred, croaking harshly; and the two beasts, noiselessly mounting the steep, stole into the shadows of the forest that clothed the high plateau.

The panthers were fierce with hunger. These two days past their hunting had been well-nigh fruitless. What scant prey they had slain had for the most part been devoured by the female; for had she not those small blind cubs at home to nourish, who soon must suffer at any lack of hers? The settlements of late had been making great inroads on the world of ancient forest, driving before them the deer and smaller game. Hence the sharp hunger of the panther parents, and hence it came that on this night they hunted together. They purposed to steal upon the settlements in their sleep, and take tribute of the enemies' flocks. Through the dark of the thick woods, here and there pierced by the moonlight, they moved swiftly and silently. Now and again a dry twig would snap beneath the discreet and padded footfalls. Now and again, as they rustled some low tree, a peewee or a nuthatch would give a startled chirp. For an hour the noiseless journeying continued, and ever and anon the two gray sinuous shapes would come for a moment into the view of the now well-risen moon. Suddenly there fell upon their ears, far off and faint, but clearly defined against the vast stillness of the Northern forest, a sound which made those stealthy hunters pause and lift their heads. It was the voice of a child crying – crying long and loud, hopelessly, as if there were no one to comfort it. The panthers turned aside from their former course and glided toward the sound. They were not yet come to the outskirts of the settlement, but they knew of a solitary cabin lying in the thick of the woods a mile and more from the nearest neighbour. Thither they bent their way, fired with fierce hope. Soon would they break their bitter fast.

Up to noon of the previous day the lonely cabin had been occupied. Then its owner, a shiftless fellow, who spent his days for the most part at the corner tavern three miles distant, had suddenly grown disgusted with a land wherein one must work to live, and had betaken himself with his seven-year-old boy to seek some more indolent clime. During the long lonely days when his father was away at the tavern the little boy had been wont to visit the house of the next neighbour, to play with a child of some five summers, who had no other playmate. The next neighbour was a prosperous pioneer, being master of a substantial frame-house in the midst of a large and well-tilled clearing. At times, though rarely, because it was forbidden, the younger child would make his way by a rough wood road to visit his poor little disreputable playmate. At length it had appeared that the five-year-old was learning unsavoury language from the elder boy, who rarely had an opportunity of hearing speech more desirable. To the bitter grief of both children, the companionship had at length been stopped by unalterable decree of the master of the frame-house.

Hence it had come to pass that the little boy was unaware of his comrade's departure. Yielding at last to an eager longing for that comrade, he had stolen away late in the afternoon, traversed with endless misgivings the lonely stretch of wood road, and reached the cabin, only to find it empty. The door, on its leather hinges, swung idly open. The one room had been stripped of its few poor furnishings. After looking in the rickety shed, whence darted two wild and hawklike chickens, the child had seated himself on the hacked threshold, and sobbed passionately with a grief that he did not fully comprehend. Then seeing the shadows lengthen across the tiny clearing, he had grown afraid to start for home. As the dusk gathered, he had crept trembling into the cabin, whose door would not stay shut. When it grew quite dark, he crouched in the inmost corner of the room, desperate with fear and loneliness, and lifted up his voice piteously. From time to time his lamentations would be choked by sobs or he would grow breathless, and in the terrifying silence would listen hard to hear if anyone or anything were coming. Then again would the shrill childish wailings arise, startling the unexpectant night and piercing the forest depths, even to the ears of those great beasts which had set forth to seek their meat from God.

The lonely cabin stood some distance, perhaps a quarter of a mile, back from the highway connecting the settlements. Along this main road a man was plodding wearily. All day he had been walking, and now as he neared home his steps began to quicken with anticipation of rest. Over his shoulder projected a double-barrelled fowling-piece, from which was slung a bundle of such necessities as he had purchased in town that morning. It was the prosperous settler, the master of the frame-house. His mare being with foal, he had chosen to make the tedious journey on foot.

The settler passed the mouth of the wood road leading to the cabin. He had gone perhaps a furlong beyond, when his ears were startled by the sound of a child crying in the woods. He stopped, lowered his burden to the road, and stood straining ears and eyes in the direction of the sound. It was just at this time that the two panthers also stopped and lifted their heads to listen. Their ears were keener than those of the man, and the sound had reached them at a greater distance.

Presently the settler realized whence the cries were coming. He called to mind the cabin, but he did not know the cabin's owner had departed. He cherished a hearty contempt for the drunken squatter; and on the drunken squatter's child he looked with small favour, especially as a playmate for his own boy. Nevertheless, he hesitated before resuming his journey.

"Poor little devil!" he muttered, half in wrath. "I reckon his precious father's drunk down at 'the Corners', and him crying for loneliness!" Then he reshouldered his burden and strode on doggedly.

But louder, shriller, more hopeless and more appealing, arose the childish voice, and the settler paused again, irresolute and with deepening indignation. In his fancy he saw the steaming supper his wife would have awaiting him. He loathed the thought of retracing his steps, and then stumbling a quarter of a mile through the stumps and bog of the wood road. He was footsore as well as hungry, and he cursed the vagabond squatter with serious emphasis; but in that wailing was a terror which would not let him go on. He thought of his own little one left in such a position, and straightaway his heart melted. He turned, dropped his bundle behind some bushes, grasped his gun, and made speed back for the cabin.

"Who knows," he said to himself, "but that drunken idiot has left his youngster without a bite to eat in the whole miserable shanty? Or maybe he's locked out, and the poor little beggar's half scared to death. Sounds as if he was scared"; and at this thought the settler quickened his pace.

As the hungry panthers drew near the cabin and the cries of the lonely child grew clearer, they hastened their steps, and their eyes opened to a wider circle, flaming with a greener fire. It would be thoughtless superstition to say the beasts were cruel. They were simply keen with hunger and alive with the eager passion of the chase. They were not ferocious with any anticipation of battle, for they knew the voice was the voice of a child, and something in the voice told them that the child was solitary. Theirs was no hideous or unnatural rage, as it is the custom to describe it. They were but seeking with the strength, the cunning, the deadly swiftness given them to that end, the food convenient for them. On their success in accomplishing that for which nature had so exquisitely designed them depended not only their own but the lives of their blind and helpless young, now whimpering in the cave on the slope of the moonlit ravine. They crept through a wet alder thicket, bounded lightly over the ragged brush fence, and paused to reconnoitre on the edge of the clearing in the full glare of the moon. At the same moment the settler emerged from the darkness of the wood road on the opposite side of the clearing. He saw the two great beasts, heads down and snouts thrust forward, gliding toward the open cabin door.

For a few moments the child had been silent. Now his voice rose again in pitful appeal, a very ecstasy of loneliness and terror. There was a note in the cry that shook the settler's soul. He had a vision of his own boy, at home with his mother, safeguarded from even the thought of peril. And here was this little one left to the wild beasts! "Thank God! Thank God I came!" murmured the settler, as he dropped on one knee to take a surer aim. There was a loud report (not the sharp crack of a rifle), and the female panther, shot through the loins, fell in a heap, snarling furiously and striking with her forepaws.

The male walked around her in fierce and anxious amazement. As the smoke lifted he discerned the settler kneeling for a second shot. With a high screech of fury, the lithe brute sprang upon his enemy, taking a bullet full in his chest without seeming to know he was hit. Ere the man could slip in another cartridge the beast was upon him, bearing him to the ground and fixing his keen fangs in his shoulder. Without a word, the man set his strong fingers desperately into the brute's throat, wrenched himself partly free, and was struggling to rise when the panther's body collapsed upon him all at once, a dead weight which he easily flung aside. The bullet had done its work just in time.

Quivering from the swift and dreadful contest, bleeding profusely from his mangled shoulder, the settler stepped up to the cabin door and peered in. He heard sobs in the darkness.

"Don't be scared, sonny," he said in a reassuring voice. "I'm going to take you home along with me. Poor little lad, *I'll* look after you if folks that ought to don't."

Out of the corner came a shout of delight, in a voice which made the settler's heart stand still. "Daddy, daddy," it said, "I knew you'd come. I was so frightened when it got dark!" And a little figure launched itself into the settler's arms and clung to him trembling. The man sat down on the threshold and strained the child to his breast. He remembered how near he had been to disregarding the far-off cries, and great beads of sweat broke out upon his forehead.

Not many weeks afterwards the settler was following the fresh trail of a bear which had killed his sheep. The trail led him at last along the slope of a deep ravine, from whose bottom came the brawl of a swollen and obstructed stream. In the ravine he found a shallow cave, behind a great white rock. The cave was plainly a wild beast's lair, and he entered circumspectly. There were bones scattered about, and on some dry herbage in the deepest corner of the den he found the dead bodies, now rapidly decaying, of two small panther cubs.

Temagami

ARCHIBALD LAMPMAN

Far in the grim Northwest beyond the lines
That turn the rivers eastward to the sea,
Set with a thousand islands, crowned with pines,
Lies the deep water, wild Temagami:
Wild for the hunter's roving, and the use
Of trappers in its dark and trackless vales,
Wild with the trampling of the giant moose,
And the weird magic of old Indian tales.
All day with steady paddles toward the west
Our heavy-laden long canoe we pressed:
All day we saw the thunder-travelled sky
Purpled with storm in many a trailing tress,
And saw at eve the broken sunset die
In crimson on the silent wilderness.

How One Winter Came in the Lake Region

WILFRED CAMPBELL

For weeks and weeks the autumn world stood still,
   Clothed in the shadow of a smoky haze;
The fields were dead, the wind had lost its will,
And all the lands were hushed by wood and hill,
   In those grey, withered days.

Behind a mist the blear sun rose and set,
   At night the moon would nestle in a cloud;
The fisherman, a ghost, did cast his net;
The lake its shores forgot to chafe and fret,
   And hushed its caverns loud.

Far in the smoky woods the birds were mute,
   Save that from blackened tree a jay would scream,
Or far in swamps the lizard's lonesome lute
Would pipe in thirst, or by some gnarlèd root
   The tree-toad trilled his dream.

Carrion Spring

WALLACE STEGNER

Often in Saskatchewan a man awakens on a winter night hearing a great wind, and his heart sinks at the prospect of more shut-in days, more cold, difficulty, discomfort, and danger. But one time in ten, something keeps him from burrowing back under his blankets, something keeps him suspiciously on his elbow, straining his ears for the sounds of hope. Repudiating his hope even while he indulges it, he may leave the warmth of bed and go to the door, bracing himself for the needles of thirty below. And one time in ten, when he opens door and storm door against the grab and bluster of the wind, the air rushes in his face as warm as milk, all but smelling of orange blossoms, and he dances a caper on his cold floor and goes back to bed knowing that in the two or three days that the chinook blows it will gulp all the snow except the heaviest drifts and leave the prairie dry enough to sit down on. Dozing off, he hears the crescendo of drip, the slump of heavied snow on the roof, the crash of loosened icicles under the eaves.

Several times every winter the harsh Saskatchewan weather is relieved by that beautiful mild wind that can raise the temperature in a half hour from zero to fifty above. It is the chinook that makes Saskatchewan bearable in winter, the chinook that clears the prairies periodically and allows cattle to feed. It was a chinook that the cattle outfits on the Whitemud waited for in vain during the winter of 1906-07.

In vain, or nearly. November, December, January, brought them only blizzards, cold snaps, freezing fogs, snow. A forkful at a time, the T-Down boys fed the hay they had stacked at Bates and Stonepile. They broke down their ponies trying to drag clear patches of hillside where the cattle could feed, only to see new snow cover their work, or the cattle flinching back from the wind to gnaw willows and starve in the snowy bottoms. Not until the end of January did the punchers at Bates and Stonepile feel on their faces that soft and strengthening blast from the southwest. They went to bed drunk on it, assured that though hundreds of cattle were dead along the river, something could be saved. When they awoke in the morning the air was still, the abortive chinook had died, the snow that had been thawed mushy was frozen hard again, the prairie was sheathed in four inches of solid ice, and cattle that had lain down in the snow were frozen in, unable to move. They dragged free as many as they could reach, threw open the gates on whatever scraps of hay were left, and retreated to the ranch, which was hoarding its few stacks for the ultimate emergency. The emergency arrived, or rather continued. Storm and cold through February; then a chinook that gave the scarecrow survivors a few days of relief; then more blizzards and cold that locked them in ice until May. During the last six weeks they could do nothing but skin out the dead.

Their story goes on too long; it is nothing but unrelieved hardship, failure, death, gloom. Even the wolfer Schulz, who had no concern about cattle, shared the ruin of that winter. The wolves that he would ordinarily have run down with his hounds on the flats were all down in the deep snow of the bottoms, where the cattle were and where their big pads would let them run while a hound floundered. They sat just out of rifle range and laughed; they were so well fed and so smart they never went near the traps Schulz set. In February, furious and frustrated, without a single wolf to show for months of effort, Schulz locked up his hounds in the Stonepile stable and poisoned a dozen carcasses up and down the river. But his great staghound, Puma, was too much of a pet to stay locked in. He broke out one afternoon when Schultz was gone, followed his master's tracks several miles upriver, stopped on the way to feed on one of the poisoned carcasses, and came upon Schulz in the middle of a white-out, a dense freezing fog, where the wolfer had built a fire on the ice to keep warm until he could get his bearings. For an hour or two the hound padded back and forth with the man as he walked to keep from freezing around the little fire of willows. Then the dog began acting strange, rolling, gaping; and at some moment during the night, lost in the whiteness of that lost river, sick and furious at his winter's failure, the wolfer looked up and saw the hound coming for him. He jumped to his gun, stuck butt down in the snow, and killed the dog with one shot in the mouth.

No one saw Schulz again. He simply vanished, disappointed or crazy or fed up. Several months later the T-Down boys, conducting their pitiful spring roundup of survivors, heard how he drowned swimming his horse across the Milk River in the spring break-up.

A casualty, a wild man defeated by the wild. But the civilized did no better. And especially Molly Henry, who on her wedding day in late October had said goodby to whatever civilization was offered by her home town of Malta, Montana, and who except for the Christmas blowout had enjoyed neither fun nor the company of another woman since. She was a tough and competent little body; she believed in work as a cure for the doldrums, and she had married with the full intention of being a good wife to a cattleman. Among the things she and Ray had talked about on their buckboard honeymoon were the future settlement of that country and the opportunities open to the young and industrious.

But six months is a long time to be shut in, too long a stretch of desperate work and hardship and shortages and unmitigated failure. The brief dream of Indian Summer would not have lasted through all that disastrous winter. In spite of the work she used as therapy, hope would have festered in her. When the long agony finally broke, and the thaw began, and the sun that had seemed gone forever came back in spells of unbelievable warmth, she would have greeted release with a tight mouth, determined to take her man and her marriage back where there was a chance for both.

The moment she came to the door she could smell it, not really rotten and not coming from any particular direction, but sweetish, faintly sickening, sourceless, filling the whole air the way a river's water can taste of weeds – the carrion smell of a whole country breathing out in the first warmth across hundreds of square miles.

Three days of chinook had uncovered everything that had been under snow since November. The yard lay discolored and ugly, gray ashpile, rusted cans, spilled lignite, bones. The clinkers that had given them winter footing to privy and stable lay in raised gray wavers across the mud; the strung lariats they had used for lifelines in blizzardy weather had dried out and sagged to the ground. Muck was knee deep down in the corrals by the sod-roofed stable, the whitewashed logs were yellowed at the corners from dogs lifting their legs against them. Sunken drifts around the hay yard were a reminder of how many times the boys had had to shovel out there to keep the calves from walking into the stacks across the top of them. Across the wan and dishevelled yard the willows were bare, and beyond them the flood-plain hill was brown. The sky was roiled with gray cloud.

Matted, filthy, lifeless, littered, the place of her winter imprisonment was exposed, ugly enough to put gooseflesh up her backbone, and with the carrion smell over all of it. It was like a bad and disgusting wound, infected wire cut or proud flesh or the gangrene of frostbite, with the bandage off. With her packed trunk and her telescope bag and two loaded grain sacks behind her, she stood in the door waiting for Ray to come with the buckboard, and she was sick to be gone. . . .

She saw Ray slumping, glooming down from the buckboard seat

with the reins wrapped around one gloved hand. Dude and Dinger were hipshot in the harness. As Rusty and Little Horn gave Molly a hand up to climb the wheel, Dude raised his tail and dropped an oaty bundle of dung on the singletree, but she did not even bother to make a face or say something provoked and joking. She was watching Ray, looking right into his gray eyes and his somber dark face and seeing all at once what the winter of disaster had done to him. His cheek, like Ed's and Rusty's, was puckered with frost scars; frost had nibbled at the lobes of his ears; she could see the strain of bone-cracking labor, the bitterness of failure, in the lines from his nose to the corners of his mouth. Making room for her, he did not smile. With her back momentarily to the others, speaking only for him, she said through her tight teeth, "Let's git!"

Promptly – he was always prompt and ready – he plucked whip from whipsocket. The tip snapped on Dinger's haunch, the lurch of the buggy threw her so that she could cling and not have to turn to reveal her face. "Goodbye!" she cried, more into the collar of her mackinaw than to them, throwing the words over her shoulder like a flower or a coin, and tossed her left hand in the air and shook it. The single burst of their voices chopped off into silence. She heard only the grate of the tires in gravel; beside her the wheel poured yellow drip. She concentrated on it, fighting her lips that wanted to blubber. . . .

Beside her Ray was silent. The horses were trotting now in the soft sand of the patrol trail. On both sides the willows were gnawed down to stubs, broken and mouthed and gummed off by starving cattle. There was floodwater in the low spots, and the sound of running water under the drifts of every side coulee.

Once Ray said, "Harry Willis says a railroad survey's coming right up the Whitemud valley this summer. S'pose that'll mean homesteaders in here, maybe a town."

"I s'pose."

"Make it a little easier when you run out of prunes, if there was a store at Whitemud."

"Well," she said, "we won't be here to run out," and then immediately, as she caught a whiff that gagged her, "Pee-you! Hurry up!"

Ray did not touch up the team. "What for?" he said. "To get to the next one quicker?"

She appraised the surliness of his voice, and judged that some of it was general disgust and some of it was aimed at her. But what did he want? Every time she made a suggestion of some outfit around Malta or Chinook where he might get a job he humped his back and looked inpenetrable. What *did* he want? To come back here and take another licking? When there wasn't even a cattle outfit left, except maybe the little ones like the Z-X and the Lazy-S? And where one winter could kill you, as it had just killed the T-Down? She felt like yelling at him, "Look at your face. Look at your hands – you can't open them even halfway, for calluses. For what? Maybe three thousand cattle left out of ten thousand, and them skin and bone. Why wouldn't I be glad to get out? Who *cares* if there's a store at Whitemud? You're just like an old bulldog with his teeth clinched in somebody's behind, and it'll take a pry-bar to make you unclinch!" She said nothing; she forced herself to breathe evenly the tainted air. . . .

A little later, accosted by a stench so overpowering that she breathed it in deeply as if to sample the worst, she looked to the left and saw a longhorn, its belly blown up ready to pop, hanging by neck and horns from a tight clump of alder and black birch where the snow had left him. She saw the wind make catspaws in the heavy winter hair.

"Jesus," Ray said, "when you find 'em in *trees!*"

His boots, worn and whitened by many wettings, were braced against the dash. From the corner of her eye Molly could see his glove, its wrist-lace open. His wrist looked as wide as a double-tree, the sleeve of his Levi jacket was tight with forearm. The very sight of his strength made her hate the tone of defeat and outrage in his voice. Yet she appraised the tone cunningly, for she did not want him somehow butting his bullheaded way back into it. There were better things they could do than break their backs and hearts in a hopeless country a hundred miles from anywhere. . . .

A high, sharp whicker came downwind. The team chuckled and surged into their collars. Looking ahead, she saw a horse – picketed or hobbled – and a man who leaned on something – rifle? – watching them. "Young Schulz," Ray said, and then here came the dogs, four big bony hounds. The team began to dance. Ray held them in tight and whistled the buggywhip in the air when the hounds got too close.

Young Schulz, Molly saw as they got closer, was leaning on a shovel, not a rifle. He had dug a trench two or three feet deep and ten or twelve long. He dragged a bare forearm across his forehead under a muskrat cap: a sullen-faced boy with eyes like dirty ice. She supposed he had been living all alone since his father had disappeared. Somehow he made her want to turn her lips inside out. A wild man, worse than an Indian. She had not liked his father and she did not like him.

The hounds below her were sniffing at the wheels and testing the air up in her direction, wagging slow tails. "What've you got, wolves?" Ray asked.

"Coyotes."

"Old ones down there?"

"One, anyway. Chased her in."

"Find any escape holes?"

"One. Plugged it."

"You get 'em the hard way," Ray said. "How've you been doing on wolves?"

The boy said a hard four-letter word, slanted his eyes sideward at Molly in something less than apology – acknowledgment, maybe. "The dogs ain't worth a damn without Puma to kill for 'em. Since he got killed they just catch up with a wolf and run alongside him. I dug out a couple dens."

With his thumb and finger he worked at a pimple under his jaw. The soft wind blew over them, the taint of carrion only a suspicion, perhaps imaginary. The roily sky had begun to break up in patches of blue. Beside her Molly felt the solid bump of Ray's shoulder as he twisted to cast a weather eye upward. "Going to be a real spring day," he said. To young Schulz he said, "How far in that burrow go, d'you s'pose?"

"Wouldn't ordinarily go more'n twenty feet or so."

"Need any help diggin'?"

The Schulz boy spat. "Never turn it down."

"Ray . . ." Molly said. But she stopped when she saw his face.

"Been a long time since I helped dig out a coyote," he said. He watched her as if waiting for a reaction. "Been a long time since I did anything for *fun*."

"Oh, go ahead!" she said. "Long as we don't miss that train."

"I guess we can make Maple Creek by noon tomorrow. And you ain't in such a hurry you have to be there sooner, are you?"

She had never heard so much edge in his voice. He looked at her as if he hated her. She turned so as to keep the Schulz boy from seeing her face, and for just a second she and Ray were all alone up there, eye to eye. She laid a hand on his knee. "I don't know what it is," she said. "Honestly I don't. But you better work it off."

Young Schulz went back to his digging while Ray unhitched and looped the tugs and tied the horses to the wheels. Then Ray took the shovel and began to fill the air with clods. He moved more dirt than the Fresno scrapers she had seen grading the railroad back home; he worked as if exercising his muscles after a long layoff, as if spring had fired him up and set him to running. The soil was sandy and came out in clean brown shovelfuls. The hounds lay back out of range and watched. Ray did not look toward Molly, or say anything to Schulz. He just moved dirt as if dirt was his worst enemy. After a few minutes Molly pulled the buffalo robe out of the buckboard and spread it on the drying prairie. By that time it was getting close to noon. The sun was full out; she felt it warm on her face and hands.

The coyote hole ran along about three feet underground. From where she sat she could look right up the trench, and see the black opening at the bottom when the shovel broke into it. She could imagine the coyotes crammed back at the end of their burrow, hearing the noises and seeing the growing light as their death dug toward them, and no way out, nothing to do but wait.

Young Schulz took the shovel and Ray stood out of the trench, blowing. The violent work seemed to have made him more cheerful. He said to Schulz, when the boy stooped and reached a gloved hand up the hole, "She comes out of there in a hurry she'll run right up your sleeve."

Schulz grunted and resumed his digging. The untroubled sun went over, hanging almost overhead, and an untroubled wind stirred the old grass. Over where the last terrace of the floodplain rolled up to the prairie the first gopher of the season sat up and looked them over. A dog moved, and he disappeared with a flirt of his tail. Ray was rolling up his sleeves, whistling loosely between his teeth. His forearms were white, his hands blackened and cracked as the charred ends of sticks. His eyes touched her – speculatively, she thought. She smiled, making a forgiving, kissing motion of her mouth, but all he did in reply was work his eyebrows, and she could not tell what he was thinking.

Young Schulz was poking up the hole with the shovel handle. Crouching in the trench in his muskrat cap, he looked like some digging animal; she half expected him to put his nose into the hole and sniff and then start throwing dirt out between his hind legs.

Then in a single convulsion of movement Schulz rolled sideward. A naked-gummed thing of teeth and gray fur shot into sight, scrambled at the edge, and disappeared in a pinwheel of dogs. Molly leaped to the heads of the horses, rearing and wall-eyed and yanking the light buckboard sideways, and with a hand in each bridle steadied them down. Schulz, she saw, was circling the dogs with the shotgun, but the dogs had already done it for him. The roaring and snapping tailed off. Schulz kicked the dogs away and with one quick flash and circle and rip tore the scalp and ears off the coyote. It lay there wet, mauled, bloody, with its pink skull bare – a little dog brutally murdered. One of the hounds came up, sniffed with its neck stretched out, sank its teeth in the coyote's shoulder, dragged it a foot or two.

"Ray . . ." Molly said.

He did not hear her; he was blocking the burrow with the shovel blade while Schulz went over to his horse. The boy came back with a red willow stick seven or eight feet long, forked like a small slingshot at the end. Ray pulled away the shovel and Schulz twisted in the hole with the forked end of the stick. A hard grunt came out of him, and he backed up, pulling the stick from the hole. At the last moment he yanked hard, and a squirm of gray broke free and rolled and was pounced on by the hounds.

This time Ray kicked them aside. He picked up the pup by the tail, and it hung down and kicked its hind legs a little. Schulz was down again, probing the burrow, twisting, probing again, twisting hard.

Again he backed up, working the entangled pup out carefully until it was in the open, and then landing it over his head like a sucker from the river. The pup landed within three feet of the buckboard wheel, and floundered, stunned. In an instant Molly dropped down and smothered it in clothes, hands, arms. There was snarling in her very ear, she was bumped hard, she heard Ray yelling, and then he had her on her feet. From his face, she thought he was going to hit her. Against her middle, held by the scruff and grappled with the other arm, the pup snapped and slavered with needle teeth. She felt the sting of bites on her hands and wrists. The dogs ringed her, ready to jump, kept off by Ray's kicking boot.

"God a'mighty," Ray said, "you want to get yourself killed?"

"I didn't want the dogs to get him."

"No. What are you going to do with him? We'll just have to knock him in the head."

"I'm going to keep him."

"In Malta?"

"Why not?"

He let go his clutch on her arm. "He'll be a cute pup for a month and then he'll be a chicken thief and then somebody'll shoot him."

"At least he'll have a little bit of a life. Get *away*, you dirty, murdering . . . !" She cradled the thudding little body along one arm under her mackinaw, keeping her hold in the scruff with her right hand, and turned herself away from the crowding hounds. "I'm going to tame him," she said. "I don't care what you say."

"Scalp's worth three dollars," Schulz said from the edge of the ditch.

Ray kicked the dogs back. His eyes, ordinarily so cool and gray, looked hot. The digging and the excitement did not seem to have taken the edge off whatever was eating him. He said, "Look, maybe you have to go back home to your folks, but you don't have to take a menagerie along. What are you going to do with him on the train?"

But now it was out. He did blame her. "You think I'm running out on you," she said.

"I just said you can't take a menagerie back to town."

"You said *maybe* I had to go home. Where else would I go? You're going to be on roundup till July. The ranch is going to be sold. Where on earth *would* I go but home?"

"You don't have to stay. You don't have to make me go back to ridin' for some outfit for twenty a month and found."

His dark, battered, scarred face told her to be quiet. Dipping far down in the tight pocket of his Levis he brought up his snap purse and took from it three silver dollars. Young Schulz, who had been probing the den to see if anything else was there, climbed out of the ditch and took the money in his dirty chapped hand. He gave Molly one cool look with his dirty-ice eyes, scalped the dead pup, picked up shotgun and twisting-stick and shovel, tied them behind the saddle, mounted, whistled at the dogs, and with barely a nod rode off toward the northeastern flank of the Hills. The hounds fanned out ahead of him, running loose and easy. In the silence their departure left behind, a clod broke and rolled into the ditch. A gopher piped somewhere. The wind moved quiet as breathing in the grass.

Molly drew a breath that caught a little – a sigh for their quarreling, for whatever bothered him so deeply that he gloomed and grumped and asked something impossible of her – but when she spoke she spoke around it. "No thanks for your digging."

"He don't know much about living with people."

"He's like everything else in this country, wild and dirty and thankless."

In a minute she would really start feeling sorry for herself. But why not? Did it ever occur to him that since November, when they came across the prairie on their honeymoon in this same buckboard, she had seen exactly one woman, for one day and a night? Did he have any idea how she felt, a bride of three weeks, when he went out with the boys on late fall roundup and was gone ten days, through three different blizzards, while she stayed home and didn't know whether he was dead or alive?

"If you mean me," Ray said, "I may be wild and I'm probably dirty, but I ain't thankless, honey." Shamed, she opened her mouth to reply, but he was already turning away to rummage up a strap and a piece of whang leather to make a collar and leash for her pup.

"Are you hungry?" she said to his shoulders.

"Any time."

"I put up some sandwiches."

"O.K."

"Oh, Ray," she said, "let's not crab at each other! Sure I'm glad we're getting out. Is that so awful? I hate to see you killing yourself bucking this *hopeless* country. But does that mean we have to fight? I thought maybe we could have a picnic like we had coming in, back on that slough where the ducks kept coming in and landing on the ice and skidding end over end. I don't know, it don't hardly seem we've laughed since."

"Well," he said, "it ain't been much of a laughing winter, for a fact." He had cut down a cheekstrap and tied a rawhide thong to it. Carefully she brought out the pup and he buckled the collar around its neck, but when she set it on the ground it backed up to the end of the thong, cringing and showing its naked gums, so that she picked it up again and let it dig along her arm, hunting darkness under her mackinaw.

"Shall we eat here?" Ray said. "Kind of a lot of chewed-up coyote around."

"Let's go up on the bench."

"Want to tie the pup in the buckboard?"

"I'll take him. I want to get him used to me."

"O.K.," he said. "You go on. I'll tie a nosebag on these nags and bring the robe and the lunchbox.". . .

Ray brought the buffalo robe and spread it, and she sat down. One-handed because she had the thong of the leash wrapped around her palm, she doled out sandwiches and hard-boiled eggs. Ray popped a whole egg in his mouth, and chewing, pointed. "There goes the South Fork of the Swift Current, out of the slough. The one this side, that little scraggle of willows you can see, empties into the Whitemud. That slough sits right on the divide and runs both ways. You don't see that very often.". . .

He sighed. He lay back and closed his eyes. After about three minutes he said, "Boy, what a day, though. I won't get through on the patrol trail goin' back. The ice'll be breakin' up before tonight, at this rate. Did you hear it crackin' and poppin' a minute ago?"

"I didn't hear it."

"Listen."

They were still. She heard the soft wind move in the prairie wool, and beyond it, filling the background, the hushed and hollow noise of the floodwater, sigh of drowned willows, suck of whirlpools, splash and guggle as cutbanks caved, and the steady push and swash and ripple of moving water. Into the soft rush of sound came a muffled report like a tree cracking, or a shot a long way off. "Is that it?" she said. "Is that the ice letting loose?"

"Stick around till tomorrow and you'll see that whole channel full of ice."

Another shadow from one of the big flat-bottomed clouds chilled across them and passed. Ray said into the air, "Harry Willis said this railroad survey will go right through to Medicine Hat. Open up this whole country."

Now she sat very still, stroking the soft bulge of the pup through the cloth.

"Probably mean a town at Whitemud."

"You told me."

"With a store that close we couldn't get quite so snowed in as we did this winter."

Molly said nothing, because she dared not. They were a couple that, like the slough spread out northwest of them, flowed two ways, he to this wild range, she back to town and friends and family. And yet in the thaw of one bright day, their last together up here north of the Line, she teetered. She feared the softening that could start her draining toward his side.

"Molly," Ray said, and made her look at him. She saw him as the country and the winter had left him, weathered and scarred. His eyes were gray and steady, marksman's eyes.

She made a wordless sound that sounded in her own ears almost a groan. "You want awful bad to stay," she said.

His long fingers plucked a strand of grass, he bit it between his teeth, his head went slowly up and down.

"But how?" she said. "Do you want to strike the Z-X for a job, or the Lazy-S, or somebody? Do you want to open a store in Whitemud for when the railroad comes through, or what?"

"Haven't you figured that out yet?" he said. "Kept waitin' for you to see it. I want to buy the T-Down."

"You *what?*"

"I want us to buy the T-Down and make her go."

She felt that she went all to pieces. She laughed. She threw her hands around so that the pup scrambled and clawed at her side. "Ray Henry," she said, "you're crazy as a bedbug. Even if it made any sense, which it doesn't, where'd we get the money?"

"Borrow it."

"Go in debt to stay up *here?*"

"Molly," he said, and she heard the slow gather of determination in his voice, "when else could we pick up cattle for twenty dollars a head with sucking calves thrown in? When else could we get a whole ranch layout for a few hundred bucks? That Goodnight herd we were running was the best herd in Canada, maybe anywhere. This spring roundup we could take our pick of what's left, including bulls, and put our brand on 'em and turn 'em into summer range and drive everything else to Malta. We wouldn't want more than three-four hundred head. We can swing that much, and we can cut enough hay to bring that many through even a winter like this last one."

She watched him; her eyes groped and slipped. He said, "We're never goin' to have another chance like this as long as we live. This country's goin' to change; there'll be homesteaders in here soon as the railroad comes. Towns, stores, what you've been missin'. Women folks. And we can sit out here on the Whitemud with good hay land and good range and just make this God darned country holler uncle.". . .

She escaped his eyes, looked down, shifted carefully to accom-

Trapper

PHIL DESJARDINS

I'm thinking how the cabin was
the wicker chair
still soft for dozing
before the logs I left full
fired to keep the room
and bed warm as a woman.
I set my boots to dry
a cup of hot rum
and sorted the traps for one more line trip
three silver fox would bring
enough for new sled
runners and good strong harnesses
for the team.
God   the wind cuts deep tonight but
it pushes me on
across the frozen lake.

Snow Story

L. A. MACKAY

Suddenly light shone out from the dark window
and he moved more cautiously over the creaking snow.
Low boughs laid on his lips a cold finger
and sprang back, as the silence dropped, with a soft whir.
The shadow mink, by his moving step startled
skimmed like a thrown stone over the glitter. Cold
sucked at his muscles; powdery breath bit in his nostrils.
He listened at the clearing's edge. The house was still.
Deep in the cold dunes he swung north, in a cautious
drifting down, stealthily, on the blind side of the house.
Unheard he hid by the chimney, crept past the corner,
and laid stiff fingers on the capped latch of the door.
Suddenly thrust. The door swung; the snow tumbled
in from the banked drift, and the swift light spread
over the level swells, blank. The new-comer
stepped stiffly into the house; and the soft air
lapped at his eyelids. The last ember shivered,
flared in the cold gust, fell. Not a spark stirred.
He closed the door, stood for a heavy instant
listening in the soft dark, then with a grunt
squirmed out of his coat, and turned towards the dead embers.
There was a gliding rustle in the frosty firs
or so he thought. But already the sharp bramble
slipped snake-toothed from the earthy edge of the hearth-sill
had trapped his ankles; the hard searching root-tip
plunged in his heart, as the fresh leaves brushed his lip.

From

Sacred Legends
of the Sandy Lake Cree

JAMES R. STEVENS

The Windigo Spirit
The dreaded windigo is the most horrible creature in the lands of
the Cree and Ojibwa Indians. Nothing strikes more terror in the
hearts of the Anishinabek than the thoughts of windigo.

The cannibalistic windigos strike from the north during the five
moons of winter and restlessly haunt our lands searching for food
as far to the south as the snow belt extends. Windigos have been
known to attack during the summer but this is very rare.

The windigo was once a normal human being but has been
possessed by a savage cannibalistic spirit. When a human is possessed
by windigo, ice forms inside the human body, hair grows profusely
from the face, arms and legs and an insatiable craving for human
flesh develops.

When the ugly creature attacks, it shows no mercy. This monster
will kill and devour its own family to try and satisfy its lust for
human flesh. The windigo is inhuman because of the powerful spirit
of cannibalism and destruction residing in its body. When a windigo
has destroyed its own people it will travel in a straight line across
the forest until it finds the next group of victims. Usually high winds
and blizzards accompany the windigo in its travels. It is said that
the scream of a windigo will paralyze a man, preventing him from
protecting himself. Sometimes an attack by a windigo can be turned
away by a powerful medicine man and this has occurred.

There is a place at Sandy Lake called Ghost Point that was
marauded and destroyed by a windigo in the old days. The remains
of the village are still there today.

The Windigo at Berens River
The mighty Berens River flows westerly from the country of the
Swampy Cree into Lake Winnipeg – Winnipeg means dirty water in
our language. In the old days the Berens River was an important
fur-trading route. Our people paddled down the river in canoes
laden with valuable furs that were traded at the Hudson's Bay post
at the mouth of the Berens.

About a hundred years ago a small camp of Indians were living near the post. One of the Indians from this camp went out trapping with his wife and children. After a few days the people in the camp heard the trapper screaming and howling in the forest. They knew from their own strange feelings that the man had turned into a windigo. One of the Indians from the camp went to the man's trap line and found the half-devoured corpses of his wife and three children. When the people heard what had occurred, they were panic stricken. It would only be a short time before the windigo would be attacking their camp and something must be done before the monster was upon them.

Meeting together in the council circle, the people chose their most powerful ma-mandowin-ninih, Rotten Log, to destroy the windigo.

"I must have a man to accompany me on this venture and he must be a man without fear," Rotten Log told the frightened people.

One man rose from the council circle after a long silence. He was a half-breed, or wessa-ko-day-wininih, who had been accepted by the people.

"I am a man without fear of man or beast," the half-breed stated softly.

The great council dispersed and the Rotten Log and the half-breed were left alone to plan the destruction of the windigo. After much discussion, they decided to capture the windigo alive.

The half-breed went around the scattered lodges of the camp and captured eight of the largest and strongest dogs that he could find and returned with them to the council circle where the ma-mandowin-ninih had constructed a huge wooden toboggan. They hitched the snarling dogs to the great sled and loaded it with lengths of thick braided ropes and other provisions for their journey.

With eight brutish dogs howling, the two brave men trekked into the frozen snow-clad forest toward the camp of the murderous windigo. The men crossed one large lake, then through a portage to the edge of a smaller lake. Here they camped because darkness began to cover the land. They built a huge fire, using eight-foot logs to feed the flames. On two sides of the roaring fire they made soft beds of green pine branches on the snow. During the night tibiki-geesis crawled across the frozen sky and the two men huddled close to the fire.

In the morning, the half-breed went out on the ice and laid a trail of branches across the lake in order to lure the windigo to their camp. When all was prepared, the two Indians sat beside the fire and waited nervously.

"Do not be afraid unless you see I have fear," Rotten Log told his partner. They threw more logs on the fire because the intense cold was making their bodies turn numb and stiff.

Then, across the lake, they saw the windigo striding boldly over the branch trail toward them. As the hairy monster approached, they noticed it had chewed off its own lips. Its face was hideous; the teeth and gums of the creature were caked with blood. The fingers of the creature were also gone; it had eaten them to satisfy an insatiable craving for flesh. The windigo sat down opposite the two stunned men at the campfire. It sat there muttering, watching the men across the roaring fire. Suddenly the creature leaped over the flames, pouncing on Rotten Log. Windigo wrestled him, trying to bite his throat, but Rotten Log called on his guardian spirit, the great turtle, mis-qua-day-sih, to help in the struggle. Mis-qua-day-sih did not fail the Indian; he gave him the supernatural power and physical strength to subdue the windigo.

The half-breed and Rotten Log tied up the windigo and rolled it on the sled. The dogs started to drag the raving windigo back to the settlement. Pulling the toboggan through the deep snow was a difficult task for the animals, because of the weight of the struggling windigo. Again the ma-mandowin-ninih called on his guardian, mis-qua-day-sib, and his sacred turtle gave him strength to shove the heavy load. The huge dogs strained in their harnesses several more times and the toboggan stopped; but each time the sacred turtle gave them the power to continue with their prisoner. Finally, they reached their camp by the Berens River with the lunatic windigo.

At the camp the people placed the captive in a large building and built a huge fire to melt the ice from his body. After several hours near the heat of the fire, the windigo finished sweating the ice from his body. Then he vomited. In front of him, in his own spew were the eyes and hair of his wife and children.

This windigo never regained normality and it died in the camp. The people there burned the corpse to destroy its windigo spirit.

To Build a Fire

JACK LONDON

Day had broken cold and grey, exceedingly cold and grey, when the man turned aside from the main Yukon trail and climbed the high earth-bank where a dim and little-travelled trail led eastward through the fat spruce timberland. It was a steep bank, and he paused for breath at the top, excusing the act to himself by looking at his watch. It was nine o'clock. There was no sun nor hint of sun, though there was not a cloud in the sky. It was a clear day, and yet there seemed an intangible pall over the face of things, a subtle gloom that made the day dark, and that was due to the absence of sun. This fact did not worry the man. He was used to the lack of sun. It had been days since he had seen the sun, and he knew that a few more days must pass before that cheerful orb, due south, would just peep above the sky-line and dip immediately from view.

The man flung a look back along the way he had come. The Yukon lay a mile wide and hidden under three feet of ice. On top of this ice were as many feet of snow. It was all pure white, rolling in gentle undulations where the ice-jams of the freeze-up had formed. North and south, as far as his eye could see, it was unbroken white, save for a dark hair-line that curved and twisted from around the spruce-covered island to the south, and that curved and twisted away into the north, where it disappeared behind another spruce-covered island. This dark hair-line was the trail – the main trail – that led south five hundred miles to the Chilcoot Pass, Dyea, and salt water; and that led north seventy miles to Dawson, and still on to the north a thousand miles to Nulato, and finally to St. Michael on Bering Sea, a thousand miles and half a thousand more.

But all this – the mysterious, far-reaching hair-line trail, the absence of sun from the sky, the tremendous cold, and the strangeness and weirdness of it all – made no impression on the man. It was not because he was long used to it. He was a newcomer in the land, a chechaquo, and this was his first winter. The trouble with him was that he was without imagination. He was quick and alert in the things of life, but only in the things, and not in the significances. Fifty degrees below zero meant eighty-odd degrees of frost. Such fact impressed him as being cold and uncomfortable, and that was all. It did not lead him to meditate upon his frailty as a creature of temperature, and upon man's frailty in general, able only to live within certain narrow limits of heat and cold; and from there on it did not lead him to the conjectural field of immortality and man's place in the universe. Fifty degrees below zero stood for a bite of frost that hurt and that must be guarded against by the use of mittens, ear-flaps, warm moccasins, and thick socks. Fifty degrees below zero was to him just precisely fifty degrees below zero. That there should be anything more to it than that was a thought that never entered his head.

As he turned to go on, he spat speculatively. There was a sharp, explosive crackle that startled him. He spat again. And again, in the air, before it could fall to the snow, the spittle crackled. He knew that at fifty below spittle crackled on the snow, but this spittle had crackled in the air. Undoubtedly it was colder than fifty below – how much colder he did not know. But the temperature did not matter. He was bound for the old claim on the left fork of Henderson Creek, where the boys were already. They had come over across the divide from the Indian Creek country, while he had come the roundabout way to take a look at the possibilities of getting out logs in the spring from the islands in the Yukon. He would be in to camp by six o'clock; a bit after dark, it was true, but the boys would be there, a fire would be going, and a hot supper would be ready. As for lunch, he pressed his hand against the protruding bundle under his jacket. It was also under his shirt, wrapped up in a handkerchief and lying against the naked skin. It was the only way to keep the biscuits from freezing. He smiled agreeably to himself as he thought of those biscuits, each cut open and sopped in bacon grease, and each enclosing a generous slice of fried bacon.

He plunged in among the big spruce trees. The trail was faint. A foot of snow had fallen since the last sled had passed over, and he was glad he was without a sled, travelling light. In fact, he carried nothing but the lunch wrapped in the handkerchief. He was surprised, however, at the cold. It certainly was cold, he concluded, as he rubbed his numb nose and cheekbones with his mittened hand. He was a warm-whiskered man, but the hair on his face did not protect the high cheek-bones and the eager nose that thrust itself aggressively into the frosty air.

At the man's heels trotted a dog, a big native husky, the proper wolf-dog, grey-coated and without any visible or temperamental difference from its brother, the wild wolf. The animal was depressed by the tremendous cold. It knew that it was no time for travelling. Its instinct told it a truer tale than was told to the man by the man's judgement. In reality, it was not merely colder than fifty below zero; it was colder than sixty below, than seventy below. It was seventy-five below zero. Since the freezing-point is thirty-two above zero, it meant that one hundred and seven degrees of frost obtained. The dog did not know anything about thermometers. Possibly in its brain there was no sharp consciousness of a condition of very cold such as was in the man's brain. But the brute had its instinct. It experienced a vague but menacing apprehension that subdued it and made it slink along at the man's heels, and that made it question eagerly every unwonted movement of the man as if expecting him to go into camp or to seek shelter somewhere and build a fire. The dog had learned fire, and it wanted fire, or else to burrow under the snow and cuddle its warmth away from the air.

The frozen moisture of its breathing had settled on its fur in a fine powder of frost, and especially were its jowls, muzzle, and eye-lashes whitened by its crystalled breath. The man's red beard and moustache were likewise frosted, but more solidly, the deposit taking the form of ice and increasing with every warm, moist breath he exhaled. Also, the man was chewing tobacco, and the muzzle of ice held his lips so rigidly that he was unable to clear his chin when he expelled the juice. The result was that a crystal beard of the colour and solidity of amber was increasing its length on his chin. If he fell down it would shatter itself, like glass, into brittle fragments. But he did not mind the appendage. It was the penalty all tobacco-chewers paid in that country, and he had been out before in two cold snaps. They had not been so cold as this, he knew, but by the spirit thermometer at Sixty Mile he knew they had been registered at fifty below and at fifty-five.

He held on through the level stretch of woods for several miles, crossed a wide flat of nigger-heads, and dropped down a bank to the frozen bed of a small stream. This was Henderson Creek, and he knew he was ten miles from the forks. He looked at his watch. It was ten o'clock. He was making four miles an hour, and he calculated that he would arrive at the forks at half-past twelve. He decided to celebrate that event by eating his lunch there.

The dog dropped in again at his heels, with a tail drooping discouragement, as the man swung along the creek-bed. The furrow of the old sled-trail was plainly visible, but a dozen inches of snow covered the marks of the last runners. In a month no man had come up or down that silent creek. The man held steadily on. He was not much given to thinking, and just then particularly he had nothing to think about save that he would eat lunch at the forks and that at six o'clock he would be in camp with the boys. There was nobody to talk to; and, had there been, speech would have been impossible because of the ice-muzzle on his mouth. So he continued monotonously to chew tobacco and to increase the length of his amber beard.

Once in a while the thought reiterated itself that it was very cold and that he had never experienced such cold. As he walked along he rubbed his cheekbones and nose with the back of his mittened hand. He did this automatically, now and again changing hands. But rub as he would, the instant he stopped his cheekbones went numb, and the following instant the end of his nose went numb. He was sure to frost his cheeks; he knew that, and experienced a pang of regret that he had not devised a nose-strap of the sort Bud wore in cold snaps. Such a strap passed across the cheeks, as well, and saved them. But it didn't matter much, after all. What were frosted cheeks? A bit painful, that was all; they were never serious.

Empty as the man's mind was of thoughts, he was keenly observant, and he noticed the changes in the creek, the curves and bends and timber-jams, and always he sharply noted where he placed his feet. Once, coming around a bend, he shied abruptly, like a startled horse, curved away from the place where he had been walking, and retreated several paces back along the trail. The creek he knew was frozen clear to the bottom – no creek could contain water in that arctic winter —but he knew also that there were springs that bubbled out from the hillsides and ran along under the snow and on top of the ice of the creek. He knew that the coldest snaps never froze these springs, and he knew likewise their danger. They were traps. They hid pools of water under the snow that might be three inches deep, or three feet. Sometimes a skin of ice half an inch thick covered them, and in turn was covered by the snow. Sometimes there were alternate layers of water and ice-skin, so that when one broke through he kept on breaking through for a while, sometimes wetting himself to the waist.

That was why he had shied in such panic. He had felt the give under his feet and heard the crackle of a snow-hidden ice-skin. And to get his feet wet in such a temperature meant trouble and danger. At the very least it meant delay, for he would be forced to stop and build a fire, and under its protection to bare his feet while he dried his socks and moccasins. He stood and studied the creek-bed and its banks, and decided that the flow of water came from the right. He reflected awhile, rubbing his nose and cheeks, then skirted to the left, stepped gingerly and testing the footing for each step. Once clear of the danger, he took a fresh chew of tobacco and swung along at his four-mile gait.

In the course of the next two hours he came upon several similar traps. Usually the snow above the hidden pools had a sunken, candied appearance that advertised the danger. Once again, however, he had a close call; and once, suspecting danger, he compelled the dog to go on in front. The dog did not want to go. It hung back until the man shoved it forward, and then it went quickly across the white, unbroken surface. Suddenly it broke through, floundered to one side, and got away to firmer footing. It had wet its forefeet and legs, and almost immediately the water that clung to it turned to ice. It made quick efforts to lick the ice off its legs, then dropped down in the snow and began to bite out the ice that had formed between the toes. This was a matter of instinct. To permit the ice to remain would mean sore feet. It did not know this. It merely obeyed the mysterious prompting that arose from the deep crypts of its being. But the man knew, having achieved a judgement on the subject, and he removed the mitten from his right hand and helped tear out the ice-particles. He did not expose his fingers more than a minute, and was astonished at the swift numbness that smote them. It certainly was cold. He pulled on the mitten hastily, and beat the hand savagely across his chest.

At twelve o'clock the day was at its brightest. Yet the sun was too far south on its winter journey to clear the horizon. The bulge of the earth intervened between it and Henderson Creek, where the man walked under a clear sky at noon and cast no shadow. At half-past twelve, to the minute, he arrived at the forks of the creek. He was pleased at the speed he had made. If he kept it up, he would certainly be with the boys by six. He unbuttoned his jacket and shirt and drew forth his lunch. The action consumed no more than a quarter of a minute, yet in that brief moment the numbness laid hold of the exposed fingers. He did not put the mitten on, but, instead, struck the fingers a dozen sharp smashes against his leg. Then he sat down on a snow-covered log to eat. The sting that followed upon the striking of his fingers against his leg ceased so quickly that he was startled. He had had no chance to take a bite of biscuit. He struck the fingers repeatedly and returned them to the mitten, baring the other hand for the purpose of eating. He tried to take a mouthful, but the ice-muzzle prevented. He had forgotten to build a fire and thaw out. He chuckled at his foolishness, and as he chuckled he noted the numbness creeping into the exposed fingers. Also, he noted that the stinging which had first come to his toes when he sat down was already passing away. He wondered whether the toes were warm or numb. He moved them inside the moccasins and decided that they were numb.

He pulled the mitten on hurriedly and stood up. He was a bit frightened. He stamped up and down until the stinging returned into the feet. It certainly was cold, was his thought. The man from Sulphur Creek had spoken the truth when telling how cold it sometimes got in the country. And he had laughed at him at the time! That showed one must not be too sure of things. There was no mistake about it, it *was* cold. He strode up and down, stamping his feet and threshing his arms, until reassured by the returning warmth. Then he got out matches and proceeded to make a fire. From the undergrowth, where high water of the previous spring had lodged a supply of seasoned twigs, he got his firewood. Working carefully from a small beginning, he soon had a roaring fire, over which he thawed the ice from his face and in the protection of which he ate his biscuits. For the moment the cold of space was outwitted. The dog took satisfaction in the fire, stretching out close enough for warmth and far enough away to escape being singed.

When the man had finished, he filled his pipe and took his comfortable time over a smoke. Then he pulled on his mittens, settled the earflaps of his cap firmly about his ears, and took the creek trail up the left fork. The dog was disappointed and yearned back toward the fire. This man did not know cold. Possibly all the generations of his ancestry had been ignorant of cold, of real cold, of cold one hundred and seven degrees below freezing-point. But the dog knew; all its ancestry knew, and it had inherited the knowledge. And it knew that it was not good to walk abroad in such fearful cold. It was the time to lie snug in a hole in the snow and wait for a curtain of cloud to be drawn across the face of outer space whence this cold came. On the other hand, there was no keen intimacy between the dog and the man. The one was the toil-slave of the other, and the only caresses it had ever received were the caresses of the whiplash and of harsh and menacing throat-sounds that threatened the whiplash. So the dog made no effort to communicate its apprehension to the man. It was not concerned in the welfare of the man; it was for its own sake that it yearned back toward the fire. But the man whistled, and spoke to it with the sound of whiplashes, and the dog swung in at the man's heels and followed after.

The man took a chew of tobacco and proceeded to start a new amber beard. Also, his moist breath quickly powdered with white his moustache, eyebrows, and lashes. There did not seem to be so many springs on the left fork of the Henderson, and for half an hour the man saw no signs of any. And then it happened. At a place where there were no signs, where the soft, unbroken snow seemed to advertise solidity beneath, the man broke through. It was not deep. He wet himself halfway to the knees before he floundered out to the firm crust.

He was angry and cursed his luck aloud. He had hoped to get into camp with the boys at six o'clock, and this would delay him an hour, for he would have to build a fire and dry out his foot-gear. This was imperative at that low temperature – he knew that much; and he turned aside to the bank, which he climbed. On top, tangled in the underbrush about the trunks of several small spruce trees, was a high-water deposit of dry firewood – sticks and twigs, principally, but also larger portions of seasoned branches and fine, dry, last-year's grasses. He threw down several large pieces on top of the snow. This served for a foundation and prevented the young flame from drowning itself in the snow it otherwise would melt. The flame he got by touching a match to a small shred of birch-bark that he took from his pocket. This burned even more readily than paper. Placing it on the foundation, he fed the young flame with wisps of dry grass and with the tiniest dry twigs.

He worked slowly and carefully, keenly aware of his danger. Gradually, as the flame grew stronger, he increased the size of the twigs with which he fed it. He squatted in the snow, pulling the twigs out from their entanglement in the brush and feeding directly to the flame. He knew there must be no failure. When it is seventy-five below zero, a man must not fail in his first attempt to build a fire – that is, if his feet are wet. If his feet are dry, and he fails, he can run along the trail for half a mile and restore his circulation. But the circulation of wet and freezing feet cannot be restored by running when it is seventy-five below. No matter how fast he runs, the wet feet will freeze the harder.

All this the man knew. The old-timer on Sulphur Creek had told him about it the previous fall, and now he was appreciating the advice. Already all sensation had gone out of his feet. To build the fire he had been forced to remove his mittens, and the fingers had quickly gone numb. His pace of four miles an hour had kept his heart pumping blood to the surface of his body and to all the extremities. But the instant he stopped, the action of the pump eased down. The cold of space smote the unprotected tip of the planet, and he, being on that unprotected tip, received the full force of the blow. The blood of his body recoiled before it. The blood was alive, like the dog, and like the dog it wanted to hide away and cover itself up from the fearful cold. So long as he walked four miles an hour, he pumped that blood, willy-nilly, to the surface; but now it ebbed away and sank down into the recesses of his body. The extremities were the first to feel its absence. His wet feet froze the faster, and his exposed fingers numbed the faster, though they had not yet begun to freeze. Nose and cheeks were already freezing, while the skin of all his body chilled as it lost its blood.

But he was safe. Toes and nose and cheeks would be only touched by the frost, for the fire was beginning to burn with strength. He was feeding it with twigs the size of his finger. In another minute he would be able to feed it with branches the size of his wrist, and then he could remove his wet footgear, and, while it dried, he could keep his naked feet warm by the fire, rubbing them at first, of course, with snow. The fire was a success. He was safe. He remembered the advice of the old-timer on Sulphur Creek, and smiled. The old-timer had been very serious in laying down the law that no man must travel alone in the Klondike after fifty below. Well, here he was; he had had the accident; he was alone; and he had saved himself. Those old-timers were rather womanish, some of them, he thought. All a man had to do was to keep his head, and he was all right. Any man who was a man could travel alone. But it was surprising, the rapidity with which his cheeks and nose were freezing. And he had not thought his fingers could go lifeless in so short a time. Lifeless they were, for he could scarcely make them move together to grip a twig, and they seemed remote from his body and from him. When he touched a twig, he had to look and see whether or not he had hold of it. The wires were pretty well down between him and his finger-ends.

All of which counted for little. There was the fire, snapping and crackling and promising life with every dancing flame. He started to untie his moccasins. They were coated with ice; the thick German socks were like sheaths of iron halfway to the knees; and the moccasin strings were like rods of steel all twisted and knotted as by some conflagration. For a moment he tugged with his numb fingers, then, realizing the folly of it, he drew his sheath-knife.

But before he could cut the strings, it happened. It was his own fault or, rather, his mistake. He should not have built the fire under the spruce tree. He should have built it in the open. But it had been easier to pull the twigs from the brush and drop them directly on the fire. Now the tree under which he had done this carried a weight of snow on its boughs. No wind had blown for weeks, and each bough was fully freighted. Each time he had to pull a twig he had communicated a slight agitation to the tree – an imperceptible agitation, so far as he was concerned, but an agitation sufficient to bring about the disaster. High up in the tree one bough capsized its load of snow. This fell on the boughs beneath, capsizing them. This process continued, spreading out and involving the whole tree. It grew like an avalanche, and it descended without warning upon the man and the fire, and the fire was blotted out! Where it had burned was a mantle of fresh and disordered snow.

The man was shocked. It was as though he had just heard his own sentence of death. For a moment he sat and stared at the spot where the fire had been. Then he grew very calm. Perhaps the old-timer on Sulphur Creek was right. If he had only had a trail-mate he would have been in no danger now. The trail-mate could have built the fire. Well, it was up to him to build the fire over again, and this second time there must be no failure. Even if he succeeded, he would most likely lose some toes. His feet must be badly frozen by now, and there would be some time before the second fire was ready.

Such were his thoughts, but he did not sit and think them. He was busy all the time they were passing through his mind. He made a new foundation for a fire, this time in the open, where no treacherous tree could blot it out. Next, he gathered dry grasses and tiny twigs from the high-water flotsam. He could not bring his fingers together to pull them out, but he was able to gather them by the handful. In this way he got many rotten twigs and bits of green moss that were undesirable, but it was the best he could do. He worked methodically, even collecting an armful of the larger branches to be used later when the fire gathered strength. And all the while the dog sat and watched him, a certain yearning wistfulness in its eyes, for it looked upon him as the fire-provider, and the fire was slow in coming.

When all was ready, the man reached in his pocket for a second piece of birch-bark. He knew the bark was there, and, though he could not feel it with his fingers, he could hear its crisp rustling as he fumbled for it. Try as he would, he could not clutch hold of it. And all the time, in his consciousness, was the knowledge that each instant his feet were freezing. This thought tended to put him in a panic, but he fought against it and kept calm. He pulled on his mittens with his teeth, and threshed his arms back and forth, beating his hands with all his might against his sides. He did this sitting down, and he stood up to do it; and all the while the dog sat in the snow, its wolf-brush of a tail curled around warmly over its forefeet, its sharp wolf-ears pricked forward intently as it watched the man. And the man, as he beat and threshed with his arms and hands, felt a great surge of envy as he regarded the creature that was warm and secure in its natural covering.

After a time he was aware of the first far-away signals of sensation in his beaten fingers. The faint tingling grew stronger till it evolved into a stinging ache that was excruciating, but which the man hailed with satisfaction. He stripped the mitten from his right hand and fetched forth the birch-bark. The exposed fingers were quickly going numb again. Next he brought out his bunch of sulphur matches. But the tremendous cold had already driven the life out of his fingers. In his effort to separate one match from the others, the whole bunch fell in the snow. He tried to pick it out of the snow, but failed. The dead fingers could neither touch nor clutch. He was very careful. He drove the thought of his freezing feet, and nose, and cheeks, out of his mind, devoting his whole soul to the matches. He watched, using the sense of vision in place of that of touch, and when he saw his fingers on each side the bunch, he closed them – that is, he willed to close them, for the wires were down, and the fingers did not obey. He pulled the mitten on the right hand, and beat it fiercely against his knee. Then, with both mittened hands, he scooped the bunch of matches, along with much snow, into his lap. Yet he was no better off.

After some manipulation he managed to get the bunch between the heels of his mittened hands. In this fashion he carried it to his mouth. The ice crackled and snapped when by a violent effort he opened his mouth. He drew the lower jaw in, curled the upper lip out of the way, and scraped the bunch with his upper teeth in order to separate a match. He succeeded in getting one, which he dropped on his lap. He was no better off. He could not pick it up. Then he devised a way. He picked it up in his teeth and scratched it on his leg. Twenty times he scratched before he succeeded in lighting it. As it flamed he held it with his teeth to the birch-bark. But the burning brimstone went up his nostrils and into his lungs, causing him to cough spasmodically. The match fell into the snow and went out.

The old-timer on Sulphur Creek was right, he thought in the moment of controlled despair that ensued: after fifty below, a man should travel with a partner. He beat his hands, but failed in exciting any sensation. Suddenly he bared both hands, removing the mittens with his teeth. He caught the whole bunch between the heels of his hands. His arm-muscles not being frozen enabled him to press the hand-heels tightly against the matches. Then he scratched the bunch along his leg. It flared into flame, seventy sulphur matches at once! There was no wind to blow them out. He kept his head to one side to escape the strangling fumes, and held the blazing bunch to the birch-bark. As he so held it, he became aware of sensation in his hand. His flesh was burning. He could smell it. Deep down below the surface he could feel it. The sensation developed into pain that grew acute. And still he endured it, holding the flame of the matches clumsily to the bark that would not light readily because his own burning hands were in the way, absorbing most of the flame.

At last, when he could endure no more, he jerked his hands apart. The blazing matches fell sizzling into the snow, but the birch-bark was alight. He began laying dry grasses and the tiniest twigs on the flame. He could not pick and choose, for he had to lift the fuel between the heels of his hands. Small pieces of rotten wood and green moss clung to the twigs, and he bit them off as well as he could with his teeth. He cherished the flame carefully and awkwardly. It meant life, and it must not perish. The withdrawal of blood from the surface of his body now made him begin to shiver, and he grew more awkward. A large piece of green moss fell squarely on the little fire. He tried to poke it out with his fingers, but his shivering frame made him poke too far, and he disrupted the nucleus of the little fire, the burning grasses and tiny twigs separating and scattering. He tried to poke them together again, but in spite of the tenseness of the effort, his shivering got away with him, and the twigs were hopelessly scattered. Each twig gushed a puff of smoke and went out. The fire-provider had failed. As he looked apathetically about him, his eyes chanced on the dog, sitting across the ruins of the fire from him, in the snow, making restless, hunching movements, slightly lifting one forefoot and then the other, shifting its weight back and forth on them with wistful eagerness.

The sight of the dog put a wild idea into his head. He remembered the tale of the man, caught in a blizzard, who killed a steer and crawled inside the carcass, and so was saved. He would kill the dog and bury his hands in the warm body until the numbness went out out of them. Then he could build another fire. He spoke to the dog, calling it to him; but in his voice was a strange note of fear that frightened the animal, who had never known the man to speak in such a way before. Something was the matter, and its suspicious nature sensed danger – it knew not what danger, but somewhere, somehow, in its brain arose an apprehension of the man. It flattened its ears down at the sound of the man's voice, and its restless, hunching movements and the liftings and shiftings of its forefeet became more pronounced; but it would not come to the man. He got on his hands and knees and crawled toward the dog. This unusual posture again excited suspicion, and the animal sidled mincingly away.

The man sat up in the snow for a moment and struggled for calmness. Then he pulled on his mittens, by means of his teeth, and got upon his feet. He glanced down at first in order to assure himself that he was really standing up, for the absence of sensation in his feet left him unrelated to the earth. His erect position in itself started to drive the webs of suspicion from the dog's mind; and when he spoke peremptorily, with the sound of whiplashes in his voice, the dog rendered its customary allegiance and came to him. As it came within reaching distance, the man lost his control. His arms flashed out to the dog, and he experienced genuine surprise when he discovered that his hands could not clutch, that there was neither bend nor feeling in the fingers. He had forgotten for the moment that they were frozen and that they were freezing more and more. All this happened quickly, and before the animal could get away, he encircled its body with his arms. He sat down in the snow, and in this fashion held the dog, while it snarled and whined and struggled.

But it was all he could do, hold its body encircled in his arms and sit there. He realized that he could not kill the dog. There was no way to do it. With his helpless hands he could neither draw nor hold his sheath-knife nor throttle the animal. He released it, and it plunged wildly away, with tail between its legs, and still snarling. It halted forty feet away and surveyed him curiously, with ears sharply pricked forward. The man looked down at his hands in order to locate them, and found them hanging on the ends of his arms. It struck him as curious that one should have to use his eyes in order to find out where his hands were. He began threshing his arms back and forth, beating the mittened hands against his sides. He did this for five minutes, violently, and his heart pumped enough blood up to the surface to put a stop to his shivering. But no sensation was aroused in the hands. He had an impression that they hung like weights on the ends of his arms, but when he tried to run the impression down, he could not find it.

A certain fear of death, dull and oppressive, came to him. This fear quickly became poignant as he realized that it was no longer a mere matter of freezing his fingers and toes, or of losing his hands and feet, but that it was a matter of life and death with the chances against him. This threw him into a panic, and he turned and ran up the creek-bed along the old, dim trail. The dog joined in behind and kept up with him. He ran blindly without intention, in fear such as he had never known in his life. Slowly, as he ploughed and floundered through the snow, he began to see things again – the banks of the creek, the old timber-jams, the leafless aspens, and the sky. The running made him feel better. He did not shiver. Maybe, if he ran on, his feet would thaw out; and, anyway, if he ran far enough, he would reach camp and the boys. Without doubt he would lose some fingers and toes and some of his face; but the boys would take care of him, and save the rest of him when he got there. And at the same time there was another thought in his mind that said he would never get to the camp and the boys; that it was too many miles away, that the freezing had too great a start on him, and that he would soon be stiff and dead. This thought he kept in the background and refused to consider. Sometimes it pushed itself forward and demanded to be heard, but he thrust it back and strove to think of other things.

It struck him as curious that he could run at all on feet so frozen that he could not feel them when they struck the earth and took the weight of his body. He seemed to himself to skim along above the surface, and to have no connection with the earth. Somewhere he had once seen a winged Mercury, and he wondered if Mercury felt as he felt when skimming over the earth.

His theory of running until he reached camp and the boys had one flaw in it: he lacked the endurance. Several times he stumbled, and finally he tottered, crumpled up, and fell. When he tried to rise, he failed. He must sit and rest, he decided, and next time he would merely walk and keep on going. As he sat and regained his breath, he noted that he was feeling quite warm and comfortable. He was not shivering, and it even seemed a warm glow had come to his chest and trunk. And yet, when he touched his nose or cheeks, there was no sensation. Running would not thaw them out. Nor would it thaw out his hands and feet. Then the thought came to him that the frozen portions of his body must be extending. He tried to keep this thought down, to forget it, to think of something else; he was aware of the panicky feeling that it caused, and he was afraid of the panic. But the thought asserted itself, and persisted, until it produced a vision of his body totally frozen. This was too much, and he made another wild run along the trail. Once he slowed down to a walk, but the thought of the freezing extending itself made him run again.

And all the time the dog ran with him, at his heels. When he fell down a second time, it curled its tail over its forefeet and sat in front of him, facing him, curiously eager and intent. The warmth and security of the animal angered him, and he cursed it till it flattened down its ears appeasingly. This time the shivering came more quickly upon the man. He was losing in his battle with the frost. It was creeping into his body from all sides. The thought of it drove him on, but he ran no more than a hundred feet, when he staggered and pitched headlong. It was his last panic. When he had recovered his breath and control, he sat up and entertained in his mind the conception of meeting death with dignity. However, the conception did not come to him in such terms. His idea of it was that he had been making a fool of himself, running around like a chicken with its head cut off – such was the simile that occurred to him. Well, he was bound to freeze anyway, and he might as well take it decently. With this new-found peace of mind came the first glimmerings of drowsiness. A good idea, he thought, to sleep off to death. It was like taking an anaesthetic. Freezing was not so bad as people thought. There were lots worse ways to die.

He pictured the boys finding his body next day. Suddenly he found himself with them, coming along the trail and looking for himself. And, still with them, he came round a turn in the trail and found himself lying in the snow. He did not belong with himself any more, for even then he was out of himself, standing with the boys and looking at himself in the snow. It certainly was cold, was his thought.

When he got back to the States he could tell the folks what real cold was. He drifted on from this to a vision of the old-timer on Sulphur Creek. He could see him quite clearly, warm and comfortable, and smoking a pipe.

"You were right, old hoss; you were right," the man mumbled to the old-timer of Sulphur Creek.

Then the man drowsed off into what seemed to him the most comfortable and satisfying sleep he had ever known. The dog sat facing him and waiting. The brief day drew to a close in a long, slow twilight. There were no signs of a fire to be made, and, besides, never in the dog's experience had it known a man to sit like that in the snow and make no fire. As the twilight drew on, its eager yearning for the fire mastered it, and with a great lifting and shifting of forefeet, it whined softly, then flattened its ears down in anticipation of being chidden by the man. But the man remained silent. Later, the dog whined loudly. And still later it crept close to the man and caught the scent of death. This made the animal bristle and back away. A little longer it delayed, howling under the stars that leaped and danced and shone brightly in the cold sky. Then it turned and trotted up the trail in the direction of the camp it knew, where were the other food-providers and fire-providers.

From

The Great Bear Lake Meditations

J. MICHAEL YATES

A man, warmly dressed, in perfect health, mushing his dogs a short distance between two villages, never arrives. He has forgotten to reach down, catch a little snow in his mitten and allow it to melt in his mouth. For a reason neither he nor his dogs understand, he steps from the runners of his sled, wanders dreamily – perhaps warmly, pleasantly – through the wide winter, then sits to contemplate his vision, then sleeps. The dogs tow an empty sled on to the place at one of the two villages where they're usually fed. While those who find the frozen man suspect the circumstances of his death, always they marvel that one so close to bed, warmth, food, perhaps family, could stray so easily into danger.

The Hunters of the Deer

DALE ZIEROTH

The ten men will dress in white
to match the snow and leave the last
farmhouse and the last woman, going
north into the country of the deer. It
is from there, and from past there, that
the wind begins that can shake
every window in the house and leaves
the woman wishing she had moved away
five years and five children ago.

During the day the father of her children
will kill from a distance. With the others
he will track and drive each bush
and at least once he will kill before
they stop and come together for
coffee in scratched quart jars. And
sometimes the November sun will glint
on the rifles propped together in the snow.

In the evening, as they skin and gut,
they talk about the one that ran three
miles on a broken leg and the bitch wolf
they should have shot and how John
the bachelor likes eating more than
hunting and they pass the whiskey
around to keep warm. In the house
the woman makes a meal from pork.

These men are hunters and later,
standing in bright electrically lighted
rooms they are sometimes embarrassed with the
blood on their clothes and although the
woman nods and seems to understand,

she grows restless with their talk.
She has not heard another woman in fourteen days.

And when they leave, the man sleeps
and his children sleep while the woman
waits and listens for the howling of
wolves. And to the north, the grey
she-wolf smells the red snow and howls.
She also is a hunter of the deer.
Tonight, while other hunters sleep, she
drinks at the throat.

In the Forest

JOHN NEWLOVE

In the forest
        down the cut roads
                the sides of them
gravel rolls
        thundering down,
                each small stone
a rock waterfall
        that frightens me
                sitting in my ditch.

I smoke my last
        cigarette rolled
                with bible paper,
listen to the stone
        cascading down,
                some of it bouncing
off my hunched shoulders.

        Above me the dark grass
                hangs over the edge
like a badly-fitted wig
        10 feet above me.
I dream of the animals
        that may sulk there,
                deer snake and bear
dangerous and inviolable
        as I am not inviolable.

Even the gentle deer
scare me at midnight,
no-one else for 100 miles,
even the sucking snakes
small and lithe as syrup.

The forest is not silent,
water smashes its way,
rocks bounce, wind magnifies
its usual noise
and my shivering fear
makes something alive
move in the trees,
shift in the grass
10 feet above me.

I am too frightened
to move or to stay,
sweating in the wind.

An hour later
I convulse unthinking,
and run, run, run down the cold road.

Fear of the Landscape

IAN YOUNG

On a hot morning
walking through rough thicket,
bushes and rocks
close to the bluffs
I was uneasy and clung to things.
The sound of a cricket
or the calls of birds were shrill
lesions in the quiet air
around me, sweltering and still.
The leaves hung from the trees
dangling on thin stems.

I am walking quickly and the land
stops. The ground
drops to a beach of stones
where a silent boat leans at the shore
into a sandy mound,
its stiff poled oars
outstretched.
The lake gulls circling it
cry out in the heat.
The sound of dry breath clings to me.
I hear the sun's core burn.
Have I been too long in cities
that I have such fear
of the landscape?

Cyclops

MARGARET ATWOOD

You, going along the path,
mosquito-doped, with no moon, the flashlight
a single orange eye

unable to see what is beyond
the capsule of your dim
sight, what shape

contracts to a heart
with terror, bumps
among the leaves, what makes
a bristling noise like a fur throat

Is it true you do not wish to hurt them?

Is it true you have no fear?
Take off your shoes then,
let your eyes go bare,
swim in their darkness as in a river

do not disguise
yourself in armour.

They watch you from hiding:
you are a chemical
smell, a cold fire, you are
giant and indefinable

In their monstrous night
thick with possible claws
where danger is not knowing,

you are the hugest monster.

Four

Crooked Nerves Made Straight:
The Benign Wilderness

INTRODUCTION

Reactions to the wilderness vary widely. Some observers, as we have seen, feel it to be threatening and malevolent. To them, it may be a source of terror. Others, as we shall see, feel it to be congenial and benevolent. For them, it is a source of joy.

Writers who experience one or other of these extreme reactions frequently attribute intent to the wilderness, interpreting it as a thinking, feeling presence or being which either welcomes them or sets out to do them harm. While this often makes for effective writing, one is tempted to say that they flatter themselves. Man, either individually or collectively, is of no concern to wild nature. The wilderness is impersonal and uncaring.

There is another sense, however, in which the wild may be viewed as a positive, even benign, force. This is the evolutionary sense, which has to do with the profusion, variety, and continuance of all life. Wilderness has a vital and creative role to play here, for it is not only the refuge of many threatened forms of being, but also the fundamental matrix of life. The product of millenia of evolutionary forces, it is the ultimate repository of genetic materials of astonishing diversity. It is in this diversity that it differs markedly from the monocultures and urban environments shaped by man. In a sense, it is a gene bank from which the evolutionary process can draw. John Livingston, a Canadian naturalist of note, has written that "nature existed long before there was man, and nature needs at least a vestigial reservoir of wilderness from which once again to populate the planet in wonderful diversity – in the due passage of time." It is from the wilderness that life springs in its most elegant complexity and variety. Such thoughts are rarely given detailed expression in poetry or fictional prose; however, the sense of fecundity and renewal and diversity frequently emerges, as it does in some selections from this theme.

Also of importance is the more immediate impact of wilderness on our own kind. For many it is a fountainhead of aesthetic pleasure and inspiration, a source of peace and much-needed solitude, a vehicle for physical and emotional rejuvenation, a touchstone of spiritual emotion and comfort.

Such ideas, distinguished by the special character of the Canadian wilderness, are the stuff of this theme. Douglas Le Pan writes of orchids along the portage, the proud exuberance of the land, and the therapeutic quality of immersion in the wild. Ethel Wilson paints a picture of "lonely lakes, great and small, shining like mercury, lying as mirrors to the clouds and the blue sky, and reflecting the rose and flame of the maple woods." For Archibald Lampman, the still woods is a place of infinite peace. And In Malcolm Lowry's "The Forest Path to the Spring" we are given a magnificent prose rendering of our West Coast wilderness and its healing effect on a troubled man. Finally, Sheila Burnford writes of pleasure in the bush and the promise of a northland spring. This, then, is the benign wilderness.

From

The Innocent Traveller

ETHEL WILSON

The forests bordered the railway tracks and ran away up the hills. The forests were more brilliant in colour than any that the travellers had ever imagined. Sunlight was reflected from the gold and flame of each leaf of each tree. The forests seemed to blaze with harmless fire. The traveller's vision was intent on the rose, flame, and yellow that shot towards them, passed them, and fell behind them, remaining stationary and identifiable only on the distant hills; they could not see and did not know that away towards the north (and southwards too) beyond and beyond the northern horizon there was a still world of red, rose, and yellow trees, and they did not think that in a few weeks these forest branches would be thin and bare. And because Time was bounded by yesterday, today, and tomorrow as the train slid and rocked along paralleling Time, they could not know that, decades later, a young grandson of the Grandmother's (not yet imagined, not yet born) would be a bush pilot and would fly in a slow, rather rackety plane above such forests. He would fly above the brilliant woods of the Maritime Provinces, and of Quebec, and of Ontario, and would see below him a flaming earth of boundless maple trees, coloured the tender warm rose and fabulous crimson of a carpet of Ispahan; and he would see small and great rivers shining like steel, widely curving through the bright trees; and he would look down on lonely lakes, great and small, shining like mercury, lying as mirrors to the clouds and the blue sky, and reflecting the rose and flame of the maple woods. The grandson would see all this in a newly discovered dimension as old as Time; yet it would be the same brilliance which they now saw with amazement, and which had transformed autumnal Canadian forests for centuries unknown.

En Route

DUNCAN CAMPBELL SCOTT

The train has stopped for no apparent reason
In the wilds;
A frozen lake is level and fretted over
With rippled wind lines;
The sun is burning in the South; the season
Is winter trembling at a touch of spring.
A little hill with birches and a ring
Of cedars – all so still, so pure with snow –
It seems a tiny landscape in the moon.
Long wisps of shadow from the naked birches
Lie on the white in lines of cobweb-grey;
From the cedar roots the snow has shrunk away,
One almost hears it tinkle as it thaws.
Traces there are of wild things in the snow –
Partridge at play, tracks of the foxes' paws
That broke a path to sun them in the trees.
They're going fast where all impressions go
On a frail substance – images like these,
Vagaries the unconscious mind receives
From nowhere, and lets go to nothingness
With the lost flush of last year's autumn leaves.

Canadian Spring

SHEILA BURNFORD

Our heralds of spring in northwest Canada bear no resemblance to the traditional and seldom inspire the poet within us: no primroses, lambs, or forsythia here, no tender green over the earth and soft unfolding buds. Instead we have the icebreaker battering a channel through the ice cap, smelt running in snow-swollen creeks, frost boils erupting on the roads, municipal drains backing up, and finally an inch-by-inch clearing of the snowdrifts in the garden until the exhausted daffodils push their way through the ironbound earth at last – in June. One's whole soul cries out for spring hats and blossom, new-mown grass, the mayfly hatch, the first young tender morels; instead one pokes ineffectually with a stick at overflowing gutters, yearns over the etiolated narcissus brought up from the cellar, and plucks not primroses but long-lost overshoes and last year's oyster shells from the snow receding at the porch.

In the first week of May, Susan and I reach the peak of delayed-spring frustration, and on a morning when the returning geese fly low over the city in an exultant, baying, clamorous pack, we receive their message especially loud and clear, for we are on our way to Whitefish, to the little hunting cabin on the shore of a lonely, hill-ringed lake, peaceful and timeless: Susan to paint and I to potter; Raimie, my Labrador, to escort us and investigate possible strange noises in the night. We have discarded our families for the weekend.

The track down the hillside to the cabin turns into a fast-running creek at this time of year, carrying off the melting snow from the hills, but the ground is hard and frozen, and the car coasts down in a childishly satisfying welter of flying spray. We leave it in a clearing, load ourselves up like pack mules, then walk or stagger the last quarter of a mile. The trail winds through spruce and poplar, the branches interlaced overhead, and always I come upon the little cabin crouched by the water's edge long before I am prepared for it, so secretly does it seem to camouflage itself against the background of trees. Weather-beaten and gray, wearing its roof and chimney slightly askew, its one half-lidded eye bleary from the winter's gales, it huddles like some shabby, eccentric old woman on a park bench in spring, blinking in the sunshine; and around her skirts, instead of cheeping sparrows, the peaty brown snow creeks make little murmurous singing sounds.

We open the door, and then, as quickly as possible, the window, when the familiar stuffy, sun-baked smell of mouse nests, straw, waders, and mud-encrusted gunnysacks hits us. The boats are stored there, and we haul out the light punt, then the heavy freight canoe, and a tangled mass of decrepit reed blinds – all the paraphernalia of last fall's hunting; sweep out the first layer of powdered mud and little fluffy piles of duck and partridge feathers; then, lastly, after tossing for the victim, out go all the visible mouse corpses, hurled into the bush, from where they are conscientiously retrieved by the dog and returned to the steps. We leave the door and windows open to the cold sweet northern air; then, mutually unenthusiastic about housework at any time, we call it a day and sit on the wooden steps, at peace with the world, a bottle of beer apiece, so sheltered from the wind and warm in the noon sun that we take off our heavy sweaters and roll up our shirt sleeves. . . .

The ice is going out on the lake, and there is open water before us for about a hundred yards from the shoreline, edged by a new high bank of turf and reeds built up through the winter by ice pressure. The marsh water close in reflects a sky pierced with reed stalks and patterned with a faint constant movement of infinitesimal bubble rings, but out beyond the channel little rippling waves lap greedily against the ice stretching across the lake to the far shore – gray, sodden ice, heavy with age, the darkness of the imprisoned water lying shadowlike a few inches below the surface. There is no hint of green yet in the hills beyond – rather, a quickening of purple; and the three long plumes of the waterfall are vivid and white even at this distance.

The first frog chorus tunes up in the bulrushes a few feet from where we sit, and the mallards who were disturbed at our coming return in quacking pairs to the open water. Four whistlers pass like children's bath toys drawn on a string, line astern, three drakes and a demure little hen leading. One drake is courting extravagantly, head bobbing and turning from side to side to a slow beat of six, then a fantastic arching of neck to twist his head back down the length of his body; but the little hen is not impressed by these contortions and swims on unheeding. The other two watch admiringly, then suddenly rise in unison and fly off with faint despondent cries; and so relieved by their departure apparently is the hen that she turns and acknowledges at last her exhibitionist suitor. They glide and posture in an endless fascinating ritual, the handsome drake in shining black and white, the drab little hen.

A long raft of ice and twigs sails by in a sudden gust of wind, with six mallard passengers aboard; sober and serious as priests on a cruise ship, they stare solemnly as they glide by, all heads turning together. The dog, inquisitive about our laughter, picks his way on heaving planks down to the water's edge, but is taken off guard by the sudden splash of an equally surprised muskrat and slips on the precarious plank, so that his hindquarters slide into the water and he hangs on with scrabbling forepaws. I help him up, because he is nine years old and not so agile, but I laugh so much that he is offended; he shakes his coat, soaking us with moody satisfaction, then disappears into the bush. I know that he will not go far, but will return stealthily and take up position concealed by some bush or tree so that he can keep me within range; and I know that if I turn suddenly I will be able to catch him at it, to his embarrassment – but not this time, for I am feeling a little guilty.

I make amends with a piece of cheese when we settle down on the steps again to eat our lunch – satisfying hunks of homemade bread and cheese, dill pickles, and another bottle of beer to celebrate our weekend emancipation. Redwings chatter in the mountain ash above, chatter in a desultory way, rather as we do ourselves, with long silences savored peacefully between their observations. The frog activity is dying down, but the muskrats are suddenly busy, the V of their wake spreading in the still water close to shore, preoccupied, bewhiskered little faces forging through the reeds. More ducks flight in and settle on the larger ice floes, preening themselves, their cheerful garrulity suddenly silenced when an osprey appears over-head and hovers watchfully. They rise in a body and circle, rising and falling uneasily, until the hawk drifts off down the shoreline on an eddy of wind, effortless as a feather.

Now the wind rises and falls too, sighing through the topmost pine branches, and all around is a chorus of protesting creaks and groans of trees bearing the chafing weight of others uprooted in the winter gales and fallen against them. I am very content; lambs, primroses, and sprays of blossoms are suddenly revealed as banal, hackneyed manifestations before this northland subtlety. I find myself filled with pity for the unfortunate masses who must wait another year before picking their next daffodil.

Susan settles down in a protected dip with easel and paint box and all the colorful clutter of a painter. She will be lost to the world for the next three hours. I whistle to Raimie, and we strike off from the trail into the bush, where the snow has receded, walking softly on a carpet of damp brown leaves; through the willow and alder clumps, whippy with new life, striking like a lash across the unwary face; over the mossy, rotting deadfalls; and around the impenetrable branches of new-fallen jack-pine, the needles still dark green, the last desperate growth of cones in rubbery clusters like brown sea snails; between towering spruce and white pine; through enchanting sunlit clearings of terraced rock slabs, covered in pinky-gray lichen and long trailing tendrils of twinflower – the stems and leaves are brown now, but at the angle of each geometrically perfect pair is a minuscule of green. The surrounding moss is ankle deep, beautiful hummocky moss, and however soggy it may be within, I cannot resist it; I throw myself down and try to count the uncountable flowerets in a quarter inch. My eyes are on a level with a ledge of rock; caught below an overhang is a papery garter-snake skin, old, yet still clearly patterned and wonderfully supple, over two feet long. I tie it in a neat bow on Raimie's tail; he is not amused, but suffers it as a collar instead.

I meander along the banks of a trout-brown creek, sun-dappled until it winds through the dark gloom of a cedar swamp, the twisted, agonized roots and branches of the giant fallen trees forming a dark dramatic frieze against the new vivid green of the living spruce beyond. The cold strikes suddenly, for the sun cannot penetrate the intertwined vaulting, and even the creek contributes to the brooding eeriness with weird shapes and fantastic grottoes sculptured from the overhanging ledges of ice. . . .

I leave the creek to come out from the darkness of the bush at the edge of a field, part of a long abandoned fox farm, and there, less than a hundred yards away, in a dip before the sagging barn, is a black bear. We stare at one another in mutual horror for a long second; then he turns and bolts across the field, galloping so fast that his back legs cross over his front ones, and disappears into the far trees. But that is the direction I want to go in as well, back to the lake, and I don't feel entirely happy about bears, and however antisocial this one may be, perhaps he has a mother or a cousin or a sister (with cubs) who isn't. I call my moral support away from his rabbit hunting and hear the reassuring sounds of his coming almost immediately. He arrives, panting, with beaming eyes and half a yard of pink tongue lolling out of a grinning mouth; I gather he has had a wonderful time. I am delighted, even more than usual, to see him. I am interested to see him sniff the wind as we cross the field, and the ridge of hair rise along his back, but he trots along beside me unconcerned; and so, of course, am I – now.

Susan has had a satisfying afternoon as well; two canvases are propped against the backs of chairs, she has found the glove she lost last fall in the bush, and has seen two deer, one mink, and a flock of geese. We sit on the steps again before dinner, loath to come in until the last possible moment, and watch a spectacular sunset flaming in wild, windblown ragged clouds. The air below is still and soft and full of evening sounds: wings whistling overhead, throbbing frog chorus from the reeds, chickadees, and the solitary falling cadence of a white-throated sparrow far back in the bush; little whispers of wind rustling the dead brown bulrush spikes; and always the soft melodious tinkling of shifting ice in the background; coy bridling giggles of mallard hens in the next bay, protesting their virtue to the hoarse excited quacks of their swains; the occasional caustic comment of a raven. We sit there until the loons cry in the gathering darkness and the cold drives us into the snug, stuffy warmth of the cabin.

We have partridge for dinner, succulent gamy partridge shot in a Saskatchewan bluff last fall, marinated and cooked in homemade wine from a local Italian producer; Burgundy jelly from the Trappists in Quebec; and wild rice that grew along these shores only last year, dark and fragrant with woodsmoke from the Indians' fires across the lake. We drink the remainder of the wine – a muscatel, says the sticking-plaster label on the gin bottle, with a surprisingly pleasant though elusive bouquet (a quality enhanced perhaps by the fact that our wine-glasses once contained anchovy paste).

We play featherheaded chess until our eyes will no longer stay open and we realize that we are dozing between moves. Raimie is already asleep on a sagging cot, muzzle resting on a headless decoy, his nostrils twitching – dreaming of rabbits, probably. I lie awake in the darkness for a while, zipped into the cocoon of my sleeping bag, listening to the sighs and creaks of the wooden framework; there is a soft, intermittent scratching on the roof, which I finally identify as a scraping branch; outside there are faint little plops in the water, and a closer, intensified tinkling of the ice, which must mean that the wind is shifting.

In the middle of the night I awaken with a sudden wide-awake alertness, almost as though someone had called me by name, but I hear nothing – only the sound of Raimie's tail thumping on the cot when he hears me sit up. I get out of bed and stand by the open door, looking out across the lake; a star is hanging low over the hills, and when the moon appears from a bank of clouds the lake is bright before me, half a mile or more of shining water triumphing over the sinking ice. And as I stand there I realize that the wind is warm and soft and full of promise – the promise of the northland spring, fulfilled at last in the silent, vanquished ice.

Arctic Spring

DAVID KEENLEYSIDE

Arctic spring:
First flash of gulls against frozen sea,
Shrieks in soundless air.

Northern landscape:
Vistas of rose and mauve light
Shimmering on sea ice.

Solitude

ARCHIBALD LAMPMAN

How still it is here in the woods. The trees
Stand motionless, as if they did not dare
To stir, lest it should break the spell. The air
Hangs quiet as spaces in a marble frieze.
Even this little brook, that runs at ease,
Whispering and gurgling in its knotted bed,
Seems but to deepen, with its curling thread
Of sound, the shadowy sun-pierced silences.
Sometimes a hawk screams or a woodpecker
Startles the stillness from its fixèd mood
With his loud careless tap. Sometimes I hear
The dreamy white-throat from some far-off tree
Pipe slowly on the listening solitude,
His five pure notes succeeding pensively.

Canoe-Trip

DOUGLAS LE PAN

What of this fabulous country
Now that we have it reduced to a few hot hours
And sun-burn on our backs?
On this south side the countless archipelagoes,
The slipway where titans sent splashing the last great glaciers;
And then up to the foot of the blue pole star
A wilderness,
The pinelands whose limits seem distant as Thule,
The millions of lakes once cached and forgotten,
The clearings enamelled with blueberries, rank silence about
      them;
And skies that roll all day with cloud-chimeras
To baffle the eye with portents and unwritten myths,
The flames of sunset, the lions of gold and gules.
Into this reservoir we dipped and pulled out lakes and rivers,
We strung them together and made our circuit.
Now what shall be our word as we return,
What word of this curious country?

It is good,
It is a good stock to own though it seldom pays dividends.
There are holes here and there for a gold-mine or a hydro-
      plant.
But the tartan of river and rock spreads undisturbed,
The plaid of a land with little desire to buy or sell.
The dawning light skirls out its independence;
At noon the brazen trumpets slash the air;
Night falls, the gulls scream sharp defiance;
Let whoever comes to tame this land, beware!
Can you put a bit to the lunging wind?
Can you hold wild horses by the hair?
Then have no hope to harness the energy here,
It gallops along the wind away.
But here are crooked nerves made straight,

The fracture cured no doctor could correct.
The hand and mind, reknit, stand whole for work;
The fable proves no cul-de-sac.
Now from the maze we circle back;
The map suggested a wealth of cloudy escapes;
That was a dream, we have converted the dream to act.
And what we now expect is not simplicity,
No steady breeze, or any surprise,
Orchids along the portage, white water, crimson leaves.
Content, we face again the complex task.

And yet the marvels we have seen remain.
We think of the eagles, of the fawns at the river bend,
The storms, the sudden sun, the clouds sheered downwards.
O so to move! With such immaculate decision!
O proudly as waterfalls curling like cumulus!

The Forest Path to the Spring

MALCOLM LOWRY

To Margerie, my wife

At dusk, every evening, I used to go through the forest to the spring for water.

The way that led to the spring from our cabin was a path wandering along the bank of the inlet through snowberry and thimbleberry and shallon bushes, with the sea below you on the right, and the shingled roofs of the houses, all built down on the beach beneath round the little crescent of the bay.

Far aloft gently swayed the mastheads of the trees: pines, maples, cedars, hemlocks, alders. Much of this was second growth but some of the pines were gigantic. The forest had been logged from time to time, though the slash the loggers left was soon obliterated by the young birch and vines growing up quickly.

Beyond, going toward the spring, through the trees, range beyond celestial range, crowded the mountains, snow-peaked for most of the year. At dusk they were violet, and frequently they looked on fire, the white fire of the mist. Sometimes in the early mornings this mist looked like a huge family wash, the property of Titans, hanging out to dry between the folds of their lower hills. At other times all was chaos, and Valkyries of storm-drift drove across them out of the ever-reclouding heavens.

Often all you could see in the whole world of the dawn was a huge sun with two pines silhouetted in it, like a great blaze behind a Gothic cathedral. And at night the same pines would write a Chinese poem on the moon. Wolves howled from the mountains. On the path to the spring the mountains appeared and disappeared through the trees.

And at dusk, too, came the seagulls, returning homeward down the inlet from their daily excursion to the city shores – when the wind was wailing through the trees, as if shot out of a catapult.

Ceaselessly they would come flying out of the west with their angelic wings, some making straight down the inlet, others gliding over the trees, others slower, detached, staggering, or at a dreadfully vast height, a straggling marathon of gulls.

On the left, half hidden among the trees in monolithic attitudes of privacy, like monastic cells of anchorites or saints, were the wooden backhouses of the little shacks.

This was what you could see from the path, which was not only the way to the spring but a fraction of the only footpath through the forest between the different houses of Eridanus, and when the tide was high, unless you went by boat, the only way round to your neighbors. . . .

Nor shall I ever forget the first time I went down that path to the spring for water. The evening was highly peculiar. In the northeast a full moon like a burning thistle had risen over the mountains. Mars hovered over the moon, the sole star. On the other side of the water a bank of fog stretched along the coastline the length of the inlet, luminous in the east opposite the house, but becoming black toward the south and west to the far right beyond the trees on the headland – that was, from our porch, from the path, the headland with the lighthouse was behind me, but it was such a strange evening I kept turning round – through which the fog showed like spirals and puffs of smoke, as though the woods were on fire. The sky was blue in the west, shading down to a pastel-like chalky sunset against which the trees were etched. A spindly water tower stood out above the fog over there. It had been dark inside the house but now I was outside on the path it was light. This was six o'clock and in spite of the blue sky to the west a patch of moonlight was reflected in the water by a diving float. The tide was high below the trees. In one instant, however, when I reached the spring, the moon went behind a cloud and it was dark: the reflection disappeared. And when I got back there was a blue fog.

"Welcome home," my wife smiled, greeting me.

"Ah yes, my darling, it really *is* home now. I love those curtains you made."

"It's good to sit by the window and look when it's beautiful outside, but when it's a gloomy twilight I like to pull the curtains, and feel from the dark night withdrawn, and full of lamp-light inside."

"None of this nonsense about love in a cottage?"

I was lighting the oil lamps as I said this, smiling as I reflected how this unprophetic and loveless remark had become a loving catchphrase, and enchanted now by the golden color of the flame of the lighted oil lamps against their pretty blue holders backed with fluted tin brackets like haloes, or a monstrance.

"But now it's night, and the Chinese Hats are on the move!" We laughed, as I turned down the flame of a wick that was smoking the chimney.

And outside the tide was sweeping in still further from the Pacific until we could hear it washing and purling under the house itself. And later we lay in bed listening to a freighter's engines as they shook the house:

> *Frère* Jacques
> *Frère* Jacques
> *Dor*mez-vous?
> *Dor*mez-vous?

But the next morning when the gulls sailed outward bound to the city shores the clear cold sun streamed right into the two rooms of our house filling it with brilliant incessant water reflections and incandescence of light as if it knew that soon the world would start rolling through the mountainous seas of winter toward inevitable spring. And that evening after the last gulls had come to rest, when the moonlight came in there was time for it to embroider the waving windows of our house with their curtains on the unresting tide of Eridanus that was both sea and river.

Thereafter at dusk, when the gulls came floating home over the trees, I used to take this cannister to the spring. First I climbed the wooden ladder set into the bank and made into steps that had replaced the Scotsman's old broken steps, that led up from our porch to the path. Then I turned right so that now I was facing north toward the mountains, white plumaged as gulls themselves with a fresh paint of snow; or rose and indigo.

Often I would linger on the way and dream of our life. Was it possible to be so happy? Here we were living on the very windrow of existence, under conditions so poverty stricken and abject in the eyes of the world they were actually condemned in the newspapers, or by the Board of Health, and yet it seemed that we were in heaven, and that the world outside – so portentous in its prescriptions for man of imaginary needs that were in reality his damnation – was hell. And for these illusory needs, in that hell of ugliness outside Eridanus, and for the sake of making it a worse hell, men were killing each other.

But a few evenings later, returning homeward along the path, I found myself possessed by the most violent emotion I had ever experienced in my life. I was so violent it took me some time to recognize what it was, and so all-embracingly powerful it made me stop in my tracks and put my burden down. A moment before I had been thinking how much I loved my wife, how thankful I was for our happiness, then I had passed to thinking about mankind, and now this once innocent emotion had become, for this is indeed what it was, hatred. It was not just ordinary hatred either, it was a virulent and murderous thing that throbbed through all my veins like a passion and even seemed to make my hair stand on end and my mouth water, and it took in everyone in its sweep, everyone except my wife. And now, again and again I would stop on the path as I came back with water, putting down my burden as I became possessed by this feeling. It was a hatred so all-consuming and so absolutely implacable that I was astounded at myself. What was all this hatred? Were these really my feelings? The world, surely, one could hate the world for its ugliness, but this was like hatred of mankind. One day, after I had been turned down again for the army, it occurred to me that in some mysterious way I had access to the fearful wrath that was sweeping the world, or that I stood at the mercy of the wild forces of nature that I had read man had been sent into the world to redeem, or something that was like the dreadful Wendigo, the avenging, man-hating spirit of the wilderness, the fire-tortured forest, that the Indians feared and believed in still.

And in my agonized confusion of mind, my hatred and suffering *were* the forest fire itself, the destroyer, which is here, there, all about; it breathes, it moves, and sometimes suddenly turns back on its tracks and even commits suicide, behaving as though it had an idiot mind of its own; so my hatred became a thing in itself, the pattern of destruction. But the movement of the forest fire is almost like a perversion of the movement of the inlet: flames run into a stand of dry inflammable cedar, yellow flames slice them down, and watching, one thinks these flames will roll over the crest of the hill like a tidal wave. Instead, perhaps an hour later, the wind has changed, or the fire has grown too big for itself, and is now sucking in a draft that opposes its advance. So the fire doesn't sweep up the hill, but instead settles back to eat the morsels of the trees it felled during its first rush. So it seemed was this hatred behaving, turning inward and back upon myself, to devour my very self in its flames.

What was wrong with me? For nearly all was unselfishness in our little settlement. Like benevolent mountain lions, I had discovered, our neighbours would wait all day, only to perform an unselfish act, to help us in some way, or bring a gift. A smile, a wave of the hand, a cheery greeting was a matter of great importance here too. Perhaps they thought us a bit shiftless but they never let us know it. I remembered how Mauger, the Channel Islander, would reconnoiter in his boat, looking at our house, trying to pick the best time to bring us some crabs, or salmon, without inconvenience to us, for which he would accept no payment. To the contrary, he would pay us for the privilege of giving us the crabs by enriching us with stories and songs.

Once he told us of a salmon he saw drown an eagle. The eagle had flown away with a salmon in its claws that he had not wanted to share with a flock of crows, and rather than give up any part of its booty it had allowed itself finally to be dragged under the waves.

He told us that in the northern regions where he fished there were
two kinds of ice, blue and white: live and dead. The white was dead
so could not climb. But the blue ice would come and calmly ravish
an island of all her beauty of trees and moss, bleed her lichen to
the rock, and leave her bare as the Scotsman's door he had come to
help us mend.

Or he would tell us of Arctic visions, of winds so strong they
blew in the outgoing tide in which were found strange fish with green
bones –

When he came back in September he loved to sing:

> Oh you've got a long way to go
> You've got a long way to go
> Whether you travel by day or night
> And you haven't a port or a starboard light
> If it's west or eastward ho –
> The judge will tell you so –

Or he would sing, in his curious jerky voice with its accents of the
old English music hall, and which was more like talking:

> Farewell, farewell, my sailor boy
> This parting gives me pain . . .

And we too had grown unselfish, or at least different, away from
the tenets of the selfish world. Eternally we watched Quaggan's float
to see that it was safe and if it broke away without his knowledge, or
when he was in the city, we brought it back, no matter how bad the
weather, honestly hoping he would not know it was us, yet proud that
it had been ourselves, for had it not been, it would have been someone else.

No one ever locked their doors, nobody discussed anyone else
meanly. Canonical virtues must not be assumed for the inhabitants
of Eridanus however. Though one point should be made in regard to
the womenfolk of the fishermen. With the exception of those who
were married, there never were any women. The unmarried fishermen
often lent their shacks to their friends in the summer, but they were
sacrosanct when they returned. What they did in the city was their own
business, yet they never brought whores, for example, to their shacks.
The attitude of the solitary fisherman toward his shack, and his boat,
was not dissimilar. In effect his love for the one was like his love
for the other. Perhaps his shack was less a part of him than his boat
and his love for his shack was more disinterested; I think one reason
for this is that their little cabins were shrines of their own integrity
and independence, something that this type of human being, who
seems almost to have disappeared, realizes can only be preserved
without the evil of gossip. And actually each man's life was in es-

sence a mystery (even if it looked like an open book) to his neighbour. The inhabitants varied in political and religious beliefs and un-
beliefs and were certainly not sentimental. There was at one time,
in later years, a family with three children living in Eridanus by
necessity and not by choice and they were indeed convinced that it
was "beneath them," and that the true values were to be found in
"keeping up with the Joneses." They let themselves sink into degrada-
tion, as seeming to be the conventional counterpart of poverty, without ever having looked at a sunrise. I recall that their dishevelment
and general incapacity caused some rather sharp comment among the
fishermen and everyone was relieved when they left, to move into
a slum in the city, where they certainly did not have to carry their
water from a spring and where their only sight of a sunrise was behind warehouses. And even ourselves were not entirely absolved from
identifying such a life with "failure," something we certainly should
have outgrown. And I remember very well how we used to drift along
in our little boat in the sun, or sit by the fire in the gentle lamplight
if it was night and cold weather, and murmur together our daydreams
of "success," travel, a fine house, and so on.

And everything in Eridanus, as the saying is, seemed made out of
everything else, without the necessity of making anyone else suffer
for its possession: the roofs were of hand-split cedar shakes, the
piles of pine, the boats of cedar and vine-leaved maple. Cypress and
fir went up our chimneys and the smoke went back to heaven.

There was no room for hatred, and resuming my load of the
cannister, I resolved to banish it – after all it was not human beings
I hated but the ugliness they made in the image of their own ignorant
contempt for the earth – and I went back to my wife.

But I forgot all my hatred and torment the moment I saw my
wife. How much I owed to her! I had been a creature of the night,
who yet had never seen the beauty of the night.

My wife taught me to know the stars in their courses and seasons,
and to know their names, and how she always laughed like a peal
of merry little bells telling me again about the first time she made
me really look at them. It was early in our stay at Eridanus while
I, used to being up all night and sleeping during the day, could not
accustom myself to the change of rhythm, and the silence, and
darkness all around us. Because I found it hard to sleep, in the small
dark hours of one moonless night she took me walking deep into the
forest; she told me to put out my electric torch and then, in a
moment, she said, look up at the sky. The stars were blazing and
shooting through the black trees and I had said, "My God, I never
saw anything like that in my life!" But I never could see the patterns
she pointed out and she always had to teach me afresh each time,

until one late autumn night there was a brilliant full moon. That night there was frosted driftwood and a slow silver line of surf on the beach. Above the night itself flashed with swords and diamonds. Standing on the porch she pointed out Orion – "See, the three stars of his belt, Mintaka, Alnilam, Alnitak, there's Betelgeuse above in his right shoulder, and Rigel below in his left knee – " and when I saw it at last she said, "It's easier tonight because the moonlight drowns all but the brightest stars."

I reflected how little I had known of the depths and tides of a woman until now, her tenderness, her compassion, her capacity for delight, her wistfulness, her joy and strength, and her beauty, that happened through my wild luck to be the beauty of my wife.

She had lived in the country as a child and now returning after her years in the cities it was as if she had never left it. Walking through the forest to meet her returning from the store I would sometimes come upon her standing as still and alert as the wild creature she had seen and was watching, a doe with her fawn, a mink, or a tiny kinglet on a bough over her head. Or I would find her on her knees, smelling the earth, she loved it so much. Often I had the feeling that she had some mysterious correspondence with all nature around her unknown to me, and I thought that perhaps she was herself the eidolon of everything we loved in Eridanus, of all its shifting moods and tides and darks and suns and stars. Nor could the forest itself have longed for spring more than she. She longed for it like a Christian for heaven, and through her I myself became susceptible to these moods and changes and currents of nature, as to its ceaseless rotting into humus of its fallen leaves and buds – nothing in nature suggested you died yourself more than that, I began to think – and burgeoning toward life.

My wife was also an accomplished cook, and though the wood-burning cookstove we had reminded us of Charlie Chaplin's in *The Gold Rush,* she somehow turned our limited and humble fare into works of art.

Sometimes, when we were most troubled in heart because of the war, or fear we would be separated, or run out of money, she would lie in bed laughing in the dark and telling me stories to make me laugh too, and then we would even make up dirty limericks together.

We found we could rarely do any outside work together, like splitting wood, or making repairs, or especially when we built the pier, without singing; the jobs begat the songs, so that it was as if we had discovered the primitive beginnings of music again for ourselves; we began to make up our own songs, and I began to write them down.

But it was the accompaniment of her speech, of her *consciousness* of everything that impressed me then, half absurd, wholly perceptive, it intensified our whole life.

"See the frost on the fallen leaves, it's like a sumptuous brocade." "The chickadees are chiming like a windbell." "Look at that bit of moss, it's a miniature tropical forest of palm trees." "How do I know the cascara from the alder trees? Because the alders have eyes." "Eyes?" "Just like the eyes on potatoes. It's where the young shoots and branches drop off." "We shall have snow tonight, I can smell it on the wind." Such was our small talk, our common gossip of the forest.

My old life of the night, how far away that seemed now, my life in which my only stars were neon lights! I must have stumbled into a thousand alcoholic dawns, but drunk in the rumble seat I passed them by. How different were the few drinks we drank now, with Quaggan or Kristbjorg, when we could afford it or when there was any. Never had I really looked at a sunrise till now. . . .

That first winter in Eridanus was a difficult one for us, in many ways; used as we were to city life our primitive existence here on the beach – simple enough in summer and warm weather – propounded problems every day for which we had no answer, and yet always we solved them somehow, and it forced upon us feats of strength or endurance which we often performed without knowing how or why; and yet looking back on it now I remember much profound happiness.

In our part of the world the days are very short in winter, and often so dark and gray it is impossible to believe the sun will ever shine again; weeks of icy drenching rain, interspersed by the savage storms that sweep down the inlet from the mountains when the sea roared around and under us and battered our shack until it seemed sometimes January would never end, though once in a long while would come a day of blinding sunlight and clarity, so cold the inlet fumed and the mist rose from the water like steam from a boiling caldron, and at night my wife said of the stars, "Like splinters of ice in a sky of jet."

The wintry landscape could be beautiful on these rare short days of sunlight and frostflowers, with crystal casing on the slender branches of birches and vine-leaved maples, diamond drops on the tassels of the spruces, and the bright frosted foliage of the evergreens. The frost melted on our porch in stripes, leaving a pattern against the wet black wood like a richly beaded cape flung out, on which our little cat tripped about with cold dainty paws and then sat hunched outside on the windowsill with his tail curled round his feet.

One dark windy day deep in January, when there seemed no life or color left in a sodden world and the inlet looked like the Styx itself, black water, black mountains, low black clouds shuddering and snarling overhead, we walked down to the lighthouse.

" – And soon the crabs will bring the spring – " Sam called to us. "But crabs . . . I had a friend, a diver – thief he was in private life, never come home without somethink, even if it was only a nail. Aye. Basement like a junkyard . . . Well, this time he goes down, down, down, you know, deep. Then he gets scairt. – Why? Migrations of billions of crabs, climbing all around him, migrating in the spring, aclambering around him, aswallering and stretching their muscles."

"!"

"Aye. Perhaps they see somethink *else* down there – who knows? Because he was so crazy scairt he wouldn't speak to no one for two weeks. But after that, he sings like nightingales, and he'd talk the head off any wooden duck. . . . And soon the crabs, my dearies, and soon the birds will bring the spring. . . ."

It was about this time we began to read more. I went to the city library and took out a "country card" which entitled me to take away a shopping bag full of books at once. The city, that already, in a few hours, had begun to render our existence an almost impossible fable, so that I seemed to know with sad foresight how even its richest comforts that one day we might in cowardice yearn for, and finally have, would almost suffocate all memory of the reality and wealth of such a life as ours, the city, with its steam heat, its prison bars of Venetian blinds, its frozen static views of roofs and a few small dingy gardens with clipped shrubs that looked, in the winter dusk, like chicken croquettes covered with powdered sugar. And ah, after being away from my wife for all these hours, to return from the city to discover the house still in place and the inlet sleeked and still, the alders and the cedars high, the pier there – for we had built a little pier – the sky wide and the stars blazing! Or, making my way down the sodden slippery path with the trees tossing and groaning about me in the tempest and the darkness, to make again the port, the haven of lamplight and warmth.

But then at night sometimes the elemental despair would begin again and we would lose all hope for terror at the noise, the rending branches, the tumult of the sea, the sound of ruination under the house, so that we clung to one another like two little arboreal animals in some midnight jungle – and we were two such animals in such a jungle – until we could laugh again at the very commotion, the very extremity of duty to a house filled with an anxiety of love like that of officers for a sailing ship in a gale. Though it was in the early mornings of high tide when getting breakfast that this wild elemental menace often proved the most unnerving, with the gray sea and white caps almost level with the windows, and the rain dashing against them, the sea crashing and hissing inshore under the house, causing horrible commotions of logs, jarring thunders dithering the whole little shack so that the lamp brackets rattled with the windows, past which a drifting timber sailed threatening the pier, and beyond the smoke of the factories in Port Boden was just a rainy gray, while leaves were falling into the sea; then our boat hurling itself about down below would seem in jeopardy, at the same time there would be the sound of breaking branches in the forest, the great maple tree would seethe and roar, while the tossing floats squealed piteously, and the loops of Mauger's fishing nets hung on the porch would flap like mad ghosts; and then be motionless; and all the anxiety that had been stretched to its utmost tension repeating, would the poor boat be hurt, the pier against which a thud was like a blow at the heart, relaxed too: though only an instant, the next moment it had all started again, so that what with the wind, the thunderous boomings, the delight in the swiftness outside, the anxiety within and without, the pride that one had survived, the sense of life, the fear of death, the appetite for breakfast as the bacon and coffee smells went singing down the gale every time one opened the door – I was seized sometimes with an exuberance so great that I wanted to dive swiftly into that brimming sea to acquire a greater appetite still, either that or because the sea seemed safer than the house.

But then we went out to a morning of wild ducks doing sixty downwind and golden-crowned kinglets feeding in swift jingling multitudinous flight through the leafless bushes, and another day of winter companionship would draw down to an evening of wind, clouds, and seagulls blowing four ways at once, and a black sky above the trembling desolate alders, the heart clothed already in their delicate green jewelry I had never really seen, and the gulls whitely soaring against that darkness, where suddenly now appeared the moon behind clouds, as the wind dropped, transillumining its own soaring moonshot depths in the water, the moon reflected in the half-moonlit clouds in the water down there, and behind, in the same translunar depths, the reflection of the struts and cross-braces of our simpleminded pier, safe for another day, disposed subaqueously in some ancient complex harmony of architectural beauty, an inverse moonlight geometry, beyond our conscious knowledge.

With February the days were noticeably longer and brighter and warmer, the sunrise and sunset were sometimes bright and beautiful again, there would be a sudden warm bright noon, or even a whole day that melted the ice in the brooks and set them running, or a day of sunlight when one could look through the trees at heaven, where luminous Aconcaguas sailed God's blue afternoon.

In the evening when I went for water, which I always liked to time to coincide with the seagulls' evening return over the trees and down the inlet, the twilight was growing longer, and chickadees and kinglets and varied thrushes flitted in the bushes. How I loved their little lives, now I knew their names and something of their habits, for my wife and I had fed them all winter and some were even quite tame, regarding me fearlessly near at hand. Just past Dunwoiken the path took a sharp dip down toward the beach, at a steep gradient, then it turned to the left, up a small slope, and there was the spring that came down from the mountains, where I filled my cannister. Ah, the pathos and beauty and mystery of little springs and places where there is fresh water near the ocean. . . .

The wash from the invisible freighter, the wash still invisible itself from where we were on the path, could be heard breaking all along the curve of the beach as it approached us, and simultaneously it began, slowly at first, and gently, to rain, and as the wash of undulating silver rippling into sight transversely spent itself against the rocks we stopped to watch the rain like a bead curtain falling behind a gap in the trees, into the inlet below.

Each drop falling into the sea is like a life, I thought, each producing a circle in the ocean, or the medium of life itself, and widening into infinity, though it seems to melt into the sea, and become invisible, or disappear entirely, and be lost. Each is interlocked with other circles falling about it, some are larger circles expanding widely and engulfing others, some are weaker, smaller circles that only seem to last a short while. And smiling as I remembered my lesson I thought of that first time when we had seen the rain falling into a calm sea like a dark mirror, and we had found the cannister and decided to stay.

But last night I had seen something new; my wife had called me out of bed to the open window to see what she first thought was a school of little fishes breaking the still water just beneath, where the tide was high under the house. Then we saw that the whole dark water was covered with bright expanding phosphorescent circles. Only when my wife felt the warm mild rain on her naked shoulder did she realize it was raining. They were perfect expanding circles of light, first tiny circles bright as a coin, then becoming expanding rings growing fainter and fainter, while as the rain fell into the phosphorescent water each raindrop expanded into a ripple that was translated into light. And the rain itself was water from the sea, as my wife first taught me, raised to heaven by the sun, transformed into clouds, and falling again into the sea. While within the inlet itself the tides and currents in that sea returned, became remote, and becoming remote, like that which is called the Tao, returned again as we ourselves had done.

Now, somewhere in the unseen west where it was setting, the sun broke through the clouds, sending a flare of light across the water turning the rain into a sudden shower of pearls and touching the mountains, where the mist rising now almost perpendicularly from the black abysses fumed heavenward in pure white fire.

Three rainbows went up like rockets across the bay: one for the cat. They faded and there, in the east, a widening rift of clouds had become a patch of clear rain-washed sky. Arcturus. Spica. Procyon overhead, and Regulus in the Lion over the oil refinery. But Orion must have already set behind the sun so that, though we were Eridanus, Eridanus was nowhere to be found. And on the point the lighthouse began its beneficent signaling into the twilight.

And the spring? Here it was. It still ran, down through the jack-in-the-pulpits, down toward Hi-Doubt. It purified itself a bit as it came down from the mountains, but it always carried with it a faint tang of mushrooms, earth, dead leaves, pine needles, mud and snow, on its way down to the inlet and out to the Pacific. In the deeper reaches of the forest, in the somber damp caves, where the dead branches hang bowed down with moss, and death camass and the destroying angel grow, it was haggard and chill and tragic, unsure measurer of its path. Feeling its way underground it must have had its dark moments. But here, in springtime, on its last lap to the sea, it was as at its source a happy joyous little stream.

High above the pine trees swayed against the sky, out of the west came the seagulls with their angelic wings, coming home to rest. And I remembered how every evening I used to go down this path through the forest to get water from the spring at dusk. . . . Looking over my wife's shoulder I could see a deer swimming toward the lighthouse.

Laughing we stooped down to the stream and drank.

Description Is a Bird

MICHAEL ONDAATJE

In the afternoon while the sun twists down
they come piggle piggle piggle all around the air.
Under clouds of horses the sand swallows turn

quick and gentle as wind.
All virtuoso performances
that presume a magnificent audience.

The leader flings his neck back,
turns thinner than whims.
Like God the others follow
anticipating each twist,
the betrayals of a feather.

For them no thumping wing beat of a crow,
they bounce on a breath
scattering with the discipline of a watch.

Sea-Gulls

E. J. PRATT

For one carved instant as they flew,
The language had no simile –
Silver, crystal, ivory
Were tarnished. Etched upon the horizon blue,
The frieze must go unchallenged, for the lift
And carriage of the wings would stain the drift
Of stars against a tropic indigo
Or dull the parable of snow.

Now settling one by one
Within green hollows or where curled
Crests caught the spectrum from the sun,
A thousand wings are furled.
No clay-born lilies of the world
Could blow as free
As those wild orchids of the sea.

Five

Never Quite the Same: Wilderness and Self-Discovery

INTRODUCTION

Among the enduring themes of world literature are those of personal change, and self-discovery. The two are often interwoven. Through his involvement in some kind of experience – warfare, a love affair, a journey – the protagonist's character and attitudes are altered. Frequently, the change involves growth toward maturity and is accompanied by a sharpened understanding of self and society. Such is the case throughout the history of literature: in Sophocles' *Oedipus Rex*, in the Old English *Beowulf*, Shakespeare's *King Lear*, Dickens' *Great Expectations*, Hermann Hesse's *Siddhartha*, Albert Camus' *The Stranger*, Mark Twain's *The Adventures of Huckleberry Finn*, Ernest Hemingway's *In Our Time*. The list could be extended to include much of the literature of many times and many places.

Canadian literature is no exception. And, not surprisingly, a wilderness experience is often the catalyst of change, growth, and self-revelation for the Canadian protagonist. Sometimes the experience is associated with violence and horror, as in Hugh MacLennan's *The Watch That Ends the Night*. Here, the young boy Jerome is initiated into manhood through the murder of his mother in a remote logging camp and his night journey down a misty, tree-shrouded river to the ocean. In later life, he thinks that "every time when I've been in danger and everything seemed hopeless, some moment like this always came. Suddenly I'd hear myself saying, 'You're going to make it. You're going to make it after all.' " His wilderness ordeal, difficult as it is, teaches him to endure – at least in a physical sense.

In other cases, change and knowledge may take place in terms of emotional or psychical development. This is so with Harry Summers, who runs white water to arrive at increased self-confidence and exuberance in James Bacque's *The Lonely Ones*. "Hey, I made it," he says, and reflects that never in his life has he "gone and done such a dangerous and difficult thing before, such a beautiful thing worth doing. . . ." This is also so with the central character of Gabrielle Roy's *The Cashier*, who retreats from the city and its "barking dogs, slamming doors, clanking milk bottles." He has been a slave of time, but in his wilderness refuge, a remarkable change takes place: he feels young – not as he did at thirty or forty, but all the same, he experiences the delight of having shed a few years from his life. He also feels, importantly, a sense of love for and oneness with his fellows on earth. The metamorphosis is so strange that he becomes "an almost constant source of astonishment to himself."

Finally, in some instances, the growth and change is of a moral or ethical nature. A bear's great paws clenched in agony are remembered by Wayland Drew's hero and, afterward, Franklin is "never quite the same." Similarly, Ken Belford's hunter kills his grouse and then begins to "wonder if a law has been broken." And in Morley Callaghan's narrative, another hunting experience leads one character to think quite explicitly in terms of ethical implications. He is led to conclude that justice in civilization, as in the wilderness, resides in one's conforming to a pattern of natural law. He becomes humble and decides that life will have meaning only if he refrains from passing judgement on other people.

Growth, change, development, revelation, be it physical, emotional, or moral – this is the subject matter of the following selections.

From

The Lonely Ones

JAMES BACQUE

Down the rapids, or the portage? Stand for a minute in the woods listening. They sound high, very high. What's the date? – about June. High water. Very loud from here.

André has left it there as always. A lot of broken branches round here, footmarks on the path and now he has made room for at least two canoes, maybe three. And this one is new. High up where the bears can't eat it.

Lift it down gently, onto thc shoulder roll and take it through the woods. It'll be the rapids. No matter how high they are.

Brilliant green of the springtime woods around me. View of the world from underneath a canoe, the long dark point riding ahead like a roof over the narrow forest trail. Wide as a deer's rump, André said. Wide as a canoe's thwarts.

First time in what, four years, I have shouldered a canoe. Once the ambition to get one sent over to Ktos and paddle down from the Piraeus out to my island.

Can this be the right trail? It seems much longer than before, when we shot the rapids that time in August laughing and falling out at the end into the falls and sliding over laughing and holding a wine bottle and bouncing down the smooth long slope of the rocks full of nothing.

But it is the trail. The last long root-tangled descent to the edge. There it is twenty feet down and going fast. Branches pulled sideways in the flood, swept fast downriver now, black silent water slithering there. Long living snake of water sliding. Pulling the leaves down sideways, hissing. And halfway down the rapids, the arena, whitewater, rocks like animals in the arena snarling charging from every side, the terrible noise. Chute Bruyante they call it round here because the noise is trapped in these high red Laurentian walls and never seems to leave. Even in winter that time when we snowshoed in you could hear the soft turn of the water under the long ice and open here and there sliding past black and cold and hissing along the edge of the ice where the deer had come down to drink.

Just gently down the slope. Tie the bowline here. The two paddles, one lashed in, throw in your dunnage bag and get in gently so. The little red canoe rocking on the fast water with the bowline hanging on to the cedar trunk. Is it strong enough? I really should walk the water first.

It is at least intelligent and not afraid to do this walking down the trail on the steep bank hardly ever used because no one ever comes this way. Everyone uses the portage, Harry. The Chute Bruyante is impassable.

And from here in June in a high sun, they certainly look bad. White everywhere, roaring everywhere spring flood.

Jesus, maybe I should portage. But I have never done this, I have never in my life gone and done such a dangerous and difficult thing before, such a beautiful thing worth doing but not I admit worth dying for but then I intend to do it and not die for it: did I intend to die for the asparagus job at the ad agency in Toronto? No I did not and there I might have had a heart attack and it was not even worth doing let alone worth thinking about dying for, and this at least is a sensationally beautiful thing to do and the water is leaping at me full of joy, come in Harry come on in and try us and see what we're like, impossible, I can't believe that, and there is the water racing and roaring and yelling come come come Harry, those waves don't know Daddy drowned, drowned in June in 1944 off France on D-Day June dying and drowning and gone. But I will not die here I'll get through walking back to the canoe looking at all that and knowing I am about to do it, it is impossible and here we are one.

Going fast now knees up water roaring, grab water sideways, paddle, grab, too fast, water too fast, can't control can't keep up to it must dig, catch up to the river still alive pointing down not sideways get going paddle faster paddle out rockahead gonepast left, left there deep trout pool past the gravel now again steep rapids, more downrace crazy can't stop mile of white water here racing past me wind in ears roar in ears mile of white water racing under me canoe too fast racing under me rocks past bounce crash god rock through bottom not through, saw the ribs bulge, now ahead dark turning place after the long race and the falls ahead, make it round the fast roaring corner here steep trees high over me reach far out to the right black deep water backed up racing here pulling me over the falls I'll die here, this is my death pulling falls coming oh God we're high fly out flying out flying down, sliding oh beautiful falling sliding never stop sliding down all my life sliding down the falls crashing into water. Crashed onto flat black water whirlpooling turning dizzy watching falls turn round and round above me, the falls go by the woods go by the stream goes by the falls go by there is water in the canoe but it is not growing we are not sinking.

What did I do?

Did I come down there? Paddle to the bank. Hold on and watch. The huge white roaring falls. Looking back up over the pool, the rapids falling down from above like huge white stairs towards me constantly moving better get back or they'll slide all the way down here and get me the spray rising into the sunlight and birds flying through it trees falling and leaning and growing into that wet sunlight over the river. My God that's a steep rapids, did I really come down all that race of water and rock? the huge falls here swaying and falling, water bulging over the edge shining swinging like hair falling. Height of falls approximately eight feet, reason I got over it the solid pour of water racing me down. Safest time of year to shoot is now.

In the explosion of white water beating at the smoothed rocks, one sandpiper stands on a rock on legs like two hairs watching the scene around.

Hey, I made it, hey I made it André. Where are you now, waiting at the cabin? No one has built on the lake I hope. Just us again out here, all alone.

A warm summer day to come back Harry. Yes indeed. Down the long river two miles now deep in June full of bugs sweeping back and forth the birds flying and nesting. Bluejay there, sharp singing in the woods, whitethroat, song sparrow, maybe a hermit thrush later on. The hummingbird at that portage once just in there passing the landing place. I've at least saved myself that long boring portage. But the balsam smells nice on that trail. Little coloured bird hanging over the portage resting place at the end by the water, always seen in country gardens and never in the bush before. Canada jay there calling. Lovely place here André. You picked well.

It is elegant to float down this river under the trees joined above your head. I am sweating wet, or is it spray or is it both? Should stop and bail this sloshing canoe. Really should. Shine of a little beach down there. Watch the bottom, no rocks all sand. In autumn come the moose, trumpeting through here, and it is dangerous to come down this drybed stream only three feet deep then instead of eight as now with trout shining all around, because they just charge through the water looking for the does and if you are in the way, bam, like a rock in the rapids, it just goes right through you and goodbye you in the cold water one October night.

Yesterday I was in Paris today I am on the river remembering moose stories pulling into shore to bail my canoe after the rough passage down the Chute Bruyante. Incredible. Did my jet pass this far north circling to land at Dorval?

Slide the bow gently up there and step forth to lift the rest of us up and stand in the sun drying a bit as we tip her over on her side and let the water and accumulated sanddust of last fall spill out the gunwales. Through the gunwale holes nails of water stab the sand leaving craters in line, of mysterious origin to archaeologists. Sixteen spotted sandpipers pissing in formation.

Nearly to the marsh here. Might see a heron or two. Or is that a heronry in the dead tree there. Black bushes of nests hanging in the old dead grey tree. Maybe so. Probably beaver runs in there and the herons are standing in the runs stiff-legged fishing.

I thought I turned right here and went on out into the lake, but I guess I go further down and yes, there they are past those little rock reefs and then right and down the long open lake towards the high hump of André's island. Yes, that's it. The last time there was fall, about what, six years ago, yes and we came down in the canoe and it was cold and grey and wet and blowing.

The final surge out the river mouth and the shallow beaches here, the sand island where you can't build for the floods of autumn and spring, the little grey remembered reefs where we came to swim and skindive those times and made our picnics naked on the rocks lying in the sun.

How far it is down the lake, I didn't remember the lake so long and wide, the hills so big. This canoe is a slow way of going. Yesterday walking up the jet cabin to my seat I stepped the length of this lake with each stride. Hills flying today, clouds blue shadows moving over them, sudden lightning of the sun on a whole range of hills green after the cloud shade, race of white water clouds in the blue river of air, green of the trees toplit by the sun blackshadowed under, covering the slopes, filling the valleys lining the lakeshore, shaved by fire far over there in a flat sloped field; on the irregular hills' high horizon, a regular line cool against the pale lower sky like fur clothing the earth.

From

The Watch That Ends the Night

HUGH MACLENNAN

Jerome put his hand on the knob of the bedroom door and pulled it open. He saw the Engineer bent double clutching his groin and he knew where his mother had hit him that last time. Beyond the Engineer's hunched body he saw his mother's legs and thighs naked in the moonlight, but the hunched man was between the boy and her face.

It was the dog who betrayed Jerome's presence. Whining into the room, the spaniel rubbed against the man's legs and made him turn. The Engineer gasped, his face came around distorted with his sick pain and was horrible with the knowledge of what he himself had just done. But he saw Jerome and recognized him, and the moment he saw him he plunged. The boy dodged back and the Engineer stumbled and hit the floor with a crash, his spanner rattling away from his right hand. Jerome saw that his pants were down about his lower legs and that it was these which had tripped him. On the floor the Engineer looked up, his mouth shut, his violence as silent as that of a fish in the sea. Jerome turned to run, escaped from the room, reached the kitchen door, felt the dog against his legs and had the presence of mind to push him back before he himself went out. He closed the door behind him and with his nightshirt fluttering and his feet bare he ran across the moonlit, chip-strewn clearing into the darkness of the forest. When he was in the trees the undergrowth began cutting his bare feet, he stopped, turned and lay flat.

Nothing moved in the clearing. The long cookhouse with the two metal pipes that served as chimneys stood silent, its sloping roof whitened by the moon, its walls dark, its windows glittering like gun metal. He heard the sigh and gurgle of the river as it poured among the tree trunks along the flooded banks, but there was no sound of men and no light in any of the bunkhouses. He could not see the bunkhouse which was still occupied, but if there had been lights in it he would have seen their glimmer through the trees.

With the instinct of an animal Jerome got up and changed his position, slinking through the shadows among the stumps at the edge of the forest-fringe to a place he knew about thirty feet away. He found it, a depression in the ground about ten feet from the edge of the moonlight, and lay down and scooped pine needles over himself to conceal the whiteness of his shirt and skin. Lying flat with his chin in his hands and his elbows in the needles, he stared at the kitchen door and listened to the pounding of his heart.

The Engineer was only ten feet away when Jerome first saw him. He was skirting the forest-fringe with the spanner in his hand, staring into the darkness of the trees and stopping to take quick looks behind him. He wore no cap, his mackinaw shirt was open and in the moonlight Jerome saw the splash of dark hair rising out of his shirt to his throat. The man stopped directly in front of him and Jerome kept his head down, pressing his face into the needles, the needles itching in his hair. Once he lifted his eyes and saw the man's feet and noticed they were small feet even in those high leather boots. There was a crunch of bracken as the man entered the woods, one of his boots came down within a yard of Jerome's head, but the engineer was staring into the total darkness of the forest and did not look down at his feet. In the cool air of the night Jerome could hear the man pant and thought he could feel the heat of his body. The boots turned and went back out of the forest into the clearing and as they crunched farther away Jerome looked up and saw the man's shoulders go around the corner of the cookhouse and down the path to the bunkhouses.

"I knew for certain that he was after me. He was putting himself between me and the men asleep in the bunkhouse. He knew I couldn't get around through the woods without making a noise. He knew the path was the only way I could hope to go."

Jerome wondered if he ought to call out, but he knew how hard the men slept and he knew who would be the first to hear him. In any case he was too frightened to call. Except for that single jeering laugh of his mother and the man's single outburst of obscenity, what had been done that night had been done with the silence of animals killing each other in the dark.

Jerome lay still until he began to shiver and when the shivering came it was so violent it seemed to shake the ground. It was like being tied up in the cords of his own muscles shaking the earth so that everyone living on it must know where to find him.

Getting to his feet, he beat the pine needles off his nightshirt and scraped some more of them out of his hair. Others chafed the tender skin between his thighs, but these he disregarded as he stepped slowly out of the forest into the moonlight. He stopped, waiting for the man to appear and give chase, but the only sound he heard was the pounding of his own heart and the only man he saw was the man in the moon. He believed there was a man in the moon who saw everything and didn't care, who sat up there seeing and not caring and laughing to himself, and he thought he was laughing now. With his nightshirt fluttering, the boy ran across the clearing, opened the kitchen door and went in. This time he forgot about the dog, who jumped outside and ran away before Jerome could close the door.

Inside the bedroom the blind was drawn and the darkness was total. Jerome found the match box, lit the lamp and turned to look. His mother's body lay like a sack under the blankets because the engineer had covered her and pulled the blind before going out. Jerome lifted the blanket, put his hands to her face and felt the fingers of his right hand sink into a warm stickiness. He jerked them back as though he had put them into fire and stood frozen.

"The bad wound was on the left side of her head and her left eye was bruised by his fist. Her mouth was open and her clear eye was open and angry. She looked far angrier than frightened. My mother died in a rage."

Her body was not yet cold, but it had lost some of its warmth and the blood barely oozed now that the heart had ceased to pump it. Blood was dark and wet all over the pillow and wetly thick in her hair; her breasts were like chalk-white balloons when he tried to shift her body. It was only then that he knew absolutely that she was dead. He cried out to her, he beat her naked breasts with his palms to wake her and all the time he did this he understood she was dead. Knowing she was dead he called to her to come alive again and take care of him, yet all this while he was glad the Engineer had not been like the other men whom she had humiliated.

Then he froze once more, for a step creaked outside. He blew out the lamp and turned to run into the darkness of the cookhouse where there were tables to hide under, but he was too late. The kitchen door creaked open and he crawled under the bed and crouched there against the wall with the sag of the spring just over his head.

The man entered and when Jerome heard him sniff, he knew he was smelling the snuffed wick of the lamp. When the man lit a match it was like an explosion of sound and light simultaneously, but the man did not carry the match to the lamp. Jerome saw his boots standing by the bed as the light slowly died. Then darkness again. Then the Engineer let out a slow, choking sob and went away. Jerome heard his feet go away noisily, heard him bump into a chair in the kitchen, open the door and leave.

He crouched shivering with cold and fright, and he might have stayed there for hours if the dog had not returned to the room. The dog came under the bed whining and nuzzling, and Jerome felt his long, wet tongue licking his feet. The feeling of the dog's tongue horrified him and he rolled over and pushed the animal away, pressing his hands against its muzzle. The beast whined appreciatively and Jerome's hair bristled when he knew the dog was licking his mother's blood off his fingers. He hit the dog and heard him whine. He hit him as hard as he could on the muzzle and the dog let out a yelp and left him alone. Then Jerome came out from under the bed and stood up.

Years afterwards he told Catherine that this was the first of many occasions when a sudden, clear-headed coolness came to him after moments of paralyzing terror. He was only ten years old, but he knew exactly what had happened and what else would happen if his mother's murderer caught him. He knew the murderer had left the bedroom because he was in terror of what he had done there, but he also knew he would be on the watch outside. The Engineer would almost certainly be watching by the kitchen door, for that was the natural way for Jerome to get out and it would also be the shortest route to the bunkhouse where the rest of the men were sleeping.

Jerome had to escape from the horror of that room where his mother lay dead. He took his clothes from the hooks where they hung: his shirt, stockings, pants, sweater and cap, and the heelless larrigans of cowhide he wore all year round. He took them out to the kitchen and dressed beside the stove which still was warm, with the dog nuzzling and whining, and he had to push the dog away several times as he pulled on his stockings. After he was dressed he washed the remaining blood from his hands under the pump and dried them on a roller towel. Very clear in the head now, he opened the big ice chest where the food was and took out the first thing he found. It was a garland of blood sausage much too clumsy and big to carry, so he cut it into lengths and stuffed a length of sausage into each of the side pockets of his pants. He left the kitchen and entered the long eating barn where the benches and trestle tables were, heading for the door at the far end, a door rarely used, and when he reached it he found it unbarred. He guessed that the Engineer had used this door when he had first gone into the clearing to search for him.

"It must have been the dog that saved me that first time. When I ran out into the clearing, the dog must have gone into the eating barn and when the Engineer heard him moving there, he must have mistaken him for me. That was the mistake that gave me time to hide."

The dog was with Jerome now and this time Jerome made no error; he caught him by the long hairs at the back of his neck, held him while he stepped out, then pushed him inside and closed the door on him.

From this corner of the cookhouse the distance to the edge of the forest was no more than twenty yards and nobody was in sight as

Jerome ran across it and disappeared into the trees. He worked his way silently through trees and deadfalls until a quick coolness touched his cheeks and he knew he was near the water on the edge of the northwest branch where his canoe was beached. In flood time the branch invaded the forest a distance of thirty yards or so, and now it was pouring through the trunks of the trees, gurgling and sighing as it strained through the scrub and deadfalls, and Jerome saw quick flashes of light as the moon struck here and there against the living water.

He worked his way along, his oiled larrigans keeping the moisture off his soles, but once his foot sank into a hole and the icy wetness poured in through the laceholes and his foot felt cold and soon went numb. After a few minutes he reached the place where the canoes and rowboats were beached, his own little canoe among them. The camp motorboat was moored to a jetty about a hundred yards downstream in the main river, but the canoes and rowboats were moored where the current was weak, and now he saw their snouts projecting out of the blackness of the woods into the moonlight. He stepped out, looked up to see the sky a wide open dome with a moon in the middle of it and a vast circle of light shining around it.

"I knew I was going to make it. Every time afterwards when I was older, every time when I've been in danger and everything seemed hopeless, some moment like this always came. Suddenly I'd hear myself saying, 'You're going to make it. You're going to make it after all.' "

The short birch bark canoe with the air cans under the thwarts was easy to lift, he turned it over and ran it out into the water. He found his own paddle made to fit his height, and with a single movement he pushed the canoe off and swung himself over into the stern seat, then crept forward and settled down just about midships, got the paddle working and guided the canoe past a tree trunk and clear of some fallen branches. The movement of the current kept pressing him inshore, but he paddled hard on the left into a back-wash that took the canoe gently out, he changed sides and gave two hard thrusts on the right, and then the canoe floated silently out into the great wash of moonlight where the branch widened into the main course of the river. The current of the branch carried him far out from the shore and when he felt himself making leeway he knew he was in the central stream at last. He gave two more thrusts and pointed the bow downstream, and at once he began to move fast on a river wide, firm, silver and alive bearing him down past the silent camp, utterly alone for the first time in his life, bearing him down under that wide open sky through the forest to the open sea which he knew was at its end.

Jerome paddled as he had been taught to paddle in a current, slowly and evenly, making long, steady sweeps of the paddle and after each stroke taking a short rest with the blade trailing behind like a steering oar. The river at this season and place was flowing at more than five miles an hour, breaking and gurgling in the shallows and sparkling in the moon, but out in the central current the flow was so satin-smooth the eddies were like whorls of polished glass. A thin mist lay patchily over the water colder than the air, and the moon was enormous in the wide greenly-shining sky.

"When I grew older and learned how human organisms behave," he said, "I knew I was in that queer state of euphoria that often comes after shock. The response of the adrenal glands to danger. But that's a mechanic's way of looking at it. It's just as real for a man to say, after he's escaped a danger to his life, that he feels twice as alive as he ever felt before. All that night I never thought of my mother. I just thought about the canoe and the river and I was so alert that everything I saw and did – everything – I still remember."

Steadily the tiny canoe went down the river between the trees, following the curves almost by itself in the current. Now that he was secure in the canoe, Jerome eased further back against the air-can lodged under the stern seat and got the head up and sank the stern to give more purchase for the current to take him along. Often he passed floating logs and once he came up with a raft of them lodged on a hidden rock and damming the current, the water washing over and making the whole raft pitch and heave as though things were alive under it. He paddled around, touched logs once or twice and when he was clear he found himself in a flotilla of individual logs that had shredded out from the raft and were going down by themselves. He kept on paddling down occasionally rubbing against a travelling log and sometimes afraid of holing his canoe, but as the logs were going in the same direction there was little danger of this. There were no lights on the shore, no cabins or houses, there was nothing but the forest, the sky, the moon, the river, the canoe and the logs floating down to the sea.

"I had no sense of time that night, but I'd guess it was about one in the morning when I first heard the motorboat. I can still hear it. It was a primitive boat, nothing but an old high-bowed fishing boat with an engine installed. Its motor was always getting out of order and the Engineer was the only man in the camp who could do anything with it. When I first heard it, the boat was still around the bend I had just rounded, and its sound came to me muffled by trees."

Jerome was abnormally strong for his age, his shoulders powerful even then, and now fear gave him its added energy. He paddled hard toward the shore, but at this point the current was so swift that when he tried to move athwart it the canoe was swept hard a-lee, he knew it would take him minutes to reach the shore and that even if he did, the backwashes would sweep him into the current again. A hundred yards ahead was a small wooded island in the middle of the stream and he brought the bow about and paddled for his life making the featherweight birch bark craft jump to his strokes. The drub-drub-drub of the motorboat struck his ears solidly and looking back he saw its dark shape with the hunched outline of the Engineer sitting at the hand-wheel in the starboard forequarter. As Jerome drew in toward the island he saw that many logs had got there first. Instead of a beach there was a mat of logs bobbing in the press of the stream and he was panic-stricken, for the log mat spread in clear moonlight about twenty yards out from the shore, and he knew he could never get through it to hide in the trees. There were all kinds of logs there, long ones and pit-props mixed, some of them piled on top of others and the whole mat creaking in the current. "I had never seen this island before but in a vague way I knew about it. There were several islands like that in the river and they caught tons of logs every year. Once the drives had gone down, work gangs used to follow to clear the islands one by one. That was one reason why men were still left in the camp."

The canoe lifted, slid smoothly up onto some half-sunken logs, stopped dead, and there was nothing for Jerome to do but lie in the bottom and wait. He peered over the side smelling the wet logs and hearing the gurgle and lap of the stream, the canoe bobbing gently with the logs while the motorboat came straight on growing larger all the time, its drub-drub-drub filling the river and the man at the wheel looming up. Jerome was sure the man was staring straight at him, but when the boat was about twenty-five yards off the island the Engineer moved and Jerome saw the bows swing sharply off and an instant later the dark length of the boat went out of sight around the left side of the island.

"Then I knew what he was doing. He was running away. All the men knew about the railway track that crossed the river at the town just inside the estuary. It was the railway a man made for when he got into trouble or just wanted to get away. Sometimes a man left after a fight and sometimes he just left. Looking back on it, I know the Engineer was numb with his own fear. He may have been drinking and that may have been why he didn't see me. Or maybe he was just exhausted by what he had done and in the state of mind when a man can't think or see anything because he can't stand thinking or seeing anything and does one thing automatically after the other. I don't know. But he was certainly getting away as fast as he could and in the only way he knew. There was no telegraph or telephone and it would be morning by the time any of the men would find my mother and a good time would pass before they missed the Engineer and put two and two together. He'd have lots of start. He'd reach the railway long before any of the men could reach it, and once he was at the tracks he'd have his choice of trains moving east or west. I knew nothing about east or west so far as the railway was concerned, not then. I didn't know that east was down to Moncton and Halifax and a dead-end, and that west was up to Quebec and Montreal, and that he'd certainly go west. But I did know he'd be able to catch a train, for all the trains stopped in that town for water."

For a long time Jerome lay in the canoe listening to the diminishing throb of the engine. Such wind as there was came up the river and it must have been twenty minutes before the throbbing ceased. It would die away and return, die and throb up again, but at last there was no sound but the lap of the river and the slow, water-softened creak of the shifting logs.

With the passing of the motorboat Jerome's euphoria left him and he began to shiver and cry. He was chilled because at dawn the cold increased and his left foot, which he had soaked while moving through the trees, began to ache. He reached into his pocket and felt the stickiness of the blood sausage he had stored there, he took it out, washed it in the river, bit off a mouthful and ate it. The taste of blood made him feel sick but he went on eating until his shivering stopped and he felt new strength grow inside of him. He scooped water out of the river in his cupped hands and sucked it in through his teeth though it was so cold it made them ache. Meanwhile more logs from upstream were floating down and kept looming at him out of the dark water, hunching at him silently, pressing at him out of the dark as though they were the river's muscles forcing him out. The log mat was loose enough for him to get his paddle into the water and he changed position and pushed and paddled until at last the canoe gave a quick slip sideways, swerved broadside on to the stream and began to list against the mat of logs as he paddled hard to get clear toward the left-hand channel. A new log loomed at him about to ram but he fended it off, struck hard with the paddle as the canoe's bow yawed against the pressure of the stream, then the unseen hand of the current caught him, he struck with the paddle on the left, the bow shot around and again he was in the flow, passing the island so effortlessly that he was by before he knew it and now in a widening river he went on with the current pouring down through the forest to the sea.

After a time – how long he did not know for he had lost all sense of time – he became conscious that the world was lighter and opening up. Instead of seeing the forest as a dark mass on either side of him, he saw it clear and close with individual trees standing out. Now the western sky where the moon was had become darker than the east, soon there was more light in the east than there had been in the dome of moonlight under which he had sailed since leaving the camp, and looking over his shoulder he saw the moon low over the forest, its light a pallid copper-coloured lane along a river that had become steel grey. Colours appeared, a flush of pink in the east broke apart until it looked like the parallel bars of a gate across the pathway of the dawn, the bars merged, the colours grew stronger, they swelled into a cool conflagration that flushed up into the wide and real sky as the entire world opened up.

Now Jerome became aware of life all around him as birds called in the forest on either side of the river, he saw the white trunks of a stand of birch, and as the current at this point swerved in toward the shore, the carolling ring of bird calls was loud and near. A crow flew out from a pine top and its cawing racketed back and forth across the river echoing from shore to shore. The hammer of a hungry woodpecker whacked against a dead trunk while a larger bird, one of the blue herons called cranes in the Maritime Provinces, flew slant-wise across the rising dawn and turned slowly, its long legs folded in under its body and trailing behind, its snaky head hanging down as it quested for fish with slow flaps of its wings heading upstream along the right bank. Jerome heard a snick and saw the flash of a trout's belly. He paddled on through clear water with hardly a log in sight and within ten minutes there were snicking flashes all around him as trout broke the surface to feed on early flies, the first run of the season in from the sea, quick, slim fish with bellies as bright as silver coins, firm and fierce from a winter of cold salt water as they drove up against the current to the beds where they had been spawned. Jerome saw the lazy roll of a salmon about ten feet from the canoe, the little humping of water as the fish turned and went down; he heard a splash behind him but when he looked over his shoulder there was only a ruffle of broken water; he paddled a few minutes more, the trout still snicking, and then directly in front of the canoe the river broke open and a huge salmon slashed out shining, paused in the air with its hard muscles bending its body like a sickle and dropped with a drenching splash, the canoe crossed the broken water, and Jerome looking over the side saw the last twisting tail-thrust as the big fish went down.

Still the tiny canoe throbbed down the stream, the boy in the stern, and around the next bend he saw a shack but no smoke from its chimney pipe. Now he was sleepy and tired and stopped paddling;

he sat with the paddles across his knees and his head sunk forward.

"I must have slept like that for half an hour, when I woke the canoe was drifting slantwise and light was hurting my eyes."

It was the rising sun, a turmoil of gold like a tremendous excitement in heaven pouring its arrows into the forest and flashing them off the stream. His limbs dead and cold, Jerome straightened the bow of the canoe and let it drift in a current much slower now because here the river was deep and he felt the huge unseen pressure of the tide lower down. Close to the shore he passed a deer drinking on a sandpit and after a while he was afraid that if he fell asleep again he would lose his paddle. A small cape stood out with a sentinel pine, the canoe struck it with a soft crunch and Jerome crawled ashore and dragged half of it clear of the stream. Then he got back in and slept.

When he woke the sun was almost directly overhead, his nostrils were dry with heat and his body felt tired, hot, heavy and stiff. It was a May morning without a cloud in the sky and already the heat had made the balsam forest pungent.

"The time must have been somewhere between eight o'clock and nine. At that season of the year the sun rises about five, so I must have been asleep nearly three hours. If it hadn't been for the glare I suppose I'd have gone on sleeping all day. I was in the aftermath of shock. Even now I can't tell you how far I had come down the river, but I had been paddling with a fast current for at least four hours before I fell asleep.

"But I didn't think about distances when I woke up. I didn't even know what distances were. What I remember is how I felt. I felt black. I felt the way I felt that morning after I first killed a man in the war. I saw my mother's dead face hard and angry in front of mine. God, she was an angry woman, that mother of mine. I saw the Engineer with his spanner and when I tried to eat some of my sausage I nearly vomited it up. I had to get out of that forest and get off that river. Far away was where I wanted to go, and then I thought about the trains."

Though he did not know it, Jerome was now close to the sea and was paddling in a new kind of river. As it nears salt water that river becomes wide and is tidal for several miles. The town lies a distance inland and Jerome could not see the open water of the Gulf, but he could smell it and his cheeks felt a new, salty moisture in the air. He became conscious of settlement along the shores – not a town, but a scattering of frame houses and large breaks in the forest where there were fields and cattle. He also became aware that paddling had turned into heavy, leaden work, for the river was much wider here than it had been at the camp, and its current was stopped by the pressure of an incoming tide from the sea. Jerome ached all over his body as he forced the canoe forward, he sobbed with exhaustion and shock and was drowned in his own sweat, he was on the point of giving up when he rounded a final bend and there, right in front of him, was the black iron bridge that carried the main railway line between Halifax and Montreal. Beyond it was a small wooden bridge for road traffic and beyond that the river seemed enormously wide. There was a town on Jerome's left, a small, drab town built almost entirely of wood, and through his sweat he remembered having been in it before, last fall when he came down in the steamboat with his mother and some men, the time she bought him his first ice cream. As his canoe drifted in toward the bridge he backed water and tried to ease toward the shore. He was so tired he cried. Then he almost dropped his paddle in terror, for a train appeared out of nowhere almost on top of him as it crossed the bridge.

"It was only a small work-train – an old-fashioned engine with two olive-grey cars and a caboose on the end. It made an awful racket though, for it crossed that iron bridge with me almost underneath it. Its exhausts were crashing as it got up speed and it belched smoke from the soft Cape Breton coal all the engines burned in those days. The whole river seemed to shake as it crossed the bridge, but by the time I passed under it the roaring had stopped and I heard the singing drone that rails make when a train goes away down a track. I looked up and saw a man on the platform of the caboose looking down at me and his face was shiny black. He was the first Negro I ever saw and I wondered if all the people in the world outside the camp were black like him."

Jerome forced himself into a last spurt of action and paddled the canoe across the current, making heavy leeway, toward a jetty on the left bank between the two bridges. He remembered it from the time when the steamboat had landed him there. The sight of the jetty also reminded him of the motorboat and he became terrified, for what if the Engineer were waiting for him on the wharf? But there was no sign of the motorboat either at the wharf or along the shore.

"He had either beached it above town or sank it in the river. He'd have wanted to walk quietly into town at dawn before the people were up and hide somewhere near the tracks till a train stopped."

Two men in dungarees and peaked caps were sitting on the curb of the jetty watching Jerome as he paddled in, but neither of them moved as he swung against the landing stage. He climbed out and hung onto the canoe with no plan whatever. He was just doing one thing after another and the next thing he did was to take the painter and secure it to a mooring post.

"Wheer'd yew git thet canoe from, son?"

A lean, unshaven face with a chicken throat was staring down at him from the curb of the wharf.

"It's mine."

"Littlest goddam canoe I ever seen," the man said and spat into the water.

Jerome climbed the ladder stiffly and as he reached the wharf the man made a lazy half-turn in his direction.

"Wheer'd yew come from, son?"

"I bin paddlin'."

The man spat again but did not answer and continued sitting with his legs dangling and his unshaven lantern jaws working steadily on his cud of tobacco. Jerome, afraid of everything and everyone and tired in every bone, walked shakily off the dock onto a dirt track that ran along the riverside of the little town. He reached the railway, bent down and touched one of the shiny rails and found it so hot it burned. When he reached the station he saw men unloading freight out of a solitary box car and was surprised that none of them were Negroes. Jerome sat on a bench under the overhang of the station roof and ate one whole length of his blood sausage, and there he continued to sit an unknown length of time half-asleep and half-awake like the town itself, but feeling a little stronger now there was food in his stomach.

Each Mountain

SID MARTY

Each mountain
its own country
in the way a country
must be
A state of mind

News of the mountains
brought out by the horse guides
long time ago, though some old boys
live long, tell it still in legion halls
how they cut trails to the high tundra
packing a few adventurers
through deadfall of the timber bands
last of the taiga
to find their way
bright with wild cranberry
and flowers

Each mountain
where local climate
controls the shade
of paintbrush and anemone
Colours and moods
vary as the weather, suddenly.
But we belonged here too
men and women
our loving squalls
intemperate desires
wide ranging
hot and cold
like August glaciers
as we travelled for pleasure
walking above the trees
and climbing the summits

Because the smell
of wild mountain flowers
of a thousand hues
threatened the civilized monster
carried in us from the highway

Must be tempered
with the threat of loss
Thus we gain
romantics because
each mountain
made us so
would not have us
any other way

From

They Shall Inherit the Earth

MORLEY CALLAGHAN

The direction of the wind changed, and from the north and over the water came the snapping cold, and in the night the slush froze hard, and a thin, hard, glistening crust was laid over the melting snow.

Michael and Ross were driving down to the flour and feed store on the main street where they were meeting Jo Jamison, the Indian, who was going on the wolf hunt with them. They had their snowshoes and a box of canned food in the back seat of the car.

Michael looked like a lanky lumberjack in his high boots and red and black mackinaw and leather hat.

At noontime the sun was glistening on the brilliant surface of the snow crust. Little kids coming home from school, were sliding on the ice and shouting, their faces raised in the sunlight, when Ross got out of the car at the feed shop. Ross had on a long, knee-length, white woolen, French-Canadian coat, with thick red and black stripes encircling it. Ross's face was round and ruddy, and he looked almost squat as he swaggered into the store. The three old men who were sitting on the bags of chicken feed around the wall, winked at each other and stopped chewing their tobacco when Ross came in in his bright coat of many colours, but Ross was delighted to see that they were grinning at him as though he were a comic character.

One of the old men said, "Hello, doc. There's Jo over there. He's been waiting a bit."

"We're late, but I couldn't get away," Ross said.

Out of the shadow at the end of the counter came a stocky Indian wearing a brown leather windbreaker over an old grey sweater. "It's all the same," he said. His face was as round as a ball and his hard brown skin was all wrinkled up in smiles, as if he had been doing nothing for years but chuckle to himself, and yet as soon as he stopped smiling his face became as solemn and wooden as a dead Indian's face.

"This is Mike Aikenhead, Jo. He's a mighty hunter."

"Sure," Jo said. "All of us mighty hunters."

"This is the first time I've shaken hands with a big wolf hunter," Mike said.

"Two all last year," Jo grinned. "We all have good time just the same. The deer are down at that swamp and if the wolves aren't there then there're no wolves around here. Maybe we catch a rabbit and eat it." And when they went out into the sunlight Jo was grinning as if a wolf hunt in that part of the country was pretty much of a joke.

They all crowded into the front seat, then they crossed over the tracks and out to the highway and turned south from the hills and away from the lake, heading for the black ash swamp some twenty miles south. It was good the way the three of them were huddled tight together in the front seat with the car taking the hills easily, and with Jo telling in his soft and pleasant voice about the time in the Great War when he got as far as London, England, and got lost and wished he were back in the wilderness again.

The road kept climbing steadily from the lowland and once when they were on the summit of the highest hill they stopped the car. It was by the fence of the red-brick church, the fence where the yellow briar bloomed in the spring. And they looked back over the wooded hills and the shadowed valleys and the shadowed mounds that were rocky ridges, and the undulating roll of snow fields, patterned with snake fences and stark elms, the whole country sloping down to the mist line at the lake. At times when the sun was very bright the fields shone as though under glass. Mike thought, "It's like a different world. My life's a different life. We'll never have to go back to the city. It keeps getting more exciting."

Down in the valley they turned into a sideroad. In the fields along the road were big, bare snow-capped rocks jutting out of the ground. The whole country was rocky, and here there were many snow-covered ridges.

The road ended at a farm gate, and there they got out of the car and sat on the running board and tied on their snowshoes. Then they slung the blankets on their shoulders, and Jo carried the provisions, and they began to cross the farmer's field. The crust of snow was broken easily by the weight of their bodies, but they didn't sink more than two inches in the soft snow underneath.

It was easy going down the sloping field. They climbed over snake fences. Soon they could see the black-ash swamp ahead with the bush of dense spruce and cedar, and there were more rocky ridges and little gulleys.

Jo pointed, and said, "Plenty deer over there."

"Only deer?"

"No. I got a lynx there. But soon you see the deer paths. Deer yards over there. I show you," Jo said.

The fringe of the swampland did not look cold until they were out of the sunlight and close to the dense bush, and then it was desolate.

Beyond one of the ridges, and by the fringe of the bush, and by a flat stretch of snow that was a great pond in the summer time, was the old shack Jo used for trapping in that country.

It was almost twilight when they got to the shack and looked back at their tracks in the snow. With the light no longer gleaming on the snow crystals it seemed terribly cold. Jo came out of the shack with a couple of axes and said, "We got to cut wood. We got to make a fire."

While they were cutting wood at the edge of the impenetrable bush Mike was alone, and when he listened, he heard only the sound of the other axe somewhere on the other side of the hut, and when the axe was silent and he still listened, he began to feel the dreadful silence and the coldness of the bush at twilight. He began to feel that in such a silence and in such a place with it so cold and the night coming on, all his hopes and the dreadful fear he sometimes felt in the city were truly unimportant. And again he listened, and again the vastness of the country and the steadiness of the bush and the darkness began to touch his mind and he thought, "If I stayed here, I'd just function like the deer or a fox or a wolf or a rabbit. I'd just be an organism, part of the living things around here; there'd be nothing distinctive about me; there'd only be the distress of my body and there'd be no distress in my soul. I never could feel separated from things here. Here my self, my soul would be lost, but it would be found because I would just be. I'd be a part of all things just being around me. I could hear the call of a winter bird and look up innocently and say, 'Brother.' I could go on day after day like the trees. My mind would grow quick from watching, my eyes would be like a hawk's eyes."

The sound of the axe came from the other side of the hut and then Jo called. Soon they had a fire in the big cast-iron stove, and while Jo opened the cans of beans, the doctor poured whisky in tin cups. "Here we are, lads. Ready for our friend, the wolf."

"We'll be lucky to see a wolf," Jo grinned. "They never come close to me. They don't like me."

"Why are we wasting our time here looking for them, then?" Mike said.

"Sometimes you get a shot at one. They go like a bit of smoke on a windy day. Maybe you catch them in traps."

"I want to have my gun handy if I see them, anyway."

"Maybe they run from you. Wolves are all right. You hear a lot of bad stories about wolves. But they are just like you and me."

"You don't think they're the meanest things on earth?"

"If they're hungry, they kill, like you or me. They're afraid of men."

"I've read of people being thrown to the wolves. Maybe you mean that what actually happened was that the wolves got alarmed and ran away."

"I don't know. I never knew a man who was thrown to the wolves," Jo said, grinning brightly.

"If a wolf isn't just plain mean, then what among living things, in God's name, is mean?" Mike said.

"I don't know," Jo said simply.

"I'm thinking of wolves, the name wolves, like men have always thought of wolves, wolves killing and tearing and preying on weaker living things. Wolves hunting deer and hunting in packs. For God's sake, don't let's get sentimental about wolves."

"Maybe you're right," the Indian said, shrugging. "These wolves around here are small. Much farther up north you get big timber wolves. Very big. Ten feet almost. One time I was trapping in the bush. I got lost. Just a big grey sky like a piece of lead. I can't go by the sun. At night I sit by the fire with my three dogs. The wolves come up at night and make a circle around. I can see their eyes shining, and my dogs howl, and run round and round the fire all night. But they don't come near me and my fire and my dogs. Then, next day, my best dog gets lost. He's my best fighter, too. He lick any two dogs. Then we find him and the wolves have torn him to pieces. Maybe they were hungry. They ate him."

"The wolf has a bad reputation, all right," the doctor said. "But maybe it's an undeserved reputation."

"Don't you see, Ross. A wolf is an individualist," Mike said. "They kill out of the sheer lust of killing, and they kill without sense." Both the doctor and the Indian were looking at Mike and wondering why he was so excited. He was jerking his arm up and down trying to emphasize every point he was making, and there was an intense indignation in his face. "If you want it to be clear that a man is ruthless and an enemy of society you call him a wolf, don't you?" he went on. "Any enemy of the race you call a wolf because he knows no moral law, and that's why you can't organize society, because it's full of wolves, and they don't know justice, and don't want it. The financial brigands and labour exploiters and the war profiteers and the Wall Street sharks and nearly anybody who tries to put his head up a world of private profit, what are they? Wolves I tell you."

While Mike talked like this, he was really crying out against the meaningless confusion of whatever he had known of living, and his search for peace, and he wanted most of all, even without quite knowing how much he wanted it, to justify his preservation of his own bit of happiness and his own life.

But the doctor and the Indian only looked at each other and

shrugged their shoulders. They went on eating their food. When they were finished, and they had all started to smoke, the doctor said a bit irritably, "After all, you don't know much about it, Mike. What do you know about wolves? They may be all you say, just useless marauders. But I thought you were a man with a scientific education, a man full of the spirit of scientific inquiry."

"What you're asking me to do is give the wolves a break, eh?" Mike mocked him.

"I'm only saying you don't understand anything about it."

"I can feel pretty keenly about it just the same," Mike said. While the Indian listened and watched impassively and smoked, Mike and the doctor grew more irritated with each other. Mike felt that the doctor wanted to be patient and understanding about something that did not require much understanding, and he began to feel, while they sat there smoking in the shack with the woods behind them and the darkness beginning to fall on the stretch of snow they could see through the window, that he and the doctor would never truly understand each other while they lived, because the doctor had never had any experience with the tough, harsh, brutal power that was the power men used to survive. Ross was a happy man, with peace and unity in his soul, who had never been pulled and pushed close to death in the riotous struggle to live. He was a simple man and was willing to believe the wolf only wanted to live. So Mike said passionately, though he kept his voice low, "I understand the wolf better than you think. Listen to me. A little while ago when we were chopping wood I felt I might stay up here and lose my personality and become one with the silence and the woods and the natural life around here. It was a good feeling and I wanted to keep it because it made me feel peaceful, but as soon as I start talking to another human being, and I mean you, I feel how different we are, and how we can never really understand each other, and that we each have a world inside us."

"That's just because we disagree. Supposing we agreed?"

"It isn't just about the wolves. It goes a lot deeper than that," Mike said impatiently.

"The trouble with you, Mike, is that you're bogged down with a lot of nineteenth-century notions about science that have been discarded long ago."

"I'm the popular scientist, is that it?"

"Your notion of your scientific training has always been a red rag to me," the doctor said. "Sometimes I can't help thinking that scientists don't know anything. They all work their own little gardens and they all hoe their own little patches. They specialize. They refuse even to consider the relation of one thing to another. If you ask them to, they apologize and say, 'Excuse me, that isn't my field.' Yet the whole world worships them. I'll respect science that's first-hand observation, just the same as I'd respect your observation on life among the wolves if it was worth a damn, but it isn't."

"What am I to say?"

"I haven't any idea."

"You know how I felt about you, Ross. I always thought you were a swell guy, who felt everything in the right way, but was absolutely wrong in his ideas about everything."

"And knowing you felt that way never worried me in the slightest, did it?"

But then Jo said, "Listen."

And while they sat there, and felt the stillness of the night coming on, they heard a lonely, wailing howl. They got up and went outside and looked over the stretch of flat snow-covered pond and beyond that to the first ridge, and beyond that to a gulley and a second higher ridge. Over there the shadow was deeper, and the falling darkness made a misty light where it became one with the snow and the sky. "There's something moving over there on that ridge. Look over there," Jo said, pointing. "Just three specks moving in a circle, little specks." And they looked over there, and Mike was sure he could see the three specks moving, moving round and round in some kind of a dance, and then the three specks were still, as though they knew they were being watched, and then they were gone, and no one could see how they had gone.

"Maybe that's as close as we get to them," Jo said.

"You're sure they were wolves?"

"Pretty sure."

But they stayed out there watching till the heavy darkness came, and the bush seemed to open up and envelop them, and the stars came out. "I keep thinking the wolves come closer like the night," Mike said. "Following the line of the night right up to the shack."

They bolted the door, and put out the light, and lay down on their blankets and tried to sleep. They were all wide awake and listening in the darkness, and Mike kept staring at the flickering light in the stove. It was not cold in the shack.

Then he heard Ross say very softly, "Mike, are you still awake?"

"Yes."

"How did Sheila look to you?"

"Pretty much the same as she always did."

"But did she seem to be the same? Didn't you notice how she had changed, how the core of her seemed to have changed?"

"She's a bit cynical in a kind of wearily wise way and maybe she's getting a bit affected."

"I'm afraid of her becoming neurotic," the doctor whispered. "She's afraid of life, afraid of letting it touch her. She only wants to protect herself. She'd like the two of us to be swayed only by the rise and fall of our own passion and never know anything but our own love for all eternity. And that feeling in her isn't a desire to abandon herself in love; it's just self-protection."

"Do you know what's the matter with her?"

"Sure I do. She feels her mother was mad, and she herself must never have children. And she's been worried about what the world thinks of her father too."

"She's never said anything to me about it."

"She doesn't talk about it to me either. It would be better if she did. She's turned it in on herself," Ross said.

They lay there, and they were silent, and in a little while Ross whispered, "I thought I'd ask you if you'd noticed her, that's all. Good night, Mike."

"Good night, Ross."

While Mike lay there, wide awake and worrying, he heard the howl of the wolf again, and it was closer this time, and he began to tremble. On any other night, if he had been feeling good and had been among friends, the howl of the wolf might have made him snuggle down into his blanket and feel the warmth of the shack and smile in his security, but now he was full of fear, and it was not fear of the wolf, but a fear of being alive and alone. There was just the one bit of light from the narrow window touching the floor. As he waited for the sound of the howling again, he felt he was waiting for a cry from another living thing that was alone and hostile. That moment of terror while he waited began to embrace all of his life. Quick flashes crowded into a moment that was eternity before the darkness of his despair overwhelmed him, made him dwell on his mother's madness, his sister's sorrow, his father walking through the snow, stooping and growing old and looking around with a frightened face, and the anguish in his own soul as he watched him go; and life and death kept beating in upon them all, and life brutalized them and crushed them and death awaited them, and they were living souls caught between life and death, and they resisted and longed for justice; they all became one in their common suffering. How small his own little place in the city was. There in their little place they kept their love, and it was all they had to put against life and death. "Anna, Anna, Anna," he began to mutter. If only the love between them could flow out from them and touch the world; but their love could touch no one but themselves; it could only grow more intense and become an agony, and yet how lucky, how marvellously lucky to have found it and resist with it, and deny joyously that it could perish on the earth. Then it came again, farther and farther away, the threatening wolf's moan, out of the night and the snow, deeper even than that, out of the core of the hostile world.

In the morning, when Michael and the doctor woke up, they were alone, and they looked out the window and saw Jo sitting outside on a log, with the white stretch of shining snow before him, smoking his pipe. Jo had been up early and he had made the fire and cooked the breakfast, but he had been too polite to waken them.

When they had eaten, they put on their snowshoes and took their rifles and started to cross the wide flat stretch of snow, heading for the ridge where they had seen the dark specks last night. The snow crust was thin, but very hard, and in places it was as hard as ice, and in other places the snowshoe broke through easily. The ridge was much farther away than it had looked last night. Jo was a little ahead of them, hurrying, with his head down, and the doctor and Mike were puffing. Mike looked at the doctor and laughed, for the doctor's nose was running a little and the cold air was making tiny little icicles on his wet moustache.

Jo kept bending down and staring at what seemed to Michael to be the utterly unmarked crust of the snow, and when they were on the ridge, he moved around in a circle, his face tense and his brown eyes half closed in the sunlight that made the snow crystals sparkle and tired the eyes. "Look," he said. "Two or three, maybe even four around here."

"I can't see anything," Mike said.

"There's nothing there," the doctor said.

"Just little scratches, that's all," Jo said. "No break in the surface. They have big pads. But little scratches there just the same."

The scratches on the ice went in a circle, and then they went off along the ridge. The doctor and Mike followed Jo, and they were tense and alert, for they were sure they were close to the wolves. There were places where the snow had drifted against the ridges, and if they stumbled, they were deep in the snow. They had turned into the fringe of the bush, and then out again, then on to another ridge. Then Jo threw out his hands and smiled. "No farther," he said. "No more tracks."

"They must have gone into the bush."

"Hard to say. Just like wisps of smoke. Gone now. They hunt along the fringe. Then vanish. No wolves today," Jo said.

On the way back to the shack, Jo was taking a short cut over ridges and gulleys, and when they came to a flat stretch of snow that was a strip of marsh in the summertime, with a gulley at one end, and the rocky ridges on the side, Jo said, "See, a deer yard. See the tracks, just like trails."

There were tracks out from the fringe and over as far as the gulley, and the snow in these trails was tramped down by the hoofs of the deer.

"There's something over there," Jo said, pointing to a mound off the tracks and out on the crust of the snow. "Let's see what it is."

They crossed the deer trails and were out on the hard crust, and when they had gone a little way they saw that the mound was really the carcass of a deer. There were many other carcasses and blood marks, with the snow churned up, and the carcasses stuck there in the hard crust; the sharp hoofs of the deer, piercing through the crust, had impaled them in the snow. A deer stuck stiff in the snow is very dead; there is nothing quite so dead. The carcasses were slashed at the throat, or slashed on the nose, and the flesh of the tenderloin had been torn from every one of the carcasses, just the nice juicy tenderloin torn away, and the rest of the carcass left there to bleed and freeze in the snow.

"Wolves here, all right," Jo said. "Just the other day, too, since the thaw ended and the crust formed on the snow."

"Good God, I never saw such a wanton slaughter in my life," Mike said. "Look at the way they've torn off the tenderloin and not bothered with the rest."

"The wolves hunt at the fringe and watch the deer yard here," Jo said. "Deer are all right if they keep to the paths. The wolves wait for the crust to form on the snow after the thaw, then they get the deer off the paths. The deer try to get away going across the thin hard crust. The sharp pointed hoofs of the deer break through the crust just like through thin ice. Wolves pretty lucky. They have bigger pads and go quick over the crust like we saw, making only scratches, maybe, and the deer stuck in the snow can't move their legs, stuck good and stiff. See. Snow here three feet deep. The wolves pretty swift to get them by the nose, or slash the throat, see," he said, pointing to a cracass.

"And they just tear the tenderloin," Ross said. "They don't even stop to eat them. They don't want them for food, just a little of the tenderloin. Why do they do it, Jo?"

"They like tenderloin, maybe," Jo grinned.

"There's a bit of natural justice for you, Ross," Mike said savagely. He stared out over the snow which was shining and making blue spots dance before his eyes, and he looked at the wilderness of spruce and cedar and the enormous blue sky with the heavy clouds rolling and merging and threatening to sweep over the impersonally bright sun, and then he looked down again at the slaughtered deer, stuck stiff in the snow, and he shouted, "What a god-damned useless slaughter. Useless, purposeless, wanton slaughter. You had the nerve to talk to me last night about meaning and order in life and justice and God knows what else, Ross. Look at it. Put your nose down and try and smell it. The natural history of natural justice. Don't you like that for a title to the picture? How about 'The Search for Glory.' "

"I don't know what to make of it," the doctor said, looking worried.

"It's a bit of sheer wanton slaughter. Slaughter for the sake of slaughter."

"What are you getting at?"

"That's the way it goes on the earth. The deer were alive. So are we alive. And that's the way it turns out," he said, pointing to the carcasses. "Deer, I guess, can't hope and long for things and, like the psalm singer, complain to the Lord, which is just as well."

The doctor was dejected, and he kept scraping his foot on the crust of snow and staring at the blood on the snow. "It's pretty hard to explain," he said. "But that doesn't mean I have to see it your way."

"I don't think it matters much how we see it. There it is," Mike said.

"What do you make of it, Jo?"

"You look pretty sad," Jo said. He had just lit his pipe, and the little puff of blue smoke was whisked away in the wind. Then he turned and pointed at the ridge and the bush. "Over there, there's a she wolf and a litter of pups. Over there maybe under old logs and in the rocks is the old she wolf. Pretty soon the snow begins to melt. The snow starts to go quick in the spring. It's pretty hard to catch deer when the snow goes. The wolves can't hunt them when the snow goes. Then what's going to happen to that old she wolf and her pups? They get pretty hungry by and by with no food because it's spring, and she's got to stay up there with the litter of pups. But maybe they look ahead like you and me. They kill the deer here, and they leave it here because it's not far away from the litter and the she wolf. You say cold storage, eh? They have something to eat when the snow goes. Maybe then the young don't starve. Then the she wolf looks after the pups."

"Mike, did you hear that?" the doctor said, pushing Mike by the shoulder, "Did you hear it? Doesn't it mean anything to you?" and the doctor, standing there in the snow in his coat of many colours, was beaming in his excitement.

"It's pretty hard to believe," Mike said.

"He doesn't believe it, Jo."

"Many people don't believe it," Jo said. "Many old trappers don't believe it. That's all right. I'm pretty sure. You wait. In the spring the frozen meat go pretty quick. You come up again and see. I feel pretty sure."

"Can the wolves worry months ahead about their young being hungry?" Mike asked. "They'd need a chart. Who draws up the chart for them? I'm not arguing. I'm knocked over. If what you say is right, then this useless slaughter is full of meaning. But is it justice for the deer, Ross?"

"I don't know about that, but I believe that everything that happens would have just as much meaning, if we could only see it properly," Ross said.

"Maybe we go back now," Jo said. "Look. It's cloudy and the snow and the wind come. Maybe a blizzard come soon."

They began the tramp back on the snow, and the wind was getting stronger, and the light, hard snow was driven against their faces. Sometimes the sun shone, and then it was gone again, and the snow whirled around them and it was darker over the ridges. Feeling more and more deeply stirred, Mike walked with his head lowered, thinking, "What do I know about anything? What do I know about justice? Why have I thought so much about justice? Is it justice for the wolves when the deer are slain? Is it justice for the deer to wait and be slain, and can they cry out and complain, and who would hear that cry and know what it meant? My own conception of justice spares me and kills my father. Day after day I try to balance the book so I will be justified. The old Greeks talked a lot about justice. Socrates. The giving of every man his due. What is any man entitled to?"

The sun had vanished from the sky and a vast shadow fell upon the earth, over the rocky ridges and the desolate bush, and over the frozen carcasses stuck in the snow; the snow was driven hard against their faces as they leaned into it, and it covered the deer paths, and fell on the wolves, and the lynx and the rabbit and the bear and the multiplicity of life that was preserved in the winter. The wolves had their time and their seasons, and the deer fled and fattened and died in their own time, too, and when the snow had gone and the warm weather came, their carcasses lay there and rotted, and carrion picked at them, and beasts that were hungry tore at the old bones, but still there was a little left for the she wolf and her litter. Now the gusts of snow were driving hard against the faces of all human beings who were out at that hour, in the country or in the city, but when the wind had gone down at nightfall the stars would come out in the heavens and shine impartially on the agitated and the turbulent and complaining living souls.

But there might be unity in life on the earth, and it might be only vanity to try to understand the meaning of the single parts. "Maybe justice is simply the working out of a pattern," he thought. "The deer and the wolf have their place in the pattern, and they know justice when they conform to the pattern. . . . And there would be a justice for all things in terms of the things themselves. There would be justice in art, the justice of form, and there would be social justice, the logical necessity of preserving the pattern of society. If society was what it was today, and there was class striking at class, it was like a jungle, and there was no pattern and no unity and no justice. That's the best I can do," he thought, and he walked on.

Then he cried out within himself, "But what about justice for each single human being? That must be there too. I stink with pride when I judge my father's life, or Dave Choate's life." And as he walked on, closing his eyes against the biting snow, he became very humble, and he thought, "I know everything will have some meaning if I stop passing judgement on other people, and forget about myself, and let myself look at the world with whatever goodness there is in me."

Never Quite the Same

WAYLAND DREW

It was an hour's drive. He wound out on country roads past farms smug with harvest. Here and there in the twilight groups of hunters broke open their guns. Dead pheasants dangled among them, bright, rising things shorn of life in the cornfields.

Dogs frolicked. Franklin blew his horn as he approached, his fear and rage fusing with its monotone. Dear God, hadn't there been enough? Must they kill and kill every small, free thing until nothing remained that was not as trapped as they? Must they kill every wild hope, every spontaneous flight or song, every impulse they failed to understand and feared, until at last they had killed the possibilities for life itself?

Yet, he knew how they felt. He had hunted. He knew the frost under his boots, the dogs snuffling. He knew the instant of the point – the instant *before* the instant – when knowledge of the lurking covey brushed like a feather in the groin, and the gun was already coming up when the dog froze. He knew the thump of the 12-gauge in his shoulder and the gorgeous, ineffably sad falling of the bird. He had seen foxes tumble at a full run, a spurt of dust behind. He had dropped deer, and moose, and antelope, and mountain goats. And he remembered a grizzly rearing up in a spring meadow, raging at the thing which had come between her and her cub. He remembered his own calm. He had settled the sights of the 30-06 first on the fawn breast of the creature, coming at surprising speed, pausing, coming again, grunting like an engine; and he had remembered this about bears: that their adrenal glands are enormous; that they will some-times batter themselves to a rage in order to perform massive feats of strength; that such a bear would be capable, with her heart shattered, of travelling yards and rending her tormentor. He had swung the sights up to the black snout and waited, waited until he felt the ground tremble. Then he shot. The arms had gone up and out, like a furry man's, and a red haze shimmered behind the muzzle that an instant before had been coursing with blood and savagery. He remembered the great breast heaving and the great paws clenched in agony, and he had once thought that that moment was one of the finest of his life, although he could not have said why, unless it was that he had gone, at last, so close to the edge. Grizzly! Afterwards you were never quite the same on Autumn rambles through cornfields, or sitting in a blind waiting for the flocks to come. But you did it anyway. You went along. It was sport. You were among friends, and a man. And you introduced your son to it with a .22 on his fourteenth birthday and a walk through greening fields where groundhogs took the sun.

He knew. He knew how easy it was to kill, how good it was. He had done his share. He knew what it was like to come out of a cold evening and to drink with friends in the odour of sweat, and smoke, and greased leather, and gun oil, and wet dogs, and drying blood. He knew how good that was. As good as being content, as having proved yourself, as having come home after a long time wandering.

But at last a day came when he realized that whatever was in his sights was dead. He stopped hunting, then. It had been a day like this, one of the last of autumn, and the animal had been a deer, a fine buck, stepping out upwind in a clearing. He had levelled the rifle and taken up the first pull of the trigger; and suddenly he saw everything that would happen as surely as if it had already occurred – the recoil, the impact which would lift the forefeet of the animal off the ground and toss it on its side, thrashing. He saw the wild eye fix and glaze. He saw himself bend, find the jugular, draw his knife across it. He saw himself caught inexorably in these events by the shot he was about to fire. Abruptly, he dropped the muzzle and sent a bullet thudding into the dirt a dozen yards ahead of the deer's forefeet. He never hunted again. He had seen it all like a film! He had seen himself living a film, round and round, through infinite replays, trapped like a Chaplin clown!

Still Shots Echo

KEN BELFORD

Still shots echo in a deliberate land,
Almost daring me
To go too far into it.

I've squinted down gun barrels here,
And closed the other eye
When I squeezed the trigger.

There's an abnormal fusion at the other ends of my sight.
And the poles I've believed in 'till now
Come turning back upon themselves.

But I hunt the Arctic grouse.
Tho always I know that to another kind of eye,
There might be nothing here.

A small grey circle of smoke drifts away from me.
A cigarette drops at my feet.
Cold fingertips meet melt and stick to colder steel.

Hit. The startled bird lifts its already dying body
And clumsily drifts across the river
To die on the other side. No one can cross here.

There is no prize today
And a deeper silence. No echo now.
And I wonder if a law has been broken,

Feeling that I've shot more than a bird
Hung out there
At the end of a dry limb.

From

The Cashier

GABRIELLE ROY

Le Gardeur led the way, clearing a path through the raspberries and wild roses, Alexandre following as best he could; he kept stumbling, worn out by too much air and sun. Here he was – he who had thought the home of solitude to be in some faraway Pacific Isle – headed into a forest of his own country, less than a day's journey distant, with the feeling of an adventure beyond recall. The brambles tore threads out of his brown suit, which he reproached himself for having subjected to the ordeals of such an expedition. For indeed Monsieur Chenevert had set off in his best clothes; as he struggled through briary swamps and clouds of mosquitoes, he still looked as though he were on his way to his bank. And yet, after such an escapade, how ever could he go back there, even find his way back? His very reasons for suffering had been, as it were, stripped from him along the way, had become trifling, meaningless. Here whom could he touch, whom could he move? Alexandre had reached that stage on his voyage where what you feel is not yet an illusion of beginning anew, but much rather of coming to an end. Occasionally from a thick clump of bushes, from a tangle of tall grass, there would emerge just his tiny visage, furrowed with weariness, emotion, and a tearing impatience to discover whether what he here would find would at last be happiness.

They came to a cabin built of rough planking. On one side a succession of peacefully contoured little hills, on the other a vast area covered with spruce. The valley thus defined opened upon a small lake, and no other dwelling looked upon it, no travelled road led to it.

The sun was on its way down; over the most distant vista of the lake it cast a showery glow, sulphur yellow and purple. Elsewhere the sky was suffused with a diminished light just sufficient to illumine the woods which enclosed this wild bit of countryside. Over all reigned a silence that long held Alexandre captive. The peace of the valley smote him like a reproach. Vain was your restlessness, without purpose your anguish, without merit your suffering, all of it useless sad silence to this spent man. And besides, have you really suffered?

nature asked him; unable in this place to assert that he had, Alexandre bowed his head; he felt that in all the world there was no man more naked.

"How quiet it is!" he remarked in a sort of wail.

With a push of his knee the farmer shoved in the door. It creaked on its hinges. Alexandre breathed in a musty, stuffy smell. He could not yet clearly make out the interior, cocking his head a little to one side in an attitude of suspicious curiosity. The farmer pulled aside a scrap of curtain stretched over the small window set in the door, and the cabin sprang to life, yet so small that Alexandre, used as he was to confined spaces, could not help a stealthy glance of disappointment. Never would he have thought it possible that, if anyone were to take the trouble to build a house, he could have built it so tiny. Naturally it was only a single room, and yet a complete dwelling, with stove, door, and windows, so that it conveyed to a solemn Alexandre the impression of poking fun at all domestic organization. In such close quarters, would it be possible for him even to think – such was his odd fear. Too much space outside, not enough inside; the curious law of living alone put him out of countenance. And yet he already felt better here, safer than under the overwhelming sky. Throwing a hasty glance about him, he realized that one of his life's deep needs was beginning to be satisfied. For was it not of this sort that he had desired earthly possessions – things unimportant, very humble, cut to the essential, little cumbersome to him as a mere traveller toward another world?

"Yes, yes," said Alexandre, "I think all this will do me very well."

"Fine! Fine!" applauded the farmer, who had watched with a certain anxiety the reaction of the city gentleman.

His mind now at rest upon this point, he set about listing the facilities of the place: "Your cooking equipment," he remarked, tapping a small black frying pan and a chipped cup hanging from the wall.

He leaned under the bed and laughed as he pulled out a basin in which reposed a clean towel and a cake of soap. "That's to wash with," said he. "My old lady has thought of everything. She's filled your lamp with oil, and there's stove wood alongside the house. Anyway, if there's anything missing, just holler!"

Finally he took a chair and made himself at home, explaining: "We've been put in this world, the way I look at it, to give each other a helping hand. Isn't that a fact, Monsieur Chenevert? . . . Chenevert . . . Seems to me I've already run across a man with that name. . . . No, I guess it was Boisvert. You're from Montreal, eh? Quite a town, quite a town! You came by bus, of course. Lots of people. The world certainly is full of people these days!"

He was a square-built, heavy-shouldered man, dressed in coarse blue work clothes who, between questions, tried to put new life into his pipe by three or four long, sucking draughts. His hair was a bundle of reddish hemp, and under heavy eyelids of the same fibre, gay eyes were wrinkled in a perpetual smile, which allowed you to see in their deep blue only a constant crackle of curiosity. Etienne Le Gardeur was certainly as Alexandre had imagined him, except that he had neglected the likelihood that he would be so talkative.

On his way in, Alexandre had already had to put up with half a hundred questions, commingled with bits of life history which he was the last man in the world to have solicited – for instance, how he, Le Gardeur, had left the Lake Saint John region to settle here, and the labour of clearing he had undertaken. In the midst of all this, he had begun the history of the cabin, which had been erected by a Russian he referred to as the Character. And here he was beginning all over again:

"My Russian character – just imagine – was camping out here in your cabin when I bought the land. There was plenty of room for the two of us, as you can very well see, but do you think that Russian could stand living within a mile of a Christian family? Not on your life! Off he went, with his fishnets, his snares, and his woollen bonnet, and can you give a guess where he is today, Mister? . . . It's always been my opinion that the Russians are the strangest characters of all. . . ."

With a weary gesture, Alexandre indicated that perhaps that was true. His sympathies were beginning to turn definitely in the Russian's direction, who had certainly been driven into the depths of the wilderness by such a stream of loquacity. To have come so far, thought he, only to be forced to endure this discrimination between races of people, so belittling to man. He shifted from one foot to another. The day's emotions had worn him out. Indeed the only thing that kept him going was a vast, impatient curiosity: even here, would he be happy? For him there could be no question of pushing on still farther, like his predecessor.

"Strange people, all these foreigners," Le Gardeur continued, but with less animation. "Very strange; not one bit like us . . ."

In his narrator's joy, he had barely noticed before that he might as well have been talking to himself, so little encouragement did Monsieur Chenevert give him. Now, though, everything about his tenant seemed to him stiff and unfriendly – the withered little smile with which he greeted humorous remarks, the eyes travelling back and forth behind the glasses, "like a rabbit looking for cover in the woods," Le Gardeur told himself. Quite nonplussed, he felt loath to leave his tenant with an unfortunate impression. For an instant he wondered whether it might have arisen from his not having shown enough cordiality. Both he and his "old lady," ever since they had put the advertisement in the paper, had lived on tenterhooks and – it must be admitted – with a feeling of friendliness toward the guest who might come their way. Le Gardeur did not know how to break away. He seemed to be going, and then returned, announcing without conviction, as though he could not resign himself to Alexandre's lack of enthusiasm, "Perhaps you'd rather be by yourself. Some folk prefer their own company. So I guess I'll be telling you good night."

But he repeated his offers for service: "Whatever you could possibly need. Why are we in this world, if not to help each other? That's what I always say. . . ."

"Yes, yes," said Alexandre.

He heaved a sigh when Le Gardeur finally closed the door behind him. Yet only a little later, when the silence proved that the farmer had really gone, he had the feeling of having been abandoned to his fate. No sound. Not a voice. Only a great, silent reproach. He stood on the threshold of the cabin, a tiny man, his hat perched on the side of his head. In his hand he still held one of his gloves. And in all his life nothing had ever made him feel so alone as this landscape so deeply at peace and foreign, in its way, to his cares as a human being. Only the crows were stirring at this hour, and they fitfully perched on the sparse tops of spruce trees. One of them cried out and flew over the valley, beating its sooty wings.

Alexandre wandered off toward the lake; but after five or six steps he hesitated, and changed direction toward the woods, soon again coming to a halt. He had made only a tiny circle around himself. Then, stripped bare, he surveyed the vastness of the world as it had been made ready for him. Night was coming. The valley took on a grey hue of abandonment. From its centre, the lake cast a reflection like an old, pock-marked mirror. This evil radiance seemed to give the human consciousness a glance at once indifferent, without pity, and cruelly frank.

"It's beautiful, it's very beautiful," murmured Alexandre, his heart in anguish.

Suddenly the light faded. And already Alexandre was in another world. The edges of the lake had lost definition and were confused with the shadow of great fallen trees. These vast masses of shadow suggested grotesque and bewildering forms to Alexandre's imagination. He thought he could make out a mammoth bear, rearing on its hind legs and advancing toward him with a great knotted stick in its paw. He walked toward the monster, forced himself to touch it, and it turned into a huge gnarled tree with a hanging branch.

Near him twigs cracked.

Alexandre jumped, became exasperated at so many silly appre-
hensions. "It's some little animal of the woods," he told himself.

Then, above his head, the clouds spoke to him out of the void
about the unknown. Voices of distress, long sighs whispered through
the air; the invisible which had been uttering its plaints seemed to
chuckle, very high up, above the treetops.

"The wind," said Alexandre to himself.

He entered the cabin and lit the lamp. And he heard a very odd,
fragile sound, which had even followed him indoors and persisted
when he forced himself into complete immobility. At last he realized
that this disturbance was the sound of his own breathing.

He tried to smile at his terrors.

He unfastened his tie and lay down on the cot.

And then, without any further possibility of subterfuge, he knew
that he was in the presence of her who had called him, seduced
him, deceived him, whom he sometimes thought he loved, and whom
in very fact he had never encountered – solitude.

What manner of thing was this?

On spring evenings, because there was no one who thought as he
did, he had imagined he was alone; but now he saw it; what he had
taken for solitude was good and comforting: at least the streets were
illuminated; all night long the electric lights burned there; bits and
snatches of radio music stole from open windows; you could glance
inside dwellings and share in the lives of strangers; and to the sound
of Alexandre's footsteps there responded the footsteps of thousands
of other men who perhaps also thought themselves alone.

At other moments, in these same streets, elbowed and pushed aside
by others, he had complained that he lacked solitude. Oh foolish and
human pretence!

Even absorbed within her, Alexandre could not succeed in seeing
what she was. A good? An evil?

He slept even less than in the city.

On the ceiling shone the light of his lamp, and in the air current
set in motion by this tiny bit of heat, a fragment of spider web
trembled, a tenuous fragment that even the lightest breath would have
torn into nothingness.

Greater and greater grew the impression of emptiness around
Alexandre.

Solitude seemed to be absence; absence of everything – of men, of
the past, of the future, of unhappiness and of happiness – an utter
stripping. Yet, at the centre of this absence, there was something like
a glance, which overlooked no thought, no action of Alexandre
Chenevert's. Was it God Who in this deep night, far in the dark bush,
had again sought out Alexandre? What could be the reason for such
unswerving attention? What could God want with Alexandre who was

on holiday? On whom the doctor had urged rest? Here God reigned in His most ambiguous aspect.

Those dark stirrings, those clouds, this exhausted creature in this unfamiliar place – all tonight seemed to dread Him.

Close as he was to his happiness, Alexandre was very near to forswearing it, to setting out at once on foot toward the Le Gardeurs' and asking them for hospitality and succour. Yet what man can protect another against God!

As soon as the sun had risen, Alexandre hastily left the cabin.

Perhaps, in the open light, he hoped at last to wrest from solitude her secret.

But now her visage was benign, soft, and pleasant. The dew shone upon the grass, woven into a carpet of numberless little insect webs. Alexandre had to touch it, to see it dissolve at the tips of his fingers to understand that the mere condensation of water could yield this extraordinary effect. The shadowy masses on the other side of the lake were nothing more than beneficent trees, varieties which Alexandre, who was not utterly ignorant of botany, readily recognized – maples, pines, a few mountain ashes, larches, the spruce family above all. The scent of their resin was in the air. As for the mysterious reach of water, yesterday a snare to his consciousness, it was merely a small lake, about a mile long where it stretched the farthest and, at its broadest, scarcely a quarter as much. Alexandre's eyes could easily take it all in at once.

Moreover, in the morning, solitude spoke the consoling language of indifference. The trees bent over, told Alexandre that they lived for a time, died, were replaced and that this was all for the good.

The beauty of this cool morning, which already spoke some hint of autumn, said as much.

Here there was no trace of pity left . . . what rest for the weary!

Alexandre grew soothed, cut down to the measure of passing things.

He watched the grass at his feet as the wind flattened it into long paths; birds flitted to and fro, a score of species, exquisite, the like of which he had never seen, even in pictures; distant clouds drifted by; and he identified himself with a secret understanding between the heart and the innocent, tractable elements of creation. Was he himself anything more than one of these green and supple reeds? And yet autumn was already beginning to wither them. The valley lay in the sunlight, level almost throughout its length, save at one or two places where slight rises allowed Alexandre to envisage it as a whole – calm, happy, spared.

At the coming of night, his soul began to be uneasy, but rather at memories of the night before than at any expectation of the unknown. Suffocating a few brief hours before, solitude had become familiar like life itself, and like it something you could make your peace with.

"How strange," thought Alexandre. "One grows accustomed to everything. I wonder whether there is any kind of life to which men, in the long run, cannot adapt themselves?"

He noticed that he was an almost constant source of astonishment to himself. Here was Alexandre's first pleasure in solitude: to discover within himself as many promises of the unknown as he would in a stranger.

That night he slept much better, yet not altogether perfectly. His sleep had too long been fitful. It still weighed upon his bemused conscience as time stolen from all those on earth who continued to suffer and to labour.

Alexandre Chenevert dreamed. He was at the Savings Bank of the City and Island of Montreal. His gooseneck lamp was lit, the great ledger was spread before his eyes, and he was doing sums. But at the bottom of each column his memory lost the figure he must carry over into the next. So he would begin all over again. And abruptly, instead of dollars and cents, what he was adding up were the Chinese. "Don't miss a single one of them," Monsieur Fontaine kept insisting. "It's very important that not one of them be missing. The collector of income taxes has asked me to balance them up, to the very last man. You know – for the use of God the Father." But it was hard to keep the book up to date. "You can't imagine," said Alexandre, "how quickly the Chinese die, how quickly they replace themselves, what with their famines and their revolutions. I'd have to have an adding machine to keep count of the men alone, and is it absolutely necessary to keep track of these Chinese? There are so many of them. One of these days they're going to spill over the whole world. You know, the yellow peril! Would it not be more humane to let them die of their hunger, since later on we'll have to wage war against them?"

His lips, his hands, his head were all shaking. Lying in profile against his pillow, outlined by the dull glow from the rectangle of the little window, his face betrayed its suffering.

Then someone came and carried off the book, closing it and hurling it far into the lake. There was something like a slight plopping sound. Almost at once the ripples in the lake died away.

And then it was all over. Alexandre slept as it befits a man to sleep. . . .

Very likely the benign presence had not withdrawn very far from Alexandre. He had no reason to seek it in one place more than another, in this quiet countryside, or even on the face of this earth. For Alexandre had a very settled notion that Heaven can only be at some great distance. Somewhere way beyond the clouds was where his imagination placed the presence that filled him to overflowing. And who could it be if it were not God once more? For who else would have taken so much trouble with Alexandre and would so constantly have sought him out? This contentment, seeping through the valley, pierced him with a certainty of God such as he had never yet experienced.

He jumped briskly out of bed.

For twenty years, thirty years, he had suffered from city noises – barking dogs, slamming doors, clanking milk bottles. And now within three days he had grown used to waking naturally.

Another thing, and very odd too: normally, when he talked to himself, it was with bitterness, to say something derogatory about himself or about others. And now the thoughts that crossed his mind were joyous thoughts – you might almost call them trivial.

He had become a stranger to himself, and living with this stranger was far easier, a thousand times pleasanter than living with the old Alexandre.

He washed and dressed with care, just as in days gone by, when through cleanliness and discipline he tried to arm himself for a worthy, undeviating life.

Already the sun had generously invaded his tiny domain. This morning he found it sufficiently ample and very adequately furnished. Was it the Russian or was it Le Gardeur who had made it so comfortable? Someone well acquainted with Alexandre's tastes could have done no better. Everything you needed was here: an old and rusty cast-iron box stove, one of those stoves you know on sight has many a night warmed a man and his thoughts; a bucket to draw water – from inside the cabin you could hear the spring murmuring – a narrow bed, two sets of shelves, a deal table.

Alexandre looked with pity upon men who burdened themselves with the building of costly stone dwellings, not to mention country houses, which they then proceeded to hem in with iron fences, ending with gatekeepers' lodges.

He was lathering his hollow cheeks, constantly turning around, shaving brush in hand, to cast a glance of understanding at the stove and the tiny collection of pots and pans.

Gradually he, Alexandre Chenevert, was reaching the conclusion that he was happier than the greater part of mankind.

He became aware that he was hungry.

To feel hunger and satisfy it – here was a pleasure he had almost forgotten.

He puttered about at the stove. He had suddenly felt a longing to eat potatoes seared and stewed with salt pork, a dish for which he had yearned for some time, but one which, since it upset his stomach, he had flatly dismissed as unrefined. Today he seemed none the worse for it; quite the opposite, he was less uncomfortable than after his ordinary meals of dull vegetables and milk puddings.

Then, no longer hungry, and spared his habitual discomfort after eating, Alexandre felt free.

Even yesterday he had clung to his practice of dividing his day into a schedule of drudgery; he had felt obliged to do such and such a thing during the morning, something else in the afternoon. He was the slave of time.

From now on he would let his impulses rule.

With his hands clasped behind his back, he set out to circle the lake on foot. His bearing put you in mind of a city dweller strolling through the streets, but of one who, instead of other pedestrians and billboards, was scrutinizing trees, a bustling anthill, a hornets' nest. It soon occurred to him that there might be occupations better suited to the day's heat; a slightly acrid odour emanating from the water powerfully attracted him.

He looked for Le Gardeur's rowboat and found it tied to the root of a willow which leaned out over the lake.

And then it was that Alexandre discovered what morning is: the time for decision, for letting yourself go, for enthusiasm, the time which restores to man the full bloom of his will; a setting-forth, a fresh journey!

Awkwardly he tried to row a few strokes, but succeeded only in slapping the water with the flat of his oars. No matter – he was moving away from shore. He had a feeling of adventure and even – a joyful thing – of a certain peril. For Alexandre had no notion of how to swim; and indeed he had not much idea of how to manage oars. But in the morning, does not everything seem easy to learn? He progressed a little further toward open water. Then he had to ship his oars to catch his breath. A gentle current and barely perceptible breeze continued to propel him. And Alexandre attained a joy beyond belief. Something happened to him better than anything yet vouchsafed: he felt young.

Not as he had at thirty, naturally.

Nor yet as he felt at forty.

All the same, Alexandre had the delight of having shed a few years from his life. He no longer felt their weight. He still retained the wisdom, the lessons those years had taught him, but neither their weariness nor their wear and tear.

He started rowing again; almost at once the bottom of the boat struck a rocky shoal. He took advantage of this halt to light a small corncob pipe he had bought at Saint Donat. At the time he had told himself that smoking such a pipe could not be as harmful as cigarettes. And now he was pensive, basking in that self-gratification of a man who thinks it in order to grant himself a favour, as a reward for being happy.

Here is what you might have beheld that day in this remote corner of the world:

First, a sheet of water quivering with light; at its centre, barely stirring, a rowboat. In it a man sat quietly, his legs spread apart.

He was smoking.

An ancient straw hat with a frayed brim shaded his face. His pale neck was exposed by a light sport shirt which made him seem youthful.

From time to time the man cupped the bowl of his pipe in one hand and drew on it mightily. He was wholly surrounded by blue smoke, quite distinguishable in the clarity of the air.

The rowboat rocked him in its cradle.

The man glanced first at one bank, then at the other, both equally free of all intruders. And at that moment he loved all his fellows on this earth.

What other good thing befell him? In truth, nothing of extraordinary moment. He grew hungry and he ate. He was thirsty and he drank. He felt a natural, wholesome fatigue, and he lay down under the branches of a pine tree, his old hat pulled over his eyes. He thought thoughts, welling up from within him as on every other day, but they were no longer his enemies. Very few people would have seen in this something to make a man thank God that God exists. Yet for Alexandre here was a gift from Heaven which he received with thankfulness. From joy to joy the day carried him on toward evening. And then he discovered the night.

It was like a moment of motherly concern. Night bade the birds fold their tired wings, close their beaks so long busy with pecking after food. It stilled the anxious trembling of the aspens. It wandered here and there, unseen and full of heed, like a lonely woman seeking to pledge and share a secret.

A pail over his arm, Alexandre made his way toward the spring, which he could hear and which thus served him as guide through the woods.

He placed his feet in the spoor left by some large animal. In the clearing flooded with moonlight, the water shone and ceaselessly laved some curly greenery. Alexandre marvelled at this delicate stream. He turned his face toward the distant point in the heavens where he still situated his Creator, and he did not fail to thank Him. But when he had scooped up water in a cup left at hand for this purpose, since he was neither ungrateful nor stupid, he recognized that the ingenuity of man played a large part in his well-being.

He needed a little light. With a wholly automatic movement he

Six

Fellow to the Falling Leaves: Man in Accord With Nature

INTRODUCTION

The Canadian life-style has undergone a dramatic change during the past century. An obvious indicator is population growth. From a nation of about three and one-half million people in 1871, we have grown to number in excess of twenty-two millions. Most of this growth has occurred in the extreme southerly portions of the country, and especially in the Great Lakes – St. Lawrence Lowlands. During the same period there has been a marked shift to the cities: a hundred years ago, less than a quarter of our people lived in urban centres; now the cities contain more than three-quarters of our population.

This demographic revolution, together with advances in technology, has affected the quality of our lives in many ways. Among other things, it has cut most of us off from any sustained contact with wild nature. While many Canadians visit the wilderness or semi-wilderness during holidays, few live in it or adjust their actions to it. Frequently, the urbanite, as if to demonstrate his apartness from nature, will install a television set in his cottage along with electric lights and gadgets of one sort or another. The rhythms of life governed by the rising and setting of the sun give place to a pattern of living adjusted to the late movie. The physical vigour required of the wilderness life also recedes. Wood need not be split when heat is commanded by turning a dial or pressing a switch. Even here, in (but not of) a semi-wild environment, the long chain of technology insulates modern man against the real flavour and fundamental cycles of the wild world. Intimate contact is minimized.

At one time, many Canadians lived much closer to untamed nature. The Indian, the fur trader, the pioneer farmer were to a large degree governed by natural forces – whether they liked it or not. Many did not, and consequently viewed the wilderness as adversary. Some did, and found life in the context of wild nature pleasant – or at least not unpleasant. Such people tended to pattern their lives in accord with nature, to roll with its punches and take pleasure in its beauties. They accepted its timetable, rather than struggling to impose their own on it. Despite all the references to the waste and howling wilderness which mark our early literature, we find evidence of lives lived at least partially in accord with nature. Father Paul Le Jeune, a Jesuit missionary isolated in winter-bound Huronia in 1633, for example, describes his environment as being "beautiful and good." More extreme is the Montagnais-Naskapi Indian tale which tells of the marriage of a beaver and an Indian hunter. Here the relationship between man and the wild is close, to the point of intimacy.

Many years were to pass, however, before a substantial body of literature began to dwell on man in harmonious relationship with the wilderness. An example of such later writing is Charles G. D. Roberts' "The Solitary Woodsman." In this poem, the woodsman, filled with "earth's dumb patience," is "fellow to the falling leaves."

Sentiments of this sort, expressed in large quantity, came late. Conservationists and environmentalists, supported by growing ecological knowledge, continue the effort to implant them in the collective mind. Because of this, many of the selections which follow are drawn from recent decades. This is the case with Fred Bodsworth's *The Atonement of Ashley Morden,* Cameron Langford's *The Winter of the Fisher,* and Gabrielle Roy's *The Hidden Mountain.* Perhaps these focus on man in harmony with nature because the authors recognize that modern man is frequently out of step with natural rhythms, or in opposition to them. Perhaps they are attempts to balance rejection with acceptance, alienation with accord. Perhaps they set out to emphasize man's poorly-realized but ancient, powerful, and irrevocable link with nature.

From

The Jesuit Relations

FATHER PAUL LE JEUNE

On the 27th of the same month of November, the winter, which had already appeared in the distance from time to time, completely besieged us, for on that and the following days the snow fell so heavily that it deprived us of the sight of the earth for five months.

I shall tell you what sort of winter we have had here. It has been beautiful, and good, and very long. It was beautiful because it was as white as snow, without mud and without rain. I do not know that it has rained three times in four or five months, but it has often snowed.

It was good, because the cold has been severe; it is considered one of the most rigorous winters that they have had for a long time. There was everywhere four or five feet of snow, in some places, over ten, before our house, a mountain: the wind drifting it, and we, on the other hand, shovelling it away to make a little path before our door. It rose like a wall, all white, higher by one or two feet than the roof of our house. The cold was at times so violent that we heard the trees split in the woods, and in breaking make a noise like that of firearms. It happened to me that while writing very near a big fire, my ink froze; and I had to place a little pan full of hot coals near my inkstand, otherwise I should have found black ice instead of ink.

This extreme cold lasted only ten days or thereabout, not continuously, but at different times. The rest of the time, although the cold greatly exceeds that of France, it is not at all intolerable; and I can say that it is easier to work here in the woods than it is in France, where the winter rains are so penetrating. But one must be provided with good mittens, unless he wants to have his hands frozen; and yet our Savages visited us sometimes half-naked, without complaining of the cold. This teaches me that, if nature can accustom itself to this cold, nature and grace can very well give us the heart and strength to support it cheerfully. If there is cold, there is wood.

I have said that the winter has been long; from the 27th of November up to the end of April, the ground was all the time white with snow; and from the 29th of the same month of November up to the 23rd of April, our little river was frozen, but in such a way that a hundred wagons could have passed over it without shaking it. The ice is of such thickness that, when they were breaking it near Kebec, to launch a bark, sieur du Plessis told me that, being on land, it was all he could do to reach the top of a piece of ice with the rest of a musket that he held in his hand. All this should not astonish any one. All who are here say that they have suffered more from cold in France than in Canada. The Scorpion carries its own antidote: in the countries most subject to sickness, more remedies are found: if disease is there, medicine is not far away.

On the 3rd of December we began to change our footgear, and to use raquettes; when I first put these great flat skates on my feet, I thought that I should fall with my nose in the snow, at every step I took. But experience has taught me that God provides for the convenience of all nations according to their needs. I walk very freely now on these raquettes. As to the Savages, they do not hinder them from jumping like bucks or running like deer.

The Beaver

PETER DESBARATS

The Indian hunted beaver. That's all he did. He trapped the beavers and killed them.

All kinds of animals came to the Indian. They wanted to marry him.

The first animal who came was the fox. "I want to marry you," she said.

"All right," said the Indian. "Would you put up the camp?"

The fox made a camp like a fox's hole. When the Indian came home from hunting, he liked the camp and his wife very much. He liked her except for one thing: she ate his moccasins, his snowshoes, his hauling rope and everything he had that was made of leather.

"If we meet other people," the Indian thought, "I will be ashamed of her when she eats my moccasins."

So he said to the fox, "Go home. I will not marry you."

The next animal who came was the caribou.

"I want to marry you," she said.

"All right," said the Indian. "Go and make a camp."

When the Indian came home, he saw a beautiful camp made out of moss, white moss. The only thing he didn't like about his wife, the caribou, was that she didn't wear any clothes.

"If there were a lot of people around," thought the Indian, "I would be ashamed because she doesn't cover herself."

So he told the caribou, "I cannot marry you."

The third animal who came was the porcupine.

"I want to marry you," she said.

"All right," said the Indian. "Go and make a camp."

All the wood she used in the camp was very nice because the porcupine eats the bark of trees. The bark had been peeled from all the wood in the tent. When the Indian came home, he liked the tent, which was very nice. The only thing he didn't like was sleeping with the porcupine because her quills always stuck into him.

So he said, "Go home. I cannot marry you."

Then the jay came to the Indian and said, "I want to marry you."

"All right," said the Indian. "Go and make a camp."

The jay made a camp like a nest out of dry branches. The Indian killed a beaver and when he got home he asked his wife, the jay, to haul the beaver into the camp. The jay tried to but it was too heavy and she broke her legs.

The Indian strapped up the legs of the jay – that's why the jay has legs that look as if they were strapped around – and he said, "No, I cannot marry you."

So another animal came to him, the beaver, and she said, "I want to marry you."

"All right," said the Indian.

This was the one he wanted to marry so he married the beaver.

While they were living together, the beaver said, "You wanted to marry me so much but you are going to be fed up. Every time we go across a brook you will have to cut branches for a dam. No matter how small the brook is, you will have to put branches across it. Even when we are travelling, that's what you'll have to do."

They went on a journey. The Indian walked ahead and he completely forgot about the branches. Late in the evening he crossed a small brook and he didn't cut any branches to put across it. He just went on and put up the camp.

When his wife didn't appear, he turned back to look for her. He found her swimming in the brook and she said, "I told you, when you wanted to marry me, that it would be difficult. Now it's your turn to stay with me where I am living in the water."

The Indian replied, "But I cannot stay in the water. I'll be cold."

"Take off your clothes," the beaver told the Indian, "and when I turn around, start swimming along with me."

When his wife turned around to swim away, the Indian walked into the water and swam behind her. They went out to the deep water. His wife dove and the Indian followed her.

When he came to the camp where his wife lived, he was not cold or anything. He felt as if he was in a house.

So the Indian and his wife lived together under the water and they had children.

One day the Indian said, "If danger should come, how could we escape? We only live in this one place."

So he made a hidden place. That's why beavers have many places where they can go if someone breaks their house. They have many holes in different places far away from their house.

The people were still hunting beavers but they couldn't kill any. They knew that the Indian was with the beaver. When they tried to trap the beaver by blocking his house with sticks, the Indian always kicked the sticks away and the beavers escaped.

One night his brother dreamed about the Indian, and the next morning he said, "I can bring him back."

So his brother searched for the hidden places where there was a tunnel along the shore. His brother broke the tunnel and trapped the Indian in the beaver's house with his wife and children. His brother put sticks through the ice and the Indian saw that the sticks went above the water and right down to the ground.

He knew that they couldn't escape and he said to his wife, "Now they will kill us."

The Indian said to his children, "Now you can go out."

The two young beavers went out and later the Indian and his wife heard the children being killed on the ice by his brother.

His wife went out and he heard his wife being killed.

His brother broke into the beaver's house and said to the Indian, "So that's the way you wanted to be. No wonder you didn't want to marry when the women asked you to marry them."

His brother gave him clothes. He hauled him back to his camp because he couldn't walk.

He lived with his brother. But he told him, "Never give me the gravy of a female beaver to drink."

They lived together for many years. But one day, when they were running out of food, his brother killed a female beaver. And he thought, "He won't know it if I give him the gravy of this female beaver."

So the Indian drank the gravy.

After he drank it, a brook sprang up from where he was sitting, by the doorway. It sprang up and carried him from the tent to the hole in the ice that they had chopped for water.

The people followed. They went to the brook and looked through the hole in the ice and they could see the Indian swimming together with his wife. They were together again.

This time it was forever.

The Solitary Woodsman

CHARLES G. D. ROBERTS

When the grey lake-water rushes
Past the dripping alder-bushes,
   And the bodeful autumn wind
In the fir-tree weeps and hushes, –

When the air is sharply damp
Round the solitary camp,
   And the moose-bush in the thicket
Glimmers like a scarlet lamp, –

When the birches twinkle yellow,
And the cornel bunches mellow,
   And the owl across the twilight
Trumpets to his downy fellow, –

When the nut-fed chipmunks romp
Through the maples' crimson pomp,
   And the slim viburnum flushes
In the darkness of the swamp, –

When the blueberries are dead,
When the rowan clusters red,
   And the shy bear, summer-sleekened,
In the bracken makes his bed, –

On a day there comes once more
To the latched and lonely door,
   Down the wood-road striding silent,
One who has been here before.

Green spruce branches for his head,
Here he makes his simple bed,
   Couching with the sun, and rising
When the dawn is frosty red.

All day long he wanders wide
With the grey moss for his guide,
    And his lonely axe-stroke startles
The expectant forest-side.

Toward the quiet close of day
Back to camp he takes his way,
    And about his sober footsteps
Unafraid the squirrels play.

On his roof the red leaf falls,
At his door the bluejay calls,
    And he hears the wood-mice hurry
Up and down his rough log walls;

Hears the laughter of the loon
Thrill the dying afternoon;
    Hears the calling of the moose
Echo to the early moon.

And he hears the partridge drumming,
The belated hornet humming, —
    All the faint, prophetic sounds
That foretell the winter's coming.

And the wind about his eaves
Through the chilly night-wet grieves,
    And the earth's dumb patience fills him,
Fellow to the falling leaves.

Sleep

EMILY CARR

When I was a child I was staying at one of Victoria's beaches.

I was down on the point watching a school of purpoises at play off Trail Island when a canoe came round the headland. She was steering straight for our beach.

The Government allowed the Indians to use the beaches when they were travelling, so they made camp and slept wherever the night happened to fall.

In the canoe were a man and woman, half a dozen children, a dog, a cat and a coop of fowls, besides all the Indians' things. She was a West Coast canoe – dug out of a great red cedar tree. She was long and slim, with a high prow shaped like a wolf's head. She was painted black with a line of blue running round the top of the inside. Her stern went straight down into the water. The Indian mother sat in the stern and steered the canoe with a paddle.

When the canoe was near the shore, the man and the woman drove their paddles strong and hard, and the canoe shot high up onto the pebbles with a growling sound. The barefoot children swarmed over her side and waded ashore.

The man and the woman got out and dragged the canoe high onto the beach. There was a baby tucked into the woman's shawl; the shawl bound the child close to her body. She waddled slowly across the beach, her bare feet settling in the sand with every step, her fleshy body squared down onto her feet. All the movements of the man and the woman were slow and steady; their springless feet padded flatly; their backs and shoulders were straight. The few words they said to each other were guttural and low-pitched.

The Indian children did not race up and down the beach, astonished at strange new things, as we always were. These children belonged to the beach, and were as much a part of it as the drift-logs and the stones.

The man gathered a handful of sticks and lit a fire. They took a big iron pot and their food out of the canoe, and set them by the fire. The woman sat among the things with her baby – she managed the shawl and the baby so that she had her arms free, and her hands moved among the kettles and food.

The man and a boy, about as big as I was, came up the path on the bank with tin pails. When they saw me, the boy hung back and stared. The man grinned and pointed to our well. He had coarse hair hanging to his shoulders; it was unbrushed and his head was bound with a red band. He had wrinkles everywhere, face, hands and clothing. His coat and pants were in tatters. He was brown and dirty all over, but his face was gentle and kind.

Soon I heard the pad-pad of their naked feet on the clay of the path. The water from the boy's pail slopped in the dust while he stared back at me.

They made tea and ate stuff out of the iron pot; it was fish, I could smell it. The man and the woman sat beside the pot, but the children took pieces and ran up and down eating them.

They had hung a tent from the limb of the old willow tree that lolled over the sand from the bank. The bundles and blankets had been tossed into the tent; the flaps were open and I could see everything lying higgledy-piggledy inside.

Each child ate what he wanted, then he went into the tent and tumbled, dead with sleep, among the bundles. The man, too, stopped eating and went into the tent and lay down. The dog and the cat were curled up among the blankets.

The woman on the beach drew the smouldering logs apart; when she poured a little water on them they hissed. Last of all she too went into the tent with her baby.

The tent full of sleep greyed itself into the shadow under the willow tree. The wolf's head of the canoe stuck up black on the beach a little longer; then it faded back and back into the night. The sea kept on going slap-slap-slap over the beach.

From

The Atonement of Ashley Morden

FRED BODSWORTH

She picked up the packsack and tiptoed out. As soon as she threw the packsack on her back and leaned against the familiar cut of the carrying straps across her shoulders, she felt a little better, a little closer to the world she knew.

The river front was deserted. She selected a light, fourteen-foot canoe and a pair of springy spruce paddles. She would need this lighter canoe anyway, for their big, old one at Kawogamee was too heavy for her to portage. She slipped it quietly into the water. Her paddle dipped silently, the canoe lunged ahead, wavelets slapping softly on its bottom, and already the fears were lifting.

She had not thought out in detail what she was doing; she was goaded instead by a series of negative decisions that had eliminated everything else and left this as the only course. She only knew that she couldn't stay in Loonlac. She was sure she could never adjust to the noise and smells, the crowds, the rushing, the men who were always staring. And she knew that Loonlac was a small frontier town, that all of these things would be magnified and more terrorizing in any other town she might go to. . . .

She was starting out now with only the canoe and a few pieces of spare clothing in the packsack. She had no tent, bedroll, ax, food nor cooking utensils, no compass nor map of the route she must travel, for she had left Kawogamee with no expectation of needing the bush travel gear. The Loonlac stores, when she bought the dresses and shoes with Mrs. Appleyard, had terrified her, and it was easier to contemplate facing the forest without equipment than to face the Loonlac stores again buying travel gear. Besides, she couldn't have done it without tipping off the Appleyards as to what she intended to do.

Kawogamee was probably a hundred and sixty miles by canoe route. She knew the northern half of the route well, for that was the Kawogamee end that she had traveled many times winter and summer with Papa, but she had only a vague memory of the maps to guide her through this first, southern half of the route. The country was a maze of twisting rivers, lakes, and small muskeg creeks, the waterways linked with portage trails, and there were possibilities every few miles of taking a wrong turn or portage and getting lost. The trip would take at least two weeks. And to keep herself alive she had only a handful of matches and the sheath knife that had been on the belt of her jeans when she left Kawogamee.

But the long forest route ahead held no terrors, not even qualms. She was leaving the terrors behind her.

She paddled with an easy, rapid, short-stroked rhythm. An hour after sunrise she had already left behind the pulpwood booms and the last of Loonlac's outlying buildings, and she was back in wilderness country. The aspen and white birch along the river were yellowing with their first, hesitant tints of fall. The river narrowed and the forests on the banks moved in on her in a comforting embrace. Her eyes still misted periodically when she thought of Papa, but her body and mind were relaxed, the fears drained away. She was home.

About two hours out she heard the roar of a rapids ahead and turned the canoe in toward a blaze mark on a spruce marking the beginning of a portage. She stepped ashore. There were tie cords on the canoe thwarts and she tied the paddles in place so that the blades would form a carrying yoke to rest on her shoulders. She removed a heavy sweater from the packsack and rolled it across her shoulders for padding. She hitched the packsack onto her back and then tested the weight of the canoe. It was light – a fifty-five or sixty pounder. She had not portaged canoes often, for this had always been Papa's job, but she found that she could lift this one to her shoulders without too much difficulty. She was relieved to discover that it wasn't oppressively heavy – a relief indeed, because there would be scores more portages like this one before she reached Kawogamee. She began walking along the portage path.

She had to put the canoe down and rest every five or ten minutes, but she used the rest stops to gather food and the survival equipment she would need. She picked a breakfast of late blueberries and cut strips of the soft, succulent underbark from young aspens which she knew Indians sometimes used as an emergency food. The aspen bark was sweetish and had a rather pleasant flavor, and it quickly silenced the hunger rumblings in her stomach. She stopped for one rest in a grove of birches and cut off several large sheets of birch bark from which she would later make utensils. When she crossed a sand plain with a dense growth of young jack pines, she pulled up several yards of the small tough roots which, after soaking to make them pliant, would serve for lashings and for sewing the birch bark.

The portage was close to two miles long, and with all the stops it took her two hours to cross it. And she didn't push on immediately even then, for at the portage end there was a marshy backwater growing densely with cattails and arrowhead. She knew the roots of both these plants, deep down in the mud of the marsh bottom, were nutritious foods. She hid the canoe in a balsam tangle and went to the back of the marsh, where she would be hidden from anyone passing on the river. She stripped naked and waded out and began pulling up the fleshy cattail rootstalks and the round, potato-like arrowhead tubers, tossing them ashore. In five minutes she had enough for several meals.

She dressed, carried the roots back to the canoe, and pushed off again. When she reached deep water, she tied the jack-pine roots to the canoe gunwales and let them trail behind in the water so that they could be soaking and softening while she traveled.

As she paddled now, she began planning a little more carefully. She had matches enough for only one fire a day, so she would cook each night and perhaps be forced to have cold breakfasts unless she could find logs suitable without chopping to hold a fire overnight. If she had to, she could start a fire without matches, using the Indian bow-drill friction method, but she was not skilled at it, so it would be time-consuming, and she decided to conserve the matches instead and have as much time as possible for traveling.

There would be no scarcity of fruit and vegetable foods. There were still limited quantities of blueberries, raspberries, and the *Amelanchier* Juneberries and, if she needed them, a fair variety of others less tasty, like bunchberries and partridge berries. And there was almost no end of greens and other edible roots, some tasty like lousewort, the *Oxalis* sour grass, fern fiddleheads, and some like the rock tripe lichen and reindeer moss which were distasteful but still nutritious foods if she had to use them. But to maintain her strength for two weeks she must find protein foods, too, and this would be more difficult. She could catch rabbits with snares made from the jack-pine roots, and she would probably have opportunities to club and kill spruce grouse, for the grouse were stupidly tame here in wilderness country where they never saw humans, but this she was reluctant to do. The rabbits and grouse were childhood friends. She could eat game when Indians brought it to them, but she had always shrunk from the thought of killing it herself. But there were other animal foods – clams, frogs, fish, and these she could kill and eat without the qualms of conscience.

There were two more short portages around rapids that morning, and then she came out onto a lake. There was the usual beach on the east shore where storms, predominantly from the west in this region, had thrown up shingles of sand. She paddled along it, searching the rippled bottom that showed clearly through the crystalline water, and soon found a colony of clams. She went ashore, undressed again, and then waded out and began diving in chest-deep water for the clams. Back on the beach she opened the shells with her knife and scraped out the white lobes of flesh, cutting away the black liver masses which in some species in summer could be poisonous.

She didn't make a fire. She ate a lunch of berries and arrowhead tubers – a light lunch because the tubers were tough when uncooked and she could wait until evening for a good meal. The jack-pine roots were pliant now, so she made two birchbark pails for carrying food inside the packsack on the portages.

Then she began considering ways of getting fish. The simplest method would be with a spear. She wouldn't get trout or pike that way, because they were in deep water, but there were suckers and whitefish in the shallow river pools, and with a spear ready she could probably catch all she needed from the canoe while traveling, with no stopping required. Anyway, whitefish was her favorite fish, the flesh was firm and sweet, she preferred it even to trout.

She walked along the beach checking the spruces carefully for a small straight-grained one that would give her a spear about six feet long with a one-inch diameter at its small end. There were several of suitable size, but they were black spruce, and she passed them by because white spruce had more of the spring and resiliency she needed. She finally found one and brought it back to the beach. She unraveled a foot or two of yarn from the sleeve of a sweater and bound the spear tightly at a point about a foot from the small end. She split it with a knife, the split going down as far as the binding, but no farther. She could pull the two split arms five or six inches apart into a Y and, when released, the spring in the wood snapped them back together like the jaws of a trap. She whittled barbs into the inner surfaces of the arms. She cut a five-inch trigger stick to place between them and hold them apart. Then she tried it, striking it at a block of wood floating in the water. The floating block knocked out the trigger stick and the spear arms snapped like a giant snapping turtle's jaws on the piece of wood.

She paddled on across the lake, skirting its shore, looking for portages or an inflowing stream. She found a small river and paddled upstream slowly, searching for rocks that were near the surface. She found one about a hundred yards in. It had several streaks of red and green paint on it from canoes scraping over it. She paddled on rapidly now, confident again that she was still on the main canoe route north.

She passed several schools of suckers and let them go, hoping she would be able to get a whitefish, and not particularly worrying because the clams would give her a meal tonight if she had no fish. It was midafternoon when she saw the silver flash midway along the canoe. She put the paddle down silently and grasped the spear, quickly setting the trigger stick. She saw the flash again and through the distortion of the surface ripples recognized the whitefish drifting downstream tail-first in typical whitefish river-feeding behavior. The canoe lost its momentum and began drifting back slowly beside the fish. She aimed at a point slightly behind it to correct for the light refraction of the water, and thrust swiftly with the spear. The jaws snapped shut and she lifted it in the same single motion over the gunwale and into the canoe. The fish slapped violently on the canoe bottom. She gazed elatedly, for it was at least a twelve-incher.

She was tired, and she stopped on a rocky point to camp for the night when the sun was still two hours above the western skyline. She broke off dead spruce and balsam branches for firewood and lit a fire. She cut lumps of gum from the spruce trunks, melted it on a wooden paddle over the fire, and waterproofed the seams in her birch-bark pails. Since the birch bark was inflammable, she couldn't put the pails on the fire, but there was another method of using them for cooking. She gathered a dozen or so fist-sized stones and dropped them in and around the fire. While the stones were heating, she washed and cut up the cattail and arrowhead roots and cleaned the fish. She put the root chunks in water in one bark pail, the clams and whitefish fillets in the other.

She lifted a hot stone from the fire on a paddle, brushed the ashes off it with a balsam branch, and dropped it into the water of one of the pails. There was a hissing sizzle of steam. Ten minutes later, after the third stone in each pail, both of them were boiling vigorously – as quickly as metal billy cans would boil on the fire itself. She added fresh stones periodically and kept them boiling half an hour, whittling herself a wooden fork and making herself a birch-bark cup and plate as she waited. Then she ate hungrily. The roots were like sweet potatoes, and for beverage she sipped the water they had cooked in. The clams and fish were as tasty as any seafood stew she had ever eaten. She saved some of the food to eat cold for breakfast, and then finished with a dessert of berries.

She gathered several armfuls of dry, springy reindeer moss and spread it under the overturned canoe close to the fire for a mattress. She put on all the clothes she had – an extra pair of slacks and two more sweaters – because she had no bedding, then she crawled under the canoe and lay silently watching the black shadows join one by one, swallowing the last amber patches of sunlight.

She began thinking that many people lost in this northern country had let themselves starve in circumstances no different from these. Man was so ingenious at surrounding himself with artificial comforts that completely altered his environment, yet so helpless when he got out of that environment and back in the natural world where his history began. Far away, a lone wolf howled a faint and tremulous aria, and she thought of Lupe, waiting, she hoped, for her return to Kawogamee. She thought of the fight last winter when Smokey and Lupe had fought so viciously, and of that strange gallantry of the victor that prevented them from really harming one another. She thought of Papa and the militant world of men, that world of balanced terror that Papa could never bring himself to accept and rejoin as his world, too.

She lay staring out at the sky under the edge of the canoe, wondering, puzzling. The sky darkened, its velvet pricked with stars. Out at the edge of her vision she thought she saw a star move, and she jerked her eyes toward it. It *was* moving, speeding across the sky with a directness and a seemingly willed intent that set it sharply apart from the stars through which it passed. She had been watching for the American and Russian space satellites since the first one went into orbit a couple of years before with its weird and sudden extension of the cold war's dimensions, and she had never seen one of them. Now she watched for several minutes with a mingling of awe and fear until it disappeared behind a ridge in the east.

Man had come a long way from his animal beginnings. He had learned a lot along the road. But in the psychological warpings that had come out of his adjustment to the artificial world his hands and brain had fashioned, had he forgotten some of the animal instincts that may once have served him well, and could again? He had never needed them more.

From

The Hidden Mountain

GABRIELLE ROY

A fortnight later he was already a long way farther down the river, the banks of which were turning sad and bare. He had constantly been moving toward the Arctic Circle. By now such trees as had ventured thus far north from more temperate climates seemed to have suffered an ordeal not dissimilar to human wretchedness. Stripped of their inner vitality, their urge to grow, their trunks looked sickly and stunted. . . .

He pressed toward even higher latitudes. What trees now remained clung ever closer to the river. At last came the moment when Pierre believed that in this frail and tiny body, half torn from the bank, yet still resolute, with its roots gnarled and swollen like an old man's veins, he must behold the ultimate member of the poplar family in the desert North. From here on only the spruce and the dwarf white birch could manage to survive, though continuing in each other's company a long way farther, to the very delta of the Mackenzie, and almost always growing side by side. Even the trees here seemed to fraternize, clustering together in accordance with their inner similarities, or because of some strange fellow feeling.

Pierre drew close to the bank, planting his paddle upright in the shallow water near shore so that he might examine the tiny aspen at leisure, remarking its every detail. As it leaned out low over the water, the little tree gave you the impression of deeply pondering its own forthcoming demise.

Pierre plucked from his pocket a bit of pencil and a scrap of paper. The leaves of the tree were fluttering. Their gentle murmur gave voice to a song of tenderness. Pierre listened for a while. He would have loved to let some portion of that voice be heard through the lines of his drawing.

But what, indeed, was his purpose, ever more insistently exacting, more daring, the farther he himself moved onward? In such fashion how could you attain a goal? Oh, well! No matter! Perhaps there was nothing more involved than the job of making this individual tree distinct from all other trees, to be the author of its revelation.

He began his sketch with lines extraordinarily quick and nervous, despite himself probing the motive cause of what he was doing. What, more than all else, held his interest captive? The solitary, lonely, abandoned side of things? Perhaps not altogether. Then what? It upset him to be such a puzzle in his own eyes. But did he really have to dig to the very bottom of the business? Once this sickly tree had been given expression – avenged, perhaps – he would go on to other things, he would continue elsewhere. Had his life no other purpose than to hold captive along the way some portion of the frightening emptiness, the frightening loneliness through which he journeyed?

When his sketch was finished, he gave it no more than a hasty glance – for he soon lost interest in that which, after all, had cost him very little. He was not ill-pleased: upon the paper, as upon the windy bank, the tree stood alone; that you could guess from the empty space surrounding it, from some weariness to be seen in its branches. You sensed that the life of this tree was folly, as so many of our undertakings seem to be folly.

Pierre picked up his drawing anew, examining it with sudden curiosity. A creature of impulse and his own inner compulsions, he did not yet know how he achieved his own effects. The distress of the living tree was disturbing, but even more disturbing was that of the tree captured upon the paper. Pierre thought of butterflies caught in a net and then pinned to a cardboard mount. His tree seemed to him of the same sort – and yet, no, for it was living, and that was what passed explanation. He picked up and opened an improvised portfolio . . . two thin wooden panels held together by a rubber band. Within it fluttered hundreds of slips of paper: pencil drawings, pen and ink sketches, a thousand animal, vegetable, and human likenesses. Haphazardly there emerged the face of an aged Indian woman, smoking a pipe. Then he stowed the whole collection away. Pierre shoved his canoe back into the flowing current of the river.

For him, everything was still almost always as simple as that. . . .

It being evening, he made his camp along the water's edge, without fuss, with a few quick actions that by now had become as natural to him as handling his paddle. Over a few branches of balsam spruce he spread his blanket. Above, he stretched a length of canvas against any possibility of rain, carefully placed his loaded gun alongside it, and then lit a fire. That was all. Most of the time solitude was a good playmate. In the net he had been trailing from the stern of his canoe a number of fine fish were thrashing about. He set most of them free, keeping the biggest, which he killed and scaled; then, impaling it on a green stick, he set it to broil over the fire that by now had reduced itself to glowing coals. He ate; he drank some fiercely strong tea that had acquired a slight taste of wood smoke. Then he slid under his shelter, pushing the canvas back a trifle so that he might watch the sky. The stars emerged from far, far away to take their places in the bewitching night. Was this really night? Could one apply the name of night to this blue – not even a dusky blue – which hovered along that vast sparkling land's edge where, even at midnight, the sun still left its glow behind it, skirting the horizon? There lay, at the end of the earth, between the day and the night, at the foot of the heavens, a sort of illuminated plain, an in-between land, with an attraction that defies describing. This hour has varying effects upon travelers in the great north: some fall under the spell of a heart-rending melancholy. Others become as though bemused by boundless confidence . . . destiny burgeoning in their mind's eye. Today, thought Pierre, he had certainly passed the sixty-eighth parallel of north latitude. He was on the road to longer and longer days. Was it the excess of light that drove away slumber? Pierre felt that he was not going to be able to sleep.

Sometimes there would return, to harass him during his rest, the faces, the creatures, and the things noticed along the way and then left behind. On occasion he would get out of his bed, make a fresh fire, find a piece of paper, and start anew, from memory, on a drawing with which he was all at once no longer satisfied. Or else he might receive a wholly unexpected flash of understanding . . . a counsel so precious that he must seize it in full flight.

This evening, however, there was no trace of anything like this in his restlessness. It was neither remorse nor that sudden gust of inspiration that sets the creative faculties in motion. What stirred within him seemed to have no relation to things done or to be undertaken in any immediate future. This was a besetting feverishness, but with no apparent object. Perhaps it was that in the depths of him, on this particular night, some remote fulfillment was beginning to come into being. Above all he had the feeling of a far-flung stretch of countryside, strange and cold in all its splendor. He did not see it, it is true; nonetheless he knew it in the same way as the dreamer to whom, while yet awake, there may be revealed aspects of the world hitherto unknown. Surely all that was involved was a landscape; he heard, however, the summons of a beauty that did not yet exist, but which, were he ever to reach its realization, would engulf him in an incomparable happiness. At a distance quite beyond his calculating, what might then be this happiness in store for him, from which, even now, he drew such warmth into his soul?

He turned his body on the bed of branches, full to overflowing with an access of expectation. Was he going to catch by surprise the secret of this extraordinary yearning? Once more he saw in recollection those strange lakes surrounded by the Rockies on the lonely highlands of Alberta, lakes that, circled by glacial peaks, remote in their wild solitude, would intermittently give birth, in the very midst of their icy waters, to a boiling geyser. It became impossible for Pierre to stay quiet where he lay. He got up, extinguished the embers of his fire, loaded his belongings, and sped on his way over the black water.

How strange the night he lived through! Beautiful in its immediate present, with its sighing sounds as water and grass caressed the sides of the canoe, with its freak gusts of wind that abruptly scattered the clouds, opening a deep clear space, a vast lunar lake, within the very heart of a cumulus; beautiful in its ageless solitude . . . but even more beautiful for the hopes sung by every breath of air. The weaving of the grasses, the silken shimmer of the water, the valley's deep breathing – was not everything in nature throughout that soft darkness one vast summons following upon another? Without stopping anywhere, Pierre travelled the whole night long.

From

The Winter of the Fisher

CAMERON LANGFORD

The mid-May sun was magnificent, clean and ripe and indulgently warm where it spattered through the nodding branches to kiss the Indian's silver thatch. He was perched in the sentinel spruce, balancing easily on a lower bough that stretched out above the sheer point of the ridge a good fifteen feet. Sitting here overlooking the great green sea of spruce and pine he sought the pleasure the scene always gave him and found it curiously lacking. He could not conceive why. . . .

Abruptly, he straightened. He understood his trouble now. It lay not in the day or the vista before him, but in himself. For the first time in many years, he was lonely for the company of men. The knowledge made him feel very old.

The sun was lowering toward the horizon. The old man cast his eyes up to where a goshawk swept his sunset circles against a sky deepening to a sadder blue. A breeze danced off the lake, bringing a touch of Maytime chill, and he shifted his weight to ease a rheumatic twinge. Older and older still, he grumbled to himself.

He jumped slightly at a sudden rattle of claws on bark, and again when the branch jarred beside him. But his face broke into a huge grin when he swung about to see the fisher stretch out on the limb at his side, the powerful head poised just above his hand. The animal glanced up at the copper face, then with a calculated insouciance, looked out across the evergreen sea. The old Ojibway chuckled, delighted anew by the fisher's way of moving like a silent wind. His eyes caressed the beautiful body. Despite his familiarity he was impressed. Nearly three feet from nose to tail, he mused. The fisher, he knew, would grow into the biggest he had ever seen. His glance drifted over the places where a nearly imperceptible difference in the lie of the fur told of injuries, at the hip, the flanks, and of course, the rather dapper saddle of silver across the deceptively slender shoulders. It's been a tough winter, the old man muttered, scarcely aware he was speaking aloud. Tough for both of us, and you just a year old.

The fisher lifted his eyes to the Indian's, and for a moment, the old man had the startling sensation that the animal understood exactly what he had said. He knew it was impossible, though the feeling surged to a height close to empathy when the fisher dropped his head, and with great respect and delicacy, touched the old man's hand with his nose and tongue. Impulsively, the man reached out and softly scratched the bullet-gouged ear. The fisher blinked, suffered the old man's touch, then circumspectly reached around, took the ball of the hand between his jaws, and gave it a firm but very careful nip. Together, he and the old Ojibway inspected the hand, the flesh indented, but the skin unbroken. Then, as one, both looked toward the lake where the reflections of the mounting clouds sailed softly across the sunset-stilled water.

As the sun touched the western rim, they turned and climbed slowly down. Side by side they walked along the ridge and together faded beneath the eternal trees. Here and there, the man stopped to scrutinize the signs of new growth, of starflower and adder's-tongue and the unfurling veined leaves of false Solomon's-seal. The fisher waited patiently at each pause, then walked beside the Indian to the mooring rocks and watched him slip into his canoe. The man tapped the gunwale near the bow, but the fisher only cocked his ears at the sound, then whirled and trotted away around the shore. The old man shrugged and pushed off smoothly across the shimmering water.

He docked the canoe and stood a moment on the shore, waiting for the fisher to swim the mouth of the stream. The animal flowed up on the land and shook himself dry in a sparkling, bluish mist of droplets. He padded swiftly forward, then stopped. The old Ojibway looked about and saw for the first time that the tenderly viridescent trees along the promontory across from his cabin were alive with warblers. Even in the languishing light, the tiny jewel-box birds seemed to flame with vivid contrasts of color. The old man had not seen such a rush of birds since the migrations of last fall. And once again he was aware of time, of its relentless passing, its finality, and of how casually he had spent its priceless gift through so many thoughtless seasons. The weight of his own mortality lay heavily upon him as he plodded to the cabin to fetch the patient fisher his egg.

The mood was still with him when he returned and knelt to watch the precision and grace with which the fisher cracked the delicate shell. The gurgling cry of a red-winged blackbird echoed cheerfully across the bay, trilling upward through the twilit hush. The old man glanced up in time to catch a figuration of dark wings rocketing up, then flashing down beyond the trees that hid the marsh. The sky still held a touch of daytime blue, but toward the zenith it was shading swiftly into indigo. To the north and south, the first few evening stars were beginning to glimmer, while in the west, very high and breathtakingly beautiful, stood three nocti-lucent clouds. They hung like flame-washed woodsmoke, so far above the earth that, though the sun was gone, they were still steeped in sunset radiance.

Carefully, as though he were afraid to shatter something very precious, the old man breathed a quiet sigh. The mood that had pressed so heavily on him all the afternoon was gone, for he had heard at last the message that for years the silent trees had whispered to him: age is of the body. Youth lies in the mind. And a man's a fool to think on time, when timelessness encloses him on every side.

There was an old Ojibway custom, seldom honored now, that when a man grew old, when the total of forgotten years outweighed the sum of years still left ahead, he would hunt a bear and kill it, and carve upon its shoulder blade a stroke for every year he wanted yet to live. Five years ago the old Ojibway had found such a bone, and smiling at his own foolishness, had cut five marks upon it. The same smile touched his eyes now as he entered the cabin and lit a fire against the spring evening's chill. Then he lifted a flat, roughly triangular shield of brittle, grayish bone from the mantle, and choosing his sharpest chisel, began to carve five more deep, meticulously straight grooves upon the weathered surface.

Outside, the fisher stretched himself sensuously and trotted toward the trees. Before he was beneath their shelter, his trot quickened to a graceful lope, for somewhere in the future just ahead, the porcupines were waiting. And he was still very hungry.

Seven

A Canada to Call Forth Love: Wilderness as Cultural Influence

INTRODUCTION

We in Canada are, in large degree, formed by the wilderness. At one time it hemmed in the lonely log cabins of our ancestors; now it forms the immense, northern hinterland of a highly urban people. It has been our context and – in some cases – our crucible. Our truly native people, the Indians and Eskimos, are people of the wilderness. Our economy is rooted in the penetration of wilderness by fur traders, lumberjacks, prospectors and miners who have wrested from it staples which remain important. The symbols on our currency are drawn from wild nature: the beaver and the bark canoe, the moose and the mountain, the maple leaf and the rushing river. In part, we are the spiritual descendants of Etienne Brulé and David Thompson, La Vérendrye and Simon Fraser, as well as thousands of unsung wilderness *voyageurs* and frontier farmers. Our cities and towns have only recently, in historical terms, grown from tiny settlements in the bush. The epic features of our national achievement have frequently had a wilderness backdrop and flavour: the French and Indian War, the expansion and brawling competition of the fur trade, Wolseley's march through the wilds to confront Riel at Fort Garry, the construction of the C.P.R., the drawing together of small provinces into a federation – provinces separated by vast tracts of mountain, prairie, rock, and forest. The wilderness context has imprinted these events with a special character which is peculiarly Canadian and North American. And the continuing opportunity to experience wilderness – an opportunity which is rapidly diminishing for urban Canadians – aids us in understanding our historical roots and our character.

It follows that those who would comprehend and comment on our culture would do well to immerse themselves at some point in wild nature. Such experience is necessary if one is to write fully and persuasively of the explorer and fur trader, of frontier settlement, of traversing the country with pipelines, of northern development, of Canadians seeking recreation, of Indians and Eskimos, of the extractive industries, of Canadian arts and letters, or, indeed, of the general Canadian *milieu*.

Many of our finest cultural interpreters and men of letters have realized this and have attempted to articulate the Canadian heritage in writings informed by immediate knowledge of our hinterland. Poet Alfred Des Rochers explains why: all of our "fierce past," he writes, "bids me to seek the North for half the year." Historian A. R M. Lower, for another, spent student summers working and camping in the bush of northern Ontario. His canoe travelling took him through much of the near-North wilderness. Later, as those who read "Island Summers" will see, he spent much time on the Lake of the Woods. There can be little doubt that such experience has coloured Professor Lower's distinguished interpretations of Canadian history.

We *are* marked by the wild, and nowhere is its formative impact more clearly evident than in our arts and letters. From the colonial artists to Jacques de Tonnancour and Jack Shadbolt, untamed nature has inspired fine painting in this country. How diminished our artistic legacy would be without Tom Thomson's "Moose at Night" or his "Jack Pine." What a loss to be without Emily Carr's strong paintings of the western rainforest; or J. E. H. Macdonald's "The Solemn Land"; or Lawren Harris' paintings of the Arctic and the Lake Superior shore. Canada is, as A. Y. Jackson has noted, "a painter's country"; and Canada's art has been nourished and made vigorous by wild nature.

Our history, our painting, and our literature are all fundamental elements of our collective memory and imagination – of Canadian culture and identity. All have been deeply influenced by the wilderness and proclaim direct experience of it as part of our rightful heritage. Gilles Hénault amplifies the point in *Hail to Thee* when he writes of a land "helmeted with polar ice/Haloed with northern lights / And offering to future generations / The sparkling sheaf of your uranium fires." Even lacking such direct experience – assuming that we, as citizens of an industrial and urban society, never set foot in it – we should recognise that wilderness remains important to us as a people. It is, claims Bruce Hutchison, no less than "the fixed matrix of our spirit." For Blair Fraser, its imminence gives rise to "the quality that makes Canada unique and gives root to Canadian patriotism." It remains important as idea and symbol, abstraction and inspiration – as an integral element of our cultural geography.

From

Sacred Legends of the Sandy Lake Cree

JAMES R. STEVENS

When the First Light Came

When the first light came, O-ma-ma-ma, the earth mother of Crees, gave birth to the spirits of the world. O-ma-ma-ma is a beautiful Indian woman who has always remained pretty although she is older than time itself. She has long black hair and she always smiles on her children, the spirits of the world.

Her first-born was powerful Binay-sih, the thunderbird who would protect the other animals of the world from the mysterious and destructive sea serpent, Genay-big. The thunderbirds live in nests high in the mountains toward the setting sun. Clouds become black and roll across the sky when the thunderbirds are angry or are fighting with Genay-big. Often it rains and fire flashes through the air while the voices of the thunderbirds cry out in anger. We humans are worms compared to the thunderbirds.

The second creature from the womb of O-ma-ma-ma was Oma-ka-ki, the lowly frog who was given sorcerers' powers and would help control the insects of the world. Oma-ka-ki is often called upon by the other animals to help them when they are in trouble.

Third-born was the supernatural Indian, Wee-sa-kay-jac. O-ma-ma-ma gave Wee-sa-kay-jac many powers. He can change himself into any shape or form to protect himself from danger. Eventually he created the Indian people. But he is also an adventurer who likes to create mischief and play tricks on us. Sometimes he gets our people very angry; however, Wee-sa-kay-jac is to be respected by our people because he has great powers. If you ever meet him offer him some of your tobacco and he may help you.

O-ma-ma-ma's fourth child was Ma-heegun, the wolf. Because Ma-heegun is the little brother of Wee-sa-kay-jac, they often travel together in the forest. Wee-sa-kay-jac will turn himself into a little person and will ride on the hairy back of his four-legged brother. They have many adventures together.

After Ma-heegun came Amik, the beaver. Amik should also be respected by our people. It is even said that the beavers were once humans in a different world, but evil befell them and they became animals. Whenever you kill a beaver, you must throw his bones back into the pond as an offering to the spirit of the beaver.

Then, fish, rock, grass and trees on the earth, and most of the other animals eventually came from the womb of O-ma-ma-ma. It was for a long time that only animals and spirits inhabited the world because Wee-sa-kay-jac had not made any Indians.

From

Canada North

FARLEY MOWAT

The concept of the Far North as a lifeless land is another of our more grotesque illusions. Its southern fringes include the upper reaches of the taiga forests – mainly black and white spruce, larch, birch and poplar. The northward-marching trees of the taiga grow sparser and more stunted until they fade out in the vast open plains called tundra. There is no absolute line of demarcation between taiga and tundra – no real "timberline". The two regions interpenetrate like the clasped fingers of gigantic hands. There are pockets of tundra deep inside the forest, and oases of trees far out on the sweep of the tundra. Nor is the tundra all of a kind. There is alpine tundra high on mountain slopes, shrub tundra close to the taiga region, sedge tundra to the north, moss-and-lichen tundra still farther north and, on the extreme northern islands, fell-field tundra where vegetation finally gives up its stubborn attempt to occupy the remote lands that lie surrounded by unyielding polar ice. But in summertime most tundra regions boast an array of flowering plants of infinite number and delight. Although they are small, they mass in such profusion that they suffuse hundreds of square miles with shifting colour. They form a Lilliputian jungle where hunting spiders, bumblebees, small and delicate moths and butterflies abound. Black flies and mosquitoes abound too, alas, and there is no evading the fact that they are the bane of summer in the North.

Birds breed almost everywhere. Mammals of many species, ranging from squat, rotund lemmings to massive muskox occupy the lands. The seas are home to whales, seals, obese walrus and sinuous white bears. The seas are also rich in fishes as are the numberless inland lakes. For those with eyes to see, the North is vitally and vividly alive. Long, long ago, men of other races out of another time recognized this truth and learned to call the northern regions "home". . . .

The Athapaskans were not the only truly northern people. Indeed to most Canadians they are virtually unknown, having been overshadowed by the overblown image of another race – the Eskimos.

What and who is the reality behind this jolly, chunky fellow in the bulky fur clothing standing four-square to the wild winds of a wild white world? Is he real – the smiling, simple little chap who seems to spend half his time posing for pictures at the mouth of an igloo, and the other half carving or stitching up little Ookpiks for the tourist trade? Let Jonasee of Frobisher Bay speak for his own people:

"You made a picture of us in your minds, you whites. Now you believe the picture, and you know nothing of us. You don't even know our name. You call us Eskimo. That is an Indian word. We are *Innuit* – we are *the* people of this land!"

Indeed the Eskimo is exactly what he calls himself, *Inuk*, which is to say pre-eminently man. His race may well be the toughest, most enduring, most adaptable produced by half a million years of evolution.

As early as 2000 B.C. his ancestors had occupied the most northerly regions of the North from Alaska to the east coast of northern Greenland. Presumably these people originated in Asia, although some archaeologists suspect there was an admixture with Stone Age people from the west as well. Whatever their origins, they were unbelievably capable. Their descendants occupied the whole of the tundra regions, then spread south down the Labrador coast, along the north shore of the Gulf of St. Lawrence, and down the west coast of Newfoundland as far as Cabot Strait. Some may have crossed the Strait into Nova Scotia. Many of them lived by the sea and from the sea, while still others lived far inland, deep in the Ungava Peninsula and in the Keewatin and Mackenzie plains. There was no major land area north of the taiga where they could not and did not live, except for the rock-desert islands at the very top of the Arctic Archipelago where nothing more advanced than lichens can survive. In their heyday, prior to our first coming, there may have been fifty thousand of them. Fifty thousand people for whom the high northern lands were home.

The world they lived in taught them how to make a way of life by adapting to nature rather than trying to overmaster her. They developed a philosophy of existence that is at least as rational as most of our religions. They learned that society is at its best when human beings co-operate lovingly instead of competing fiercely. It is true they never learned to build high-rise apartments, could not fly (except in the imagination), could not have invented television, and were content to jog along (sometimes at fifteen miles an hour) behind a dog team. But then neither did they invent napalm bombs, devise poison gas, manufacture T.N.T. or nuclear weapons. Nor did they learn how to pollute, scarify, exploit and despoil the natural environment in which they lived. In the sense in which we use the word the Eskimos were not progressive; nor, if we make literacy the basic standard, were they civilized. They had no written language, but they had a very adequate alternative in a spoken language that experts consider one of the most expressive and subtle known – an evaluation that might also be applied to their carvings and prints.

Canada

WALTER BAUER

This earth does not bestow
The wisdom of Plato.
Aristotle did not live here.
Nor did Dante pass here through the inferno
In the fellowship of Virgil.
And Rembrandt? Not here the glamour of great lords
And then the drunken unknown king in exile.

Here you receive another kind of wisdom,
Bitter and icy and not to everybody's taste.
This earth says:
I was here long before you and the likes of you came;
Unmolested I conversed with wind and rivers,
Don't forget that, my friend.
The wind blows cold from Labrador:
I have a message for you from the ice age,
But I shall not decode it for you.
The forests of the north surge like waves:
We shall last longer than you.
The Yukon and the Mackenzie flow with quiet patience:
Son, don't make things too hard for yourself;
Different times will come when you are gone, stranger.
The arctic expresses the sum total of all wisdom:
Silence. Nothing but silence. The end of time.

Henry Beissel, (translator)

From

The Canadian Identity

W. L. MORTON

The Canadian, or Precambrian, Shield is as central in Canadian history as it is to Canadian geography, and to all understanding of Canada. It is almost one half of all Canadian territory and sweeps in a vast crescent from the Strait of Belle Isle by the St. Lawrence and the Lakes to the Canadian lakes of the Northwest and the mouth of the Mackenzie. It holds like a saucer the great inland sea of Hudson Bay. It throws up in Labrador and Baffin Island mountains that almost challenge the Rockies which balance it on the Pacific, and along its southern rim heaves up its granite and glacier-scored shoulders in geologic defiance of four Ice Ages survived and of those yet to come. So strong that not even the contraction of the globe itself has buckled its rigidity, it remains with its naked granite ridges, its multitudinous waters and sodden muskegs, an enduring contrast to the wide and fertile lands, the gentle slopes and hardwood forests of the Mississippi valley. The heartland of the United States is one of the earth's most fertile regions, that of Canada one of earth's most ancient wildernesses and one of nature's grimmest challenges to man and all his works. No Canadian has found it necessary seriously to revise Cartier's spontaneous comment as he gazed on the Labrador coast of the Shield. It was, he said in awe, "the land that God gave Cain." The main task of Canadian life has been to make something of this formidable heritage.

There has, in fact, always been something to be made of the Shield, provided a base was available on which to grow food and on which to prepare for the penetration and exploitation of the Shield. In Canadian history the St. Lawrence valley, the Ontario peninsula, and the western prairies have been the regions of settlement which have furnished and fed the men, the fur traders, the lumberjacks, the prospectors, and the miners who have traversed the Shield and wrested from it the staples by which Canada has lived. And this alternate penetration of the wilderness and return to civilization is the basic rhythm of Canadian life, and forms the basic elements of Canadian character whether French or English: the violence necessary to contend with the wilderness, the restraint necessary to preserve civilisation from the wilderness violence, and the puritanism which is the offspring of the wedding of violence to restraint. Even in an industrial and urban society, the old rhythm continues, for the typical Canadian holiday is a wilderness holiday, whether among the lakes of the Shield or the peaks of the Rockies.

I Am the Dwindled Son

ALFRED DES ROCHERS

I am the dwindled son of a race of supermen,
The violent, strong, adventurous; from this strain
I take the northland homesickness which comes
With the grey days that autumn brings again.

All the fierce past of those *coureurs de bois* –
Hunters and trappers, raftsmen, lumberjacks,
Merchant-adventurers, labourers on hire –
Bids me to seek the North for half the year.

And I dream of going there as my fathers did:
I hear within me great white spaces crying
In the wastes they roamed, haloed by hurricanes;
And, as they did, I hate a master's chains.

When the tempest of disasters beat upon them,
They cursed the valley and they cursed the plain;
They cursed the wolves which robbed them of their wool:
Their maledictions dulled their pain.

But when the memory of a distant wife
Brusquely dispelled the scenes that faced these men,
They brushed their eyelids with the back of their sleeve
And their mouths chanted *A la claire fontaine*.

So well repeated to the echoing forests
This simple lay (where the wood-warbler tunes
On the highest branches his own plaintive song),
It mingles with my own most secret thoughts:

If I bend my back beneath invisible burdens
In the hubbub of bitter leavetakings,
And if, when thwarted or constrained, I feel
That urge to strike which clenched their massive fists;

If from these men, who never knew despair
And died even while they dreamed of conquering
    nature,
I take this sickly instinct for adventure
Beneath whose spell I sometimes fall, at night –

In this degenerate age of ours, I am like
The beech whose living sap was never drawn,
And I am leafed around by dead desires,
Dreaming of going forth as my fathers did.

But the faint words emitted by my voice
Remain: a rosebush, branches and a spring,
An oak, a warbler in a sheen of leaves;
And, as it did in my forefather's day,
In the mouth of him who was *coureur de bois,*

My joy or sorrow sings the landscape still.

From

The Quest for the Peaceable Kingdom

WILLIAM KILBOURN

. . . When William Van Horne gave up his American citizenship after completing the C.P.R., he remarked, 'Building that railroad would have made a Canadian out of the German Emperor.' The inexorable land, like the Canadian climate, has always commanded the respect of those who have tried to master it. It is simply overwhelming. The voyager from Europe is not suddenly confronted by the rational outlines of a colossal liberty goddess; he is slowly swallowed, Jonah-like, by a twenty-two-hundred-mile-long river, gulf and lake system. Coming in by air, he finds himself, scarcely past Ireland, flying above the shining blue-set islands of Bonavista-Twillingate, hours before he touches down in Toronto or Montreal. Further inland, islands come by the Thousand – or the Thirty Thousand; there are more lakes than people, and more forests than lakes. Except in small pastoral slices of southern Ontario and Quebec, the original wilderness of bush or prairie presses close to the suburban edge of every Canadian town. Even Toronto surprised a recent British visitor who called it 'a million people living in a forest'. In summer the boreal lights, a shaking skyful of LSD visions, can remind the most urban of Canadians that they are a northern people, that winter will bring again its hundred-degree drop in the weather, and that their wilderness stretches straight to the permafrost, the ice pack and the pole.

Nature dreadful and infinite has inhibited the growth of the higher amenities in Canada. The living has never been easy. The need to wrestle a livelihood from a cruel land has put a premium on some of the sterner virtues – frugality and caution, discipline and endurance. Geography even more than religion has made us puritans, although ours is a puritanism tempered by orgy. Outnumbered by the trees and unable to lick them, a lot of Canadians look as though they had joined them – having gone all faceless or a bit pulp-and-papery, and mournful as the evening jack-pine round the edges of the voice, as if (in Priestley's phrase) something long lost and dear were being endlessly regretted. Or there are those who run – by car, train or plane (flying more air miles per capita than any other people), lickety-split as if the spirit of the northern woods, the *Wendigo* himself, were on their trails. Nature has not always been an enemy, but she has rarely been something to be tamed either. At best we have exploited her quickly and moved on. No wonder the atmosphere of our towns still often suggests that of the mining camp or the logging drive, the trading post or the sleeping compound. If transportation has been crucial for Canada, and our main-street towns attest the worship of train and motor car, then communications (more telephone calls than anybody else), particuuarly radio and television (the world's longest networks), have been vital. It is no surprise when some of old Rawhide's Canadian characters become so addicted to the telegraph key that they can only talk in the dah-dah-dits of Morse code.

Survival itself is a virtue and a triumph. Images of survival abound in our popular mythologies: whooping cranes and Hutterites, dwarf ponies on the Sable Island sand dunes, the Eskimo in their howling prison of ice and snow. Ask the Nova Scotian or the French Canadian what he has done in this country of his these two or three centuries and more. 'I survived,' is the answer – though neither of them is satisfied with mere survival any longer.

But Canadians have also learned to live with nature and derive strength from her. It is not just the Group of Seven who came to terms with her terrible grandeur. From the first military surveyors and the C.P.R. artists down to the abstract expressionists of post-modern Toronto, our painters have been profoundly influenced by the Canadian landscape. 'Everything that is central in Canadian writing', said our great critic, Northrop Frye, 'seems to be marked by the imminence of the natural world.' The American critic Edmund Wilson sees the most distinguishing feature of Hugh MacLennan's work to be the unique way the author places his characters in 'their geographical and even their meteorological setting'. Our historians do not argue about the amount but the kind of influence geography has had on our history – whether it has been the north-south pull of North American regionalism or the east-west thrust of the St. Lawrence and Saskatchewan river systems and the Laurentian Shield. The fur trade of the Pre-Cambrian forest was not only crucial to Canada's economic life for two centuries, but by 1867 it had literally determined the basic outlines of our political boundaries.

Hail to Thee

GILLES HENAULT

1

Redskins
Tribes consumed
in the conflagration of fire-water and tuberculosis
Hunted down by the pallor of death and the
      Palefaces
Carrying off your dreams of old spirits and the
      manitous
Dreams shattered by the fire of the arquebuses
You have left us your totemic hopes
And our sky now has the colour
of the smoke of your pipes of peace.

II

We have no limits
And abundance is our mother
Land girdled with steel
With great lake eyes
And rustling resinous beard
I salute you and I salute your laughter of waterfalls
Land helmeted with polar ice
Haloed with northern lights
And offering to future generations
The sparkling sheaf of your uranium fires.
We hurl against those who pillage and waste you
Against those who fatten upon your great body of
      humus and snow
The thunderous imprecations
That roar from the throats of storms.

III

I already hear the song of those who sing:
Hail to thee, life, full of grace
the sower is with thee
blessed art thou by all women
and the child radiant with discovery
holds thee in his hand
like the multicoloured pebble of reality.

Beautiful life, mother of our eyes
clothed in rain and sunny days
may thy kingdom come
on the roads and on the fields
Beautiful life
Praise be to love and spring.

F. R. Scott (translator)

Island Summers

A. R. M. LOWER

Island summers have not been rare for me. Two summers on an island in Lake Neboquazi, one summer on an island in Lake Nipigon, and parts of two others on Vancouver Island. But my longest and dearest island home was in the Lake of the Woods, where we had a cottage on Mackie's Island. We called our cottage 'Shining Tree', because it was placed in a beautiful grove of birches and because that is the Indian name (translated) of an equally beautiful lake where I had spent many happy hours. 'Shining Tree' was our home for the greater part of the period from May to October during fifteen years. It was just an ordinary cottage, with coal-oil lamps, wood stove, and outside privy, but when we had got the shutters pulled off in the spring, lighted big fires in the stove and fireplace, let down the mattresses onto the springs, and made our first meal, it was home; and the other comforts of civilization, such as they were, could have stayed a thousand miles away. Towards the end of our term, we went so far as to get a coal-oil cook-stove for the hotter days and to put a sink in the kitchen, with some rainwater piped into it, but the electric light and telephone awaited our departure before invading. In the interval a 'Delco' plant in the establishment of one of our neighbours made noise and nuisance in their place.

Mackie's Island lies off Keewatin Beach about three-quarters of a mile at the nearest point, but it is a paddle of about two miles from Keewatin village. Paddle: for the first ten years we had nothing but a canoe and a rowboat, although here, too, we eventually compromised on a small outboard, whose antics enabled us to reach our destination in twice the time. The canoe was the best, a craft without peer, light, safe and swift. I never encountered a wind that kept me from making that three-quarter mile stretch, though on one occasion when we had an Anglican parson and his wife aboard I thought we might have to ask them to swim for it; I do not know whether they could swim. The island is about a mile and a half long, but nowhere more than two hundred yards wide. When we first went to live there, there were seven cottages scattered around it, but when we left there were fourteen. We occupied a humble toe-hold in the midst of rich Winnipeg doctors. But in early spring and late fall, the whole island was ours! I had not at first thought of the cottage as anything more than a haven, but gradually it changed into our summer home, especially during the war when I took to writing instead of journeying.

The cottage lay on a solid piece of granite about two hundred feet from the water, to which the land sloped down gently, the granite submerged under a nice depth of good soil. From those days back in the misty 1910's when I first went into the bush I have always, when opportunity offered, begun the day with a swim. While we occupied 'Shining Tree' I hardly missed a single morning, though it took a great deal of preliminary shivering to get into the cold water in the spring, especially if there were still bits of ice in it. As the summer went on I used to swim farther and farther out, judging my distance by the amount of main shore that unrolled beyond the long north point of the island. . . .

The Lake of the Woods being the summer outlet for Winnipeg's *élite,* the northern end is filled during July and August with expensive high-speed boats of every description. These seldom, however, penetrate southwards more than a few miles, so that if one wishes to be in primitive wilderness, it takes only a short time to get there. The lake is supposed to have some eleven thousand islands in it and only those at its northern end are occupied by the summer cottager. Here and there are little farmsteads, usually abandoned, commercial fishing-camps, and tourist resorts. For the most part, however, the lake remains a wilderness, still given over to the Indian and the deer. It is as a result an interesting combination of sophistication and the primitive. Indians often used to come to our cottage door with fish for sale. Since we could catch all we wanted for ourselves, they made few sales. One day, when we had a few on hand that we could not use, we had such a visit, and my wife thinking to do the Indians a good turn took down our excess fish to give them. She poked our fish at them before they had a chance to offer their own fish wares. They had a good laugh together.

The lake, though large and empty, has not failed to suffer from the assaults of the white man. There may be eleven thousand islands in it, but to find a clear title to any one of them would be difficult, for the area offers a prime example of the carelessness and cupidity of the frontier. When we lived there the long western arm, known as Clearwater Bay (parallel to which the highway from Winnipeg was being built), was being taken up in summer cottage lots, which at that time could be obtained from the Crown at a nominal price. Arthur Phelps got one of these and he hired a surveyor from Kenora to go out and lay it off for him. He and I went along with the surveyor as handy-men. This surveyor had laid out nearly all the properties along that twenty-five-mile stretch of lakeshore, most of which consisted of bold, rocky bluffs up to a couple of hundred feet in height. Here and there the bluffs were penetrated by little valleys through which, when roads were built, it would be possible to get cars down to the water's edge. The surveyor, an old-time bush hand, said that by law he was compelled to leave a roadway to the lakeshore on an average of every two and a half miles. 'I put them all out onto the tops of the bluffs,' he said, which means that the public was forever debarred from getting to the water's edge (except by climbing down the cliffs), and that the nice little valleys were reserved for those who had acquired summer cottage lots.

Shortly after we got 'Shining Tree' my wife and I started out in our canoe to explore the lake. We went down the western channel until we reached American waters. There we camped on an island, and I am not sure to this day whether we were in the United States or in Canada. We paddled up North West Arm Inlet to the point at which the provinces of Ontario and Manitoba and the state of Minnesota all meet. There at the beginning of the old overland trail to the Red River, we came upon the home of M. Goulet, member of a family well-known in Red River French circles. M. Goulet lived in a comfortable log house and, as my wife was not very well, he insisted on having us stay with him. The only difficulty was conversation. The family spoke very little English, and M. Goulet had few teeth. He also seemed to prefer to talk with his mouth full. The resulting French was hard to understand. But he was hospitality itself. . . .

From the Goulets' we paddled down through the swamps of the Inlet to the site of La Vérendrye's fort. Until a few years before that, no white man had known just where it was, but the Indians had preserved the memory of it and it had been marked. Someone, ancient or modern, had carved on a rock *'Tombe du Père Aulneau, 1732'*. We had intended to go from it on out into the lake to Massacre Island, where the Sioux had come upon La Vérendrye's son and his party and had killed them all, but it was three miles offshore and the weather did not look settled, so we decided to play safe. Instead, we turned north again, and in one of the narrow channels we made one of the most trying camps I have ever had to make.

The cause of the trial was the special Lake of the Woods pest: a fly that looks exactly like a housefly except that, instead of a pad protruding from its mandibles, it is armed with a lance. Yes, a lance, razor sharp and able to penetrate ordinary thin summer clothing! Not only that, but it is fiendishly ingenious in finding holes in the thicker spots, as around the eyelets of a pair of running shoes. The only thing to be said for it when it attacks in force is that it usually confines itself to the neighbourhood of the shore; otherwise it could make life almost impossible. I have encountered every species of insect, I think, in this insect-ridden country: mosquitoes, blackflies, sandflies, yellow hornets, wasps, bees – bumble and otherwise – deer-flies of assorted sizes and shapes, 'bulldogs', otherwise moose-flies, or to Cree Indians, 'turkeys' (*mikissuk*) – but I have never encountered anything more incessantly painful than this biting fly of the Lake of the Woods. Every time its lance goes in, it feels exactly like that – a lance going in!

This fly may be extending its range; since moving back to southern Ontario I have been attacked by it, but never in the diabolical way in which it acts around the Lake of the Woods. I know it has got as far as Lake Michigan, for many years ago, right in the great city of Chicago itself, we were sitting at dinner at a pleasant open-air restaurant on the shore, and there Mr. Lance Fly spoiled the meal. I watched its operation on an over-elegant American woman. She was sitting with a male companion at a table near by and was displaying a tempting length of silk stocking. Too tempting for the biting fly. It went to work on it with a will and spoiled her meal, too.

We survived the fly attack in the Tug-boat Channel by getting our tent up and crawling under the mosquito netting as quickly as possible (no squirting fly-bombs in those days). My wife stood it better than I did and stayed outside to cook our supper over the open fire, which proves that the female of the species may also be more hardy than the male.

That long trip down to the southern area of the lake was by no means the last, for we often used to throw some grub and blankets into the canoe and just strike out. There are numberless channels between those eleven thousand islands, so many that a man could not hope to explore them all. Each one, though so similar to the rest, has its own character; each one retains some of the mystery of the unknown. If my fellow Canadians knew some of these northern lakes as I know a great many of them, they would not be so ready to complain everlastingly about the country that presents them with such blessings.

One favourite trip was round to Clearwater Bay, where our friends the Phelpses, the Pickersgills, and the Wheelers all had cottages, either across the neck of land through the Indian reserve into White Partridge Bay or around the peninsula and up the other side. Once, as we got out of our canoe at the beginning of the portage across the reserve, we found an Indian family encamped there. The mother was showing her daughters how to tan a mooseskin; she was a good teacher, and I had that little fair-haired girl of whom I have spoken stand close to watch. Dampen the skin, hold it over the fire, pull, flap, and stretch, dampen, heat, pull, so it went on. . . .

We gave our little girl her introduction to life under canvas by taking her all the way round to Clearwater Bay, a paddle of about twenty miles. It came on to rain, so we went ashore and put up our tent. Then it relented, and we went out again, fighting a hard west wind until we got to the turn to the north, which gave us shelter. Then we came to a magic island, just large enough to camp on, and with birch trees and pine trees arranged together just right and shining in the evening sun. After we had got settled we heard a dog barking over on the main shore, so paddled over to see what was going on. We found a camp whose sole inhabitant – if one did not count his dog – was a gaunt old man of about seventy-five. But why not count the dog, who was as much part of the show as the man was? He was almost as big as a colt and not disposed to let us get close to his master until he was reassured. Then it turned out that the master was the original Mackie after whom our island had been named. He asked where our cottage was, and when I told him 'near the northern point', he replied simply, 'Oh the point where the man is buried.' This we had never heard of. . . .

On our way home, down at the end of a bay, we saw a deer. By paddling towards it when its head was down to drink and keeping stock still when it was up, we managed to get quite close. Then we saw it was not alone. Behind it, carefully kept just within the trees, were two little forms whose spots blended perfectly with the lights and shadows, two little fawns. The excitement of our young lady over these other young things may be imagined. I hope she never forgets that day or that place! . . .

We used to have lots of fun on our island. One pleasant evening Louise and I went for a little paddle around the tip of our island while her mother walked over. As she came through the bush towards us, she began to imitate something, some kind of animal. At any rate, the sound became to us a 'moo-moo', long and ominous. Our youngster did not recognize her mother's voice and became quite frightened until she saw her, when there was a good laugh; 'the night the moo came at us', that remains. Then there was Treasure Island just a little way off shore, and on the other shore Indian Island, and a little farther on the island with the empty cottage on it, and farther still the island with the two cottages in ruins; there were a dozen places of interest for the young and the not so young.

After we left Winnipeg (1946) 'Shining Tree' seemed too far away to retain. We made one trip back there in the summer of 1947, but, after all, Kingston is something like thirteen hundred miles from Keewatin, and that is a long way to go and come. Our trip was marked by our first and last contact with a 'company town', Smooth Rock Falls. We arrived there towards evening and seeing quite a good-looking hotel, we went in to get rooms. We were surprised to find that as strangers we were distinctly not welcome. I asked the woman at the desk whether she could refer us to any private houses that might take tourists. She could not. In fact, she made it quite clear that she did not want to do so. I did not like the atmosphere at all. We pulled out, drove over the dam that formed the road at that point, and went down and camped on the shores of the Metagami River, where we were quite as comfortable as we would have been in the company town. If Smooth Rock Falls is typical of what one might expect from a foreign company in possession of a Canadian national resource, the neighbouring forest, I can understand the outcry against the foreign capitalist.

So in 1947 I closed up 'Shining Tree' for the last time and the next summer I sold it. I have never since been back to the Lake of the Woods. And how far away now it seems. But, oh, those eleven thousand islands, that myriad of channels, that mixture of the primitive – I come back to the point – that mixture of the primitive and the advanced, how they grip me! They are Canada.

From

Western Windows

BRUCE HUTCHISON

If the Department of National Revenue should happen to discover my real bank account, doubtless it would send me to jail. For I and all countrymen have amassed more treasure than we deserve or can possibly spend.

The valiant yellow banners and the wholesome smell of skunk cabbages in February, the first purple catkins dripping like wine from the March alders, the loon's eerie cry on the silent lake, the crackle of deer's footsteps and the insect buzz in the parched summer woods, the corn growing in the hot nights, the autumnal grin of pumpkin, squash and marrow, the drumbeat of winter rain, the moan of wind, the screech of torn branches and the hiss of brush fires in the snow – these are property enough for any man but he cannot buy them with his chequebook, only with his hands and senses.

Like all men who know the outdoors, I have amassed still more precious assets. Riding in the high Rockies, far above timber line, I have seen some things unsuspected by the traveller in train, automobile or airplane, unrecorded by the camera, unwritten on the tourist advertisements.

Up there the air is clean, the type legible and printed boldly, in basic English, but you cannot read it until you have climbed slowly, day by day, through caverns measureless to man (or to Coleridge) and risked your neck on many a slippery precipice. And even when you have read that gigantic typography you cannot reproduce it or convey its import to other men.

The message of the mountains is always confidential, cryptic and brief. One of their communications, a staggering headline, was written on my heart, like Calais on Queen Bloody Mary's, but I shall not try to translate it for the present reader. Enough to state the bald facts.

Fog, rain and snow had kept us battend down in camp for two days and nights. At last a narrow crack in the sky persuaded us to goad our unwilling horses up a vertical shale slide to a bare ridge of rock where we could see hardly ten feet ahead and the clouds lay above, below and around us like wet concrete. Then, for half a minute, no more, the wind struck from the west and almost blew us from our saddles. The sun bored through the concrete, the clouds were torn to fluttering rags of blue and white, the valley of gilded autumn poplar at our feet was emptied instantly of mist. Sky, earth, mountain and forest, rock and tree, were convulsed like the colours in a child's kaleidoscope. The whole planet (how else can I say it?) turned into whirling, bubbling, molten substance as on the day of creation – a sight too dizzy for human eyes to look upon.

As suddenly as they had split, the clouds closed again and we toiled blindly downward through them all day to pitch our camp in darkness under a sky now spangled with stars, beside a cliff of gleaming silver. The Rockies had written their message and sealed the envelope. In all my later journeys I could never reopen it.

Nor could I appreciate the message until I had travelled in more distant lands. The barbered English meadows, the geometrical French fields, the tidy, upright Alpine farms taught me the essential difference separating the only two kinds of men, whatever their race or colour – the outdoor men and the men of civilization, the trail men and the street men, forever separate.

In Europe the earth is domesticated and its owners with it. In America, not far from any town, the wild is still close to us and makes the stable weather, the fixed matrix of our spirit, whether we know it or not. We know it, all right, when we go abroad and see in Europe a continent long tamed, a people truly civilized, as we are not. Europe's land is a garden under man's tillage. Here, outside our few urban strongholds, it is a wilderness which we may ravish but cannot tame; and some of us are not quite tamed yet, either, though we shall be in due time.

A Canadian must see the old world before he comprehends the new. Invariably he will come home more Canadian than ever, and for myself the return to my swamp and the whispered welcome of the forest seems like release from a luxurious prison. That self-discovery is worth all the cost and exasperation of foreign travel.

Laurentian Shield

F. R. SCOTT

Hidden in wonder and snow, or sudden with summer,
This land stares at the sun in a huge silence
Endlessly repeating something we cannot hear.
Inarticulate, arctic,
Not written on by history, empty as paper,
It leans away from the world with songs in its lakes
Older than love, and lost in the miles.

This waiting is wanting.
It will choose its language
When it has chosen its technic,
A tongue to shape the vowels of its productivity.

A language of flesh and of roses.

Now there are pre-words,
Cabin syllables,
Nouns of settlement
Slowly forming, with steel syntax,
The long sentence of its exploitation.

The first cry was the hunter, hungry for fur,
And the digger for gold, nomad, no-man, a particle;
Then the bold commands of monopoly, big with machines,
Carving its kingdoms out of the public wealth;
And now the drone of the plane, scouting the ice,
Fills all the emptiness with neighbourhood
And links our future over the vanished pole.

But a deeper note is sounding, heard in the mines,
The scattered camps and the mills, a language of life,
And what will be written in the full culture of occupation
Will come, presently, tomorrow,
From millions whose hands can turn this rock into children.

From

The Search for Identity

BLAIR FRASER

It is commonplace to refer to Canada as one of the young countries of the world. In fact it is one of the oldest. Few others still look, as Canada does in about three quarters of its area, just as they did two hundred and perhaps ten thousand years ago.

More than half of it is primordial granite, the great Pre-Cambrian shield rubbed clean of soil by the glacier of the latest Ice Age. Since the glacier receded the land has recovered, at least in the milder climatic belt that in the west runs as far north as the Yukon and the Mackenzie Delta and in the east dips to south of James Bay, enough shallow humus to support a coniferous bush. Shallow lakes are everywhere upon its surface – Canada is thought to contain about one third the fresh water of the entire world.

In the main this land is still empty. Westward from Lake Superior the old Voyageur Highway is intact as far as Rainy Lake – not as busy now as it was when the freighter canoes carried the pelts down and the trade goods back between Grand Portage and the Athabaska region, but its portages still well marked, its lakes and streams still clean.

Most Canadians, of course, have never seen this wilderness area and never will. It is too far away. But it is typical, an extreme but not misleading example, of something that is within the easy reach of every Canadian, urban or rustic – an empty area of forest or plain in which a man can still enjoy the illusion of solitude. This is the quality that makes Canada unique and gives root to Canadian patriotism.

It needs no excess of optimism to believe that the social problems of nationhood will solve themselves – to be succeeded, of course, by other problems, but not by national dissolution. Already the strains of biculturalism seem to be easing off, as English Canadians rush to learn French and English-speaking provinces move, still grudgingly but definitely, toward the establishment of schools in which French is the language of instruction. Regional prejudices ebb and flow, but each high tide is a little lower (if the printed word is true evidence) than the last one was.

Meanwhile "development" continues. Canada's standard of living, second highest in the world (by North American measurement), is in no danger of losing that proud position. Washing machines and television sets abound, as in no other nation save one. Superhighways devour uncounted acres of fertile land, and the second highest incidence of automobiles achieves, in the metropolitan areas, a second highest air pollution. Ugly little towns prosper, all calling themselves cities and all looking like faithful copies of Omaha, Nebraska.

This is not a Canada to call forth any man's love. But just north of it still lies a different kind of land – too barren ever to be thickly settled, too bleak to be popular like Blackpool or Miami. There is no reason to doubt that it will always be there, and so long as it is there Canada will not die.

Eight

Farewell to Saganaga: Wilderness Lost

INTRODUCTION

Canada is a wealthy, urban, industrial nation. She has a sophisticated technology and an exceptionally high standard of living.

Canada is also young. She has only recently emerged from the pioneer stage, during which a handful of men and women set out to tame her wilderness and tap her resources. In the far North, aided by modern technology, the process still goes on.

Canada's development from sparsely-populated wilderness to modern nation has been based largely on broadscale extraction of natural resources: fur-bearing animals, fish, forests, mineral ores, oil. Their utilization has been rapid and dramatic, marked by exuberance, rapacity, waste, and material success. It has made possible the growth of our cities. It has fertilized our Gross National Product. It has bought us the security and comforts and luxuries of our high standard of living. Our success is measured in terms of automobiles and highways, bulldozers and electric can-openers, computer systems and nuclear reactors, and instant communications which inform, amuse, and stimulate our appetites.

Life has become opulent, complex, and in some ways more secure (forgetting, for the moment, some of the more ambitious products of modern defence technology). For Canadians, however, this progress towards perfection has been purchased or sustained through the rapid subjugation of wild nature. Rail lines and roads have been pushed into remote areas, connecting them to the mushrooming cities of the south. Mines, mills, drilling rigs, and logging camps have been set up in distant places: Ungava, Yellowknife, Kitimat, the Arctic islands. We now have townsites and garbage dumps where, until recently, only caribou and musk-oxen herded together. Pipelines pass through previously untouched mountain valleys and promise to spread in response to the insatiable appetite for oil. Dams alter the flow and drown the courses of once-wild rivers: we have recently celebrated the demise of Churchill Falls in Labrador; now the Eastmain, Nottaway, and La Grande are threatened in Quebec; almost any river system in British Columbia seems to be vulnerable to the hydro-power developers. At the same time, we are invited to consume more power for trivial purposes. But the wilderness has other enemies: snow-mobiles and helicopters, all-terrain vehicles and float-planes. Used without restraint, without sense, without sensitivity to the environment, they are no friends to wild places and wild beings. Even in many of our "parks," which we assume to be protected, the forests are given over to commercial logging and mechanized travel.

Perhaps our writers see this despoliation more clearly than most. The selections in this theme suggest that this is so. Poet Gaston Miron writes of ruin: for him, the land has been "despoiled," "worked out," "in its livid back the blows of heated knives." William O. Pruitt, Jr. gives us a similar picture of a landscape assaulted by bulldozers and chattering rock drills and left "exposed to the howling winds and drifting snow, as bare and sterile as when the glaciers had melted." Yorke Edwards also remarks upon the destruction of the wilderness – "one of the earth's most important creations" – by the onslaught of railways, highways, paper mills, communications towers, and the like. As Raymond Souster wryly notes, only God can create a tree, but "He'll never try it in Sudbury."

If what these writers tell us of the past and present is also pro-logue, then Joni Mitchell's bleak and visionary song is not very far-fetched: "They took all the trees / And put them in a tree museum / And they charged all the people / A dollar and a half just to see 'em / Don't it always seem to go / That you don't know what you've got / Till it's gone."

The limitless wilderness *is* gone in the sense of inviolate life and assured continuance. Andy Russell makes the point in writing of the West: "when the white man came to plow the sod and kill the buffalo, this wilderness largely disappeared forever." Today, those who value wild places are concerned with preserving remnants. We have, along with Sigurd Olson, said farewell to Saganaga, but we can still debate the future of Quetico Park, which adjoins it. Those who join in the debate should recognize that not all the agents of de-struction are as obvious as noisy resort developments, strip-mines, and timber-jacks. Some of these destructive forces are subtle, even invisible: the insidious, universal drift of pesticides which have in-fected polar bears and now threaten the falcon, eagle, and loon with extinction; the waterborne chemical effluent of industry flowing far from the source; mercury poisoning in northern fish.

Wilderness is not limitless. Like all the riches of the earth, it can be destroyed. Dorothy Livesay says as much when she imagines the pioneer, sitting complacently with folded hands and burning to see "How he has ravaged earth / Of her last stone, her last, most stub-born tree." Her pioneer does not recognize the interdependence of all life. He fails to see that man is a part of nature and imperils his own kind, as well as other species, when he arbitrarily sets himself apart from and above nature. A new ethic is surely required to combat such ignorance, one which is less anthropocentric and which reflects a respect for life in its totality. Lacking such an ethic, we must anticipate a degraded existence, a spring bereft of bird songs, a declining quality of life.

In Canada we have a rare opportunity. Despite our vigorous exploitation of nature, we still have remnants of wilderness against which to measure our ethical maturity and ecological awareness. Hopefully, we realize that man – even at his most creative peak – cannot make a bird, or the tree in which the bird sings, much less the astonishingly complex wilderness of which the bird and the tree are part. We also must know that we will never again see the like of a creature we have made extinct; that wilderness can shrink, but never grow. The fact that we are fortunate in having some wild places left should help us to recognize these fundamental facts. And so should the wealth of prose and poetry which proclaims us to be, in striking degree, marked by the wild.

It is in the wild, in what remains to us of our wilderness legacy, that we can see the purest expression of life and evolution – of beauty, power, and wonderful complexity which are not of our making. In this wilderness we can experience the awe and rejuvenation, the challenge and joy which are reflected in our literature. We can choose to destroy this dwindled legacy, or we can appreciate it in non-destructive ways. We can respect it, or rape it. The choice we make will be sign and symbol of our relationship to life and our stature as ethical, thinking, fully human beings.

The Predator

IRVING LAYTON

The little fox
was lying in a pool of blood,
having gnawed his way out to freedom.

Or the farmhand,
seeing his puny, unprofitable size
had slugged him after with a rifle butt.

And he had crawled
to the country roadside
where I came upon him, his fur dust-covered.

Hard to believe
a fox is ever dead, that he isn't
just lying there pretending with eyes shut.

His fame's against
him; one suspects him of anything,
even when there's blood oozing from the shut eyes.

His evident
self-enjoyment is against him also:
no creature so wild and gleeful can ever be done for.

But this fox was;
there's no place in the world any more
for free and gallant predators like him.

Eagle, lion,
fox and falcon: their freedom is their death.
Man, animal tamed and tainted, wishes to forget.

He prefers bears
in cages: delights to see them pace
back and forth, swatting their bars despondently.

Yet hates himself,
knowing he's somehow contemptible:
with knives and libraries the dirtiest predator of all.

Ghost of small fox,
hear me, if you're hovering close
and watching this slow red trickle of your blood:

Man sets even
more terrible traps for his own kind.
Be at peace; your gnawed leg will be well-revenged.

Railroads

DAN KENNEDY

The construction of the transcontinental railway across the Dominion's wilderness in the early eighties of the last century by the C.P.R. Company was not only an outstanding pioneering achievement, but made Confederation a reality by forging the East and the West, economically and politically, into one nation.

This romantic chapter in Western history ushered in the dawn of a new day, spearheading Western expansion and development.

But what was the reaction of the Indian? What were his reactions to this impact with civilization? We were a people whose only means of transportation was the travois. Our communication line was the moccasin telegraph. We did not sow or reap, but depended on the buffalo as the staff of life. Fires were kindled with flint and steel and game hunted with the bow and arrow. To be caught in the maelstrom of the on-rushing tidal wave of civilization was, to say the least, demoralizing.

The coming of the railroad was one of the wonders and surprises that staggered our imaginations. On the Plains we heard vague rumours of a smoke- and fire-belching monster winding its way westwards, towards the great Rockies. In our childish fancy, we youngsters wondered if it were not one of those terrible mythological monsters or even the dreaded Windigo that was on the prowl.

Our kinsmen, the Dakotas, were not the kind of people to let anyone put anything over them and get away with it – not even this new terror of the Plains. It has only one path on which it travels, coming and going. So why not set a snare to capture it, they reasoned.

They drove stout stakes in the ground on either side of the track and wove strong rawhide lariats from stake to stake, until they were satisfied it would withstand the mightiest onslaught.

They then retired some distance and hid behind the tall sage brush to await developments. They did not have to wait long. The smoke in the distance presaged its approach and in a matter of minutes it was in full view.

They were eager to spring into action as soon as the monster was caught in the coils of the snare, but they could hardly believe their eyes when the monster cut through the snare as if it were nothing but mere cobwebs.

The monster scored the first round by sheer weight and might.

Inasmuch as we would like to kid ourselves with tribal egoism, we Assiniboines fared no better in our encounters with this new mechanical wonder.

It was in the late summer of 1882, when the steel ribbons were girdling the Western Plains, that a party of Assiniboines chanced upon the railroad and saw, for the first time, the train, which to their inexperienced native mind appeared to be a fantastic monster bearing down on them. Without hesitation one of the party slipped into some nearby brush, which was conveniently near the track, took careful aim at what he thought was the vulnerable spot of the monster, and pulled the trigger as it roared past.

There wasn't even a trace of a tremor and the bullet ricocheted.

The monster scored a feather for its shining armor.

What Is Grizzly Country?

ANDY RUSSELL

It was very early in the morning in mid-June. The stars were gone, except Venus, and night shadows lingered restively in the deeper folds among the hills and mountains. The air was cool and still, smelling of new grass, wild geraniums, and the golden blooms of Indian turnip, where the prairies sweep in close before soaring up to the saw-toothed eagle aeries along the sky.

The horse carried his head low, threading the winding trail at a fast running walk on a loose rein. Having bucked the kinks out of his frame and mine back at the corral gate a half hour earlier, he was now tending to business, his ears working to pick up the bells of the pack string scheduled to leave on the first trip of the season across the Rockies to the wilds of the Flathead River in British Columbia. He did no more than cock an ear at four big mule deer bucks, their stubs of new antlers sheathed in velvet, bounding up out of a draw in the long springy leaps so typical of their kind. When I reined him after them to the top of a lookout butte not far from Indian Springs, the red sun was just breaking over the rim of the plains to the east. On the crest the horse stopped of his own will. We stood motionless, facing the sun with only a light zephyr of wind fingering his mane and the fringes of my buckskin jacket, as we watched the new day being born.

This is something of nature's witchery, when the night goes and the day comes to the living world. Nothing matches the back of a good horse as a place to watch it. No other place but here at the foot of the Rockies, where the prairies and the mountains meet, can its awesome and beautiful display be seen and felt so well. Only on a June morning, between the last of spring and the first of summer, does it impart such a feeling of sudden-bursting life. Here the Rockies are its great backdrop, a timber-topped ridge winging it to the north and the sprawling peaks of the Great Lewis Overthrust walling it off to the south. Mountain meadows, lakes, and ageless stone couple into solid magnificence. It is a marriage of light and life, a promise and a fulfillment of that promise. While the mountains light up at first sun in deep rose, swiftly changing to gold, and all shot through with deep purple shadow, it is as though the whole universe pauses for a long, heart-stretching moment, locked in a spell of deep wonder.

Not a sound broke the stillness that morning. The horse and I stood waiting, breathless. Then he gave a long sigh; the saddle creaked under me, and a spur rowel jingled. A meadow lark burst into song and was joined by a white-crowned sparrow and a solitaire. The spell was broken. The day and the whole country jumped into wakefulness, vital and alive.

No wonder the old Plains Indians worshipped the sun, for it is the root of all life. They too were aware of this moment in the morning and made a ritual of viewing it from the brow of a hill. The sun was a simple explanation of their existence, their promise of tomorrow and their reassurance of today. For some reason wild animals also sometimes stand motionless at dawn, as though listening to the first soft music of the waking day – caught in the magic. It is a thing to ponder.

The horse lifted his head, pointing his ears at a ridge between us and the sun. Like a reincarnation of the past when black hordes covered the plains, a long line of buffalo broke from a hidden fold to feed along its crest. The big animals were shaggy in half-shed winter coats. To the south a half dozen cow elk, sleek and saddle brown in their new summer coats, came trotting out of a draw and fanned out to drink at a little lake. They were perfectly reflected in its mirror surface, until the calves suddenly went gamboling through the shallows, shattering their mothers' images. Above and farther to the right, high on the face of the mountain, white rump patches heliographed the presence of a bunch of feeding bighorn rams. Still higher a golden eagle suddenly dropped from the point of a pinnacle, plummeting down for a low level pass over the grasslands in search of a ground squirrel for breakfast.

The horse swung his head sharply to the north as a musical jingle of Swiss bells gave the other horses away. They were standing on a small bench watching something above them.

Out of a patch of aspens came a big she-grizzly with two small cubs at heel. The sun glinted on her bright silver ruff and shoulder mantle and bounced off the coats of the two small replicas bounding ecstatically behind her.

Here was the living symbol of the mountain wilderness, one giving an impression of power and royalty matched by no other. She seemed to go slowly with a certain massiveness; yet she moved with smooth grace, covering the ground with surprising speed. She stopped to investigate something, and through my glasses I saw the flash of ivory-white claws as she pawed up a bit of sod. One or the other of the cubs trailing her would discover something of fascinating interest, whereupon they would poke small inquisitive snouts into a clump of grass or flowers. Then they would gallop to catch up, carefree and happy, yet disciplined and careful not to lose sight of their big mother for a moment. Apparently she had no particular destination in mind, though she traveled steadily, angling up toward a saddle where the ridge butted into the mountain.

She had the bearing of a monarch. In the old days, when unbroken wilderness stretched from here to Lake Winnipeg and the Mississippi Valley, the grizzly's kingdom was as vast as that wilderness. The grizzly was then king of all animals across the thousands of miles of his range. The big bears ate berries and buffalo meat along the Saskatchewan, the Missouri, and the Yellowstone. They wandered the country drained by the Colorado and the Rio Grande. They fed on the pine nuts and oak mast in the sierras of Arizona, Nevada, New Mexico, old Mexico, and California. They caught salmon in the tributaries of the Snake and the Columbia. They ranged from the parched mountains of the south to the frozen, barren prairies of the arctic, from the Midwest to the beaches of the Pacific Ocean.

But when the white man came to plow the sod and kill the buffalo, this wilderness largely disappeared forever. The grizzly range shrank as the big animals were harried and decimated, running for the first time from any animal, the only one ever to challenge them successfully in their environment. More cautious and much less numerous, those that remained forted up in the mountain fastnesses of the west and north, never to venture far out onto the plains again.

This was the edge of the wilderness, where I sat my horse, comparatively untouched by man save for the fence built as a sort of repentant afterthought to enclose the buffalo. Because it is wilderness protected within the boundaries of Waterton Lakes National Park, this southwest corner of Alberta is still grizzly country, and always will be grizzly country if the principles of national parks are guarded well.

Watching the mother grizzly top out on the saddle, it was evident that the female knew where safe haven lay; for had she traveled as many minutes in the opposite direction, she would have been in ranching country. There she would not be welcome, and her appearance would likely spark someone to shoot first and ask questions afterward.

But there is plenty of grizzly country in the mountains – country that is high, wild, and rugged, a place where birds and streams and wind still blend in a song of the wilderness that lifts and falls in a cadence of freedom as sweet as life and as old as time among the proud gnarled trees and the rocky pinnacles.

That same wind blows across the plains to the east; the same waters flow down the valleys there, and the birds still nest and sing in the coverts. But there the song of freedom is muted now. It is not grizzly country any more. It is man country. The grizzly I watched knew it, and she was teaching her cubs by following the sun back into the wild fastnesses among the peaks.

Wild Horses

PATRICK LANE

Just to come once alone
to these wild horses
driving out of high Cascades,
raw legs heaving the hip-high snow.
Just once alone. Never to see
the men and their trucks.

Just once alone. Nothing moves
as the stallion with five free mares
rushes into the guns. All dead.
Their eyes glaze with frost.
Ice bleeds in their nostrils
as the cable hauls them in.

Later, after the swearing
and the stamping of feet,
we ride down into Golden:

'Quit bitchin.
It's a hard bloody life
and a long week
for three hundred bucks of meat.'

That and the dull dead eyes
and the empty meadows.

The Bull Moose

ALDEN NOWLAN

Down from the purple mist of trees on the mountain,
lurching through forests of white spruce and cedar,
stumbling through tamarack swamps,
came the bull moose
to be stopped at last by a pole-fenced pasture.

Too tired to turn or, perhaps, aware
there was no place left to go, he stood with the cattle.
They, scenting the musk of death, seeing his great head
like the ritual mask of a blood god, moved to the other end
of the field, and waited.

The neighbours heard of it, and by afternoon
cars lined the road. The children teased him
with alder switches and he gazed at them
like an old, tolerant collie. The woman asked
if he could have escaped from a Fair.

The oldest man in the parish remembered seeing
a gelded moose yoked with an ox for plowing.
The young men snickered and tried to pour beer
down his throat, while their girl friends took their pictures.

And the bull moose let them stroke his tick-ravaged flanks,
let them pry open his jaws with bottles, let a giggling girl
plant a little purple cap
of thistles on his head.

When the wardens came, everyone agreed it was a shame
to shoot anything so shaggy and cuddlesome.
He looked like the kind of pet
women put to bed with their sons.

So they held their fire. But just as the sun dropped in the river
the bull moose gathered his strength
like a scaffolded king, straightened and lifted his horns
so that even the wardens backed away as they raised their rifles.
When he roared, people ran to their cars. All the young men
leaned on their automobile horns as he toppled.

From

The Great Bear Lake Meditations

J. MICHAEL YATES

The caribou are crossing. Someone has just come to town and said that from the air you can't see the ground for the animals. Twenty or thirty thousand of them. It's fifty below. Quickly the town begins to empty as the long snake of smoking vehicles moves out the highway. When they arrive at the appointed place, the animals are still behind a ridge. Cars and trucks park in a long line at the shoulder of the road, engines and heaters running; together they send a mile-long hackle of ice-fog into the flawless winter sky. The waiting begins and could last for days until something occurs to the milling animals. Always there are a few men who won't wait. They leave their automobiles, sling their rifles and make for the ridge-crest. After a while, there are shots. Then the interval to clean the kill. Those still waiting grow excited, impatient, expectant. The first to kill and clean his caribou drapes the carcass around his shoulders and begins climbing the ridge toward the road, the long antlers bouncing as he walks. The rack is higher than the hunter's head, and those waiting see this before they see the man beneath the animal against the horizon at the top of the ridge. Doors open and several race across the road. Shots. The man carrying the caribou drops the carcass, flattens himself behind it, and fires back at the line of cars. The sound of a bullet striking the metal or the glass of a vehicle is almost indistinguishable from the sound of a bullet entering the body of a caribou or a bear.

Rare and Vanishing Wildlife

YORKE EDWARDS

In many minds the wildlife of these mountains and the valleys between are typified by the grizzly bear and the mountain caribou. The grizzly has been retreating northward all the way from Mexico for two centuries. The main population has now been eliminated northward well into Canada. The extermination process is still in progress. In my short life I have seen grizzly tracks on several mountains where none will ever be seen again.

The caribou has retreated neither so far nor for so long a time. The retreat began with the fires from the first railroads in these mountains, and today the signals for the complete and hasty withdrawal of caribou from the southern half of British Columbia are the plumes of smelly smoke rising from new paper mills. Mountain caribou need old forests; forests managed for pulpwood must be young forests. I am glad that I knew these mountains when I did. I got there just before progress arrived. I saw far views from places uncluttered by beer cans, and I crossed lush meadows that had never known a helicopter. I heard geese clamouring in valleys that had never known a gasoline engine, and for whole days I walked knee deep in flowers where no woolly sheep had ever grazed. No doubt another generation is finding some of these things in the north. I knew them in the south.

There is an apparently small minority that holds these things to be priceless. I am one of them, and I have had my try at preserving some so others may know that wilderness living can be a supremely elevating experience known to few men. It is really as strong as that. My idea of heaven has no paper mills, no busy highways, no communications towers insulting the scenery for miles around. My heaven has mountains and lakes, and long green meadows where grazing caribou flush out ptarmigan and pipits from acres of coloured flowers. Things like caribou and the grizzly must be there if the place should have them; to leave them out would be to omit the important parts.

A minority is usually considered to be out of step, although it is entirely possible that it is the only group able to hear the music.

Being out of step is not often a pleasant condition. Few people are out of step on purpose, rather it is because they hear a really different beat, and this may be because they have been trained to hear it. That different beat can be real and true. Those who mourn when the grizzlies retreat from another mountain seem to be vastly outnumbered by those who do not. If this were all there was to it, the mourners could accept their minority status. But the tremendous frustration they know is due to the obvious fact that most of the non-mourners know nothing of the situation, and the few that do have no knowledge with which to assess the worth of a grizzly. About the only satisfaction allowed the mourners is their ability to see where others cannot, which is a sad accomplishment when the sight is the unconcerned destruction of one of earth's most important creations.

I speak of grizzly bears, but really I speak of all living things. My concern is not over the mere deaths of individuals but over the deaths of species. Individuals are replaceable. A species once dead is the end, forever, of something that succeeded and was perfected through time too long to comprehend.

When the last old grizzly and the last caribou in these mountains are found among the last alpine flowers to escape the herds of man, there will be efforts to save them. And there is no doubt that the strongest opposition will come from those who have not the slightest idea of what they are talking about.

But it will not matter then. It will be much too late.

The Boom

WILLIAM O. PRUITT, JR.

In the dim prehistory of North America, after the continental glacier had melted, the scoured bedrock ridges and troughs of the Canadian Shield remained bare and sterile. Many thousands of daily exposures to the sun's energy broke down the bare rock and it became covered with chips, then finer chips and eventually soil; horsetails colonized the soil and were finally superseded by a thin, struggling taiga of scattered spruce trees. Between the spruces were bushes of Labrador tea and dwarf birch, and under them the basic carpet of lichens and mosses. Because of the low summer temperatures, the fallen leaves and needles did not rot when they died and fell. They compacted and turned to peat. Eventually, after more thousands of exposures to the sun's energy, the once bare rock was hidden by a thick mat of peat, on top of which grew the taiga.

The topmost layer of peat was riddled by the tunnels and runways of red-backed voles and shrews. The Labrador tea, the dwarf birch, and the willows and alders were clipped and barked by snowshoe hares. Every few years a moose would spend the winter here, pulling down the birches and alders to strip the tender new growth. And twice each year, in autumn and in spring, the caribou came, with hoofs clacking and popping, on their migration to and from their wintering range. Each caribou walked with its muzzle close to the ground. It pulled a clump of lichens here, stripped the leaves from a stem of dwarf birch there, and pulled another clump of lichen farther on. Above the caribou a red squirrel shelled a spruce cone and the extra seeds fluttered down to the ground. Some seeds happened to fall onto the spots where the lichen cover had been broken by the caribou's feeding. These seeds were the ones that would germinate and grow to succeed the present adult trees. Not many seeds were successful, but because of the low energy budget of the taiga not many new seedlings were necessary to reproduce the forest.

One summer day a helicopter fluttered overhead. From its belly hung a cable which supported a shining cylinder. The helicopter thundered on, then turned and made other passes back and forth over the area. Later in the summer it returned. This time it landed on a small open ridge. Two men climbed out and unloaded a stack of boxes and bundles. The helicopter roared aloft and fluttered out of sight.

The men pitched a tent and set up camp. Then they unpacked the boxes and assembled a portable power drill. The roar of its engine echoed over the forest. The drill bit and chattered into the rocky ridge. Its vibrations caused bubbles of marsh gas to rise to the surface of a pond in the valley beside the ridge. After a week the helicopter returned and the men loaded into it many long rock cores, each protected in its own box.

Far to the south, in Toronto, a stock ticker clattered and spewed out a strip of tape. A perspiring young man wrote figures on a huge blackboard that covered one end of the room. In the brokers' seats one man leaned back and whispered to another, "Watch No-Ferrous; it's up three points since yesterday." His partner nodded and, later, quietly left his seat.

Next day No-Ferrous climbed five more points. Orders to buy this stock came from investors, speculators, and suckers. Some of their money lined the pockets of the brokers, some circled around among the other habitual stock-players, but some ended up in the bank account of No-Ferrous, Ltd. Thus the company was able to send another helicopter crew to the ridge in the taiga. Other companies and individuals joined the "good thing."

Helicopters roared in, dumped their loads and took off again. A small lake nearby was roiled with the floats of Beavers, Otters, and a variety of other types of aircraft.

The peaty valleys were churned to a pulp. Spruces that had taken a hundred years to grow were cut to provide corner posts for claims, for firewood, and for corduroy roads. The mining camp was booming. Rock drills roared and chattered, bulldozers scraped the thousand-year-old peat into windrows and churned the lichens into powder.

Then the inevitable happened – fire. Someone touched off the trash dump and sparks ignited a bulldozed dry spruce top nearby. Flames hissed through the dry lichens, roared up through the resinous branches of another spruce. The smoke rose thick, white, and acrid. . . .

The rock drills and bulldozers continued their work. "Cat time" was too expensive to be wasted making a firelane, although an hour's work would have contained the fire. The fire spread through the summer-dry lichen and moss, roaring whenever it turned a spruce tree to a torch. By the end of the day the flames had blackened a hundred acres; by the next day, a square mile. Unfought, the fire burned for a week, when chance rain showers dampened it out. Twenty thousand acres lay charred.

More cores were flown out. The outline of the ore body was

delimited. The prospectors whose claims lay outside this area drifted away, their tents and tools abandoned. The camp population shrank as winter approached. The boom collapsed.

The days grew shorter; willow leaves turned sere and brown. On the rocky ridges the patches of bearberry glowed scarlet. The outriders of the herds of migrating caribou arrived from the north. They encountered the huge freshly burned area and turned aside. On each previous migration five thousand caribou had spent about ten days here in the fall and ten days again in the spring. But caribou could no longer live in the burned area. Thus the total caribou lives were reduced by about a hundred thousand caribou-days per year.

Moose no longer spent the winter there; squirrels were gone; hares were gone; voles and shrews were gone. The bare rock ridges lay exposed to the howling winds and drifting snow, as bare and sterile as when the glaciers had melted. The total productivity of Canada had been reduced.

Far to the south, in Toronto, a Deputy Minister rose to address a meeting of the Board of Trade. He spoke in glowing terms of the increased annual rate of economic growth. He dwelt at length on the qualities of hard work, vision, and aggressive drive that characterized the business leaders of the industry. Then on behalf of the Board of Trade he presented its annual award to one who had done the most during the past year to exemplify these qualities, the President of No-Ferrous Ltd.

Very Short Poem

RAYMOND SOUSTER

". . . But only God can make a tree"
– He'll never try it in Sudbury.

Farewell to Saganaga

SIGURD F. OLSON

I had come a long way since leaving Lac la Croix – had heard the roar of Curtain Falls, threaded the labyrinth of islands and channels of Crooked Lake to the painted rocks at the far east end. I had made the historic portages around the rapids of the Basswood River and crossed the open reaches of the lake above. Then the sweep of Knife with its clear water and mountainous horizons, the cliffs of Otter-track, and at last the gateway to Saganaga.

There, on the afternoon of the fifth day, I lowered my canoe into the water. The last level rays of the sunset caught a stand of dark pine on the opposite shore and brushed the trunks with flame. An exploring tentacle picked out a rocky shelf miles across the open water and made it explode with light. The lake was calm and its islands floated like battleships in a sea of crimson. Far in the distance the loons called. This was Saganaga as it used to be.

I loaded in my worn packs and pushed off toward the open sweep of the lake beyond Cache Bay. My paddle all but sang as it dipped the blue-green water, and once more came the feeling of detachment I had known when I first came in many years before. Saganaga then was deep in the wilderness, a symbol of the primitive, perfect and untouched.

Until the day when I discovered it, my life had been dominated by the search for a perfect wilderness lake. Always before me was the ideal, a place not only remote, not only of great beauty, but possessed of an intangible quality and spirit that typified to me all of the un-broken north beyond all roads. Time and again I thought I had found it, but always there was something wrong, some vague, unreasoned lack of shape or size, some totally unexplainable aspect involved with the threat of accessibility. Above all, I wanted vistas that controlled not only moonrises and sunsets, but the northern lights and the white mists of the river mouths at dawn. Sometimes it was a matter of intuition and feeling, an unsettled state of mind more than any particular physical character, that made me push on. The search drew me farther and farther into the bush, and I finally began to wonder if I actually knew what I was looking for and if I would know when I had found it.

Then one golden day I came to Saganaga. My first glimpse from the western narrows was enough, and as I stood there and looked out across the broad blue reaches to the east with their fleets of rocky islands, the hazy blue hills toward the hinterlands of the Northern Light Country, I knew I had reached my goal. How I knew without having explored the lake, I cannot say, but the instant I saw the lake, I realized it was the end of my search, and that there was nothing more beyond the hills. I shall never forget the sense of peace and joy which was mine at the discovery. Perhaps I was ready for Saganaga; perhaps all the searching that had gone before had prepared me. Whatever it was, I was content at last, knowing that I would find in this lonely solitude the realization of all my dreams.

That first experience was an ecstatic one. Each camp I made there was different from and more delightful than the one before. Even the air seemed to have a clearer, more crystalline quality than elsewhere. No two days were quite the same, and I learned to know and love the moods of the great, sprawling lake and how its winds blew and where the mists came in. I had vantage points for every great event in all kinds of weather. There was one hill from which the coyotes howled on moonlit nights and a point where the loon calls echoed for many miles around. The birds and animals around my campsites became friends, and in some of the swampy bays the moose lost their shyness when my canoe drifted in. I watched the beaver build their houses, and in a rocky bay a family of otter played around me unafraid.

In the years that followed, I came to know every island and channel, every bay and cliff. In the spring, I knew where arbutus and moccasins bloomed; in the summer, places that were white with water lilies; in the fall, where oaks and maples flamed. There was never anything lacking in Saganaga, and each time I returned, it was the same. Here at last I came to feel at home.

And then one time when I was far away I heard the news. A road had come to Saganaga. I stared in disbelief at the newspaper clipping. A road to Saganaga? It did not seem possible. The article told briefly of some new mining discovery and how a new highway would open up a vast and untouched wilderness north of Lake Superior. The very matter-of-factness of the item struck me like a blow. Saganaga had come to mean far more than just another lake. It had woven itself into my consciousness, become part and parcel of all I had ever wanted, something real and true and tangible, a place secure and permanent in a world where values were always shifting and men no longer seemed to be sure of anything. I tore the little clipping into bits and crumpled them in the palm of my hand. For a long time I tried to forget, but the knowledge haunted me and I knew that some day, somehow, I must return and see for myself. I must go back to the wilderness I had known.

As time went on, there was a growing compulsion about my return which could not be denied. But, knowing that Saganaga had changed, I postponed my trip year after year and contented myself with dreaming of the place I had known, the one spot in the world which for me was perfect and untouched.

Then at last I was back, and as I paddled along and saw the old familiar reaches of blue, the islands riding at anchor in the distance, the gnarled old trees and lichen-covered cliffs, it seemed as though I had never been away. As yet I had seen no change – no cabins, no motor boats – and had heard no sounds that were strange. The loons were calling as they had always called in welcome to a voyageur.

I pitched my tent under the pine trees on my old campsite, kindled my fire with dry tinder I had left there long ago. Even there I found no sign, no evidence of a change that I could only sense. As I stood at the water's edge and looked out toward the far eastern shore, the old feeling of immensity and distance came back to me, but I was apprehensive and uneasy.

That night I paddled far into the south bay through a maze of islands toward the place where I knew the road had come. There I would see for myself. Darkness gathered and the near-by shores loomed black. I paddled through channel after channel, finally emerging into the open near the mouth of a long bay where in the past I had often come to look for moose and to listen to the sounds of the night. The dark mouth of the opening widened before me and the canoe slipped silently along the shore.

I rounded a final point and there, like the rising of a full moon, was a blaze of light over the horizon, the windows of a lodge. I dropped my paddle and sat staring. I had expected exactly that and had steeled myself, but it seemed incredible and unreal. One moment the old wilderness of Saganaga, its timelessness and solitude; then in an instant, in the space of a paddle stroke, civilization and change.

From the brightly lighted lodge a broad trail of yellow ran out into the darkness. It fascinated me, and before I realized what I was doing, the canoe was gliding down its path straight into the glare. Not until I was at the very rim of the half-moon of light did I stop. In the shadows just beyond its edge I allowed the canoe to drift. Instead of the old primeval chorus, slow, seductive music trembling across the water. Strangely enough, I was not resentful at what I saw and heard. Such things had their place. But I was saddened by the realization that something had been lost, something old and beautiful and to me beyond price; that the long silence had been broken at last and that in this loved place solitude was no more.

The music stopped suddenly. The door swung wide and above the talking sounded the high, clear laughter of a girl. A group came outside. There was a flare of matches, pinpoints of light. The door opened and closed once more. Again the music and couples drifting by the windows.

Suddenly a beam of light sliced through the black of the sky, faded for an instant, then, like a meteor, burst full upon the shore, its violent brilliance eclipsing for a moment the steady yellow glow from the lodge. There was the roar of a racing motor, then quiet and blackness. The great door opened and the new arrivals were swallowed swiftly by the warmth and music within.

In a way it was very pleasant, listening and watching from the canoe. Light and music and laughter were good after days in the bush. The warmth and gaiety invited me, and suddenly in the darkness and solitude from which I had come there seemed to be a great loneliness. At that moment I doubted myself. Perhaps I had been wrong about silence and solitude, about places where time meant nothing and where a man might stand aloof and alone and listen to his dreams. Perhaps this was what it should be, this the real goal.

But then like a flood I remembered the nights I had waited and listened in this same little bay when the only sounds were the sloshing of moose in the shallows, the whack of beaver tails, the eternal song of the swamp, music that for ages past had never changed, and I knew that for me there was no question. Now there was music of a different tempo, the heady, exciting throb of drums, the tom-toms of another wilderness.

The sudden whine of an outboard motor roused me from my reverie. Out from the shore it came, straight down the path of golden light, leaping like a wild thing from wave to wave. I grasped my paddle in readiness for the swell. The boat sped by me with a shattering roar and was lost swiftly in the blackness from which I had come. The shores crashed and re-echoed with a violence of sound, but in a moment there was only the dull, monotonous drone that merged gradually with the other sounds of night. Far out toward the open lake the fierce glare of its headlight was a giant firefly dancing fitfully against the far horizon.

I swung the canoe around and began the long paddle back to the old campsite. As I pushed through the dark, winding channels, I wondered if what I had seen could really change the Saganaga the voyageurs and Chippewas had known. Did not the ancient headlands brood as calmly then as now? Did it really matter that the silence they had known was gone? Was solitude a matter of remoteness and primitive country or was it something within myself?

I half turned once more toward the brilliance of the lodge. Faintly now, softly as a caress of the south wind itself, came the strains of melody across the water. A stroke of my paddle and it was gone and the canoe was swallowed once more by the silence and darkness of the islands.

In the north toward Cache Bay the sky was bright with the shifting lights of the Aurora, the ghost dance of the past. Toward the south I had listened to strange music, a requiem to the wilderness. Although the old music was again in the night wind and in the whispering of the waves against the rocks, for me it was farewell to the Saganaga I had known.

As my canoe slipped along the shores, I knew that for them there was no change; it was not important that the silence was broken now. To them, who had seen the great ice come and go, who had watched the passing of Indian tribes and the migration of the caribou, this was but a moment in the æons they had known.

Héritage de la Tristesse

GASTON MIRON

Sad and confused among the fallen stars
pale, silent, nowhere and afraid, a vast phantom
here is this land alone with winds and rocks
a land forever lost to its natal sun
a beautiful body drowned in mindless sleep
like water lost in a barren thirst of gravel

I see it bridled by chances and tomorrows
showing its face in the dreams of anguished men
whenever it breathes in wastes and undergrowth
    of bracken
whenever it burns, in poplars old in years and
    neglect,
the useless leaf-green of its abortive love
or whenever a will to being sleeps in the sail of its
    heart

bowed down, it awaits it knows not what redemption
among these landscapes walking through its stillness
among these rags of silence with eyes of the dying
and always this ruined smile of a poor degraded future
always this hacking at the stands of darkness
and horizons fading in a drift of promises

despoiled, its only hope is a vacant lot's
cold of cane talking with cold of bone
unease of the rust, the quick, the nerves, the nude
and in its livid back the blows of heated knives
it looks at you, worked out, from the depth of its
    quarries
and out of the tunnels of its abstraction where one
    day
it surrendered and lost forever the memory of
    man

winds that shuffle the lots of precedence by night
winds of concourse, winds with solar eyes
telluric winds, winds of the soul, universal winds
come couple, o winds, and with your river arms
embrace this face of a ruined people, give it the
    warmth
and the abundant light that rings the wake of
swallows

Fred Cogswell (translator)

Transcontinental

EARLE BIRNEY

Crawling across this sometime garden
now in our chaircars like clever nits
in a plush caterpillar should we take time
to glance from our dazzle of folders
and behold this great green girl grown sick
with man   sick with the likes of us?

Toes mottled long ago by soak of seaports
ankles rashed with stubble
belly papulous with stumps?
And should we note where maggoting miners
still bore her bones to feed our crawling host
or consider the scars across her breasts
the scum of tugs upon her lakeblue eyes
the clogging logs within her blood –
in the doze between our magazines?

For certainly she is ill   her skin
is creased with our coming and going
and we trail in her face the dark breath of her dooming

Is it true she is too big and strong to die
of this disease but she grows quickly old
this lady   old with us –
nor have we any antibodies for her aid
except our own.

Pioneer

DOROTHY LIVESAY

He laboured, starved, and ploughed:
In these last days
Cities roar where his voice
In lonely wilderness first sang out praise.

Out of the forest, walls,
From rock, the wheat:
Winters to chill the heart
That slowly withers in the summer's heat.

Out of the fight, desire
Re-born each spring
To leave some mark behind –
High harvest for the autumn's gathering.

What labourer could dream
The axe's chime
And swiftly builded house
Would mean a city in so brief a time . . .

He sits with folded hands
And burns to see
How he has ravaged earth
Of her last stone, her last, most stubborn tree.

From

Western Windows

BRUCE HUTCHISON

We know no better than our grandfathers where we are going. Indeed, we may know less than they, who at least had a confident sense of direction and faith in ultimate arrival somewhere. Perhaps, if a dangerous heresy may be ventured, it was not a fortunate day for our species when Darwin politely ushered God out of the universe, Marx invented the fiction of Economic Man and the State erected its pantheon of new gods with plastic hearts and brains of cunning clockwork.

Denied the old certainties, we must take such knowledge as we can find around us. It is not much but, so far as it goes, is reliable. We know that sap rises in the spring, buds open, leaves unfold and in autumn drop to rot and make the new soil on which all men live. Snow falls, frost splits the rock and the mountains will slide perpetually until, as in its beginning, the earth is flat once more and lifeless. But for a little time the snow will melt again, a drop of moisture will ooze from some tiny crevice, hesitating between the eastern, western and northern watersheds, a brook will seek its ancient channel, and long after man has gone the great rivers of Canada will move, unseen, to the three oceans.

This much we know on the outer fringes of truth, whose hinterland has been shut and double-barred forever – enough to tell us at least why our civilization is sick. It is sick because man has separated himself from our earth and will never be healed unless he rediscovers the flowing springs and green nutriments of his life.

Can We Not At Last Say Yes to This Land?

HUGH MACLENNAN

A culture of cities with unspoiled nature in abundance, more fresh air and water than in any other part of the earth – if only our imaginations could look both back and forward, back to the loveliness of the cities of ancient Greece and forward to what such a combination of urbanity and the wilderness promises us!

Can we not at last say yes to this land the ancient navigators discovered for us and the *voyageurs* opened up for us? Changes in the climate have made it easier for us than for the pioneers, but it still is a dramatic climate. If it becomes soft and tropical it is never for long. A storm breaks and astringent air pours in from the north to blow away the smog we still believe is allowable because there is temporary profit in it for those who make it. The sky is electric blue and old men remember their youth. This land is too precious to be put at auction.

Contributors

Margaret Atwood (1939-   ). Born in Ottawa but now lives in Toronto. Has composed four slim volumes of finely-sculpted verse. Also two novels. One of the more highly-regarded of Canada's poets. A deceptive simplicity in diction and structure always clothes a density and complexity of meaning in her poetry.

James Bacque (1929-   ). Born and lives in Toronto. Educated at Upper Canada College and the University of Toronto. A poet, novelist, and editor, he has worked for newspapers, magazines, and in publishing. Recently spent a year in France working on a second novel. With his family, he seeks recreation in canoe-tripping and withdrawing to a cottage on Georgian Bay.

Walter Bauer (1904-   ). Born in Germany and began writing there. Books banned by the Nazi government in the thirties. Emigrated to Canada in 1952 and worked as a dishwasher and labourer. Author of several books, including one awarded the Albert Schweitzer Prize. Now teaches at the University of Toronto.

Ken Belford (1946-   ). Born in British Columbia where he lives in a cabin in the wilderness near Hazelton. Hunts, fishes, traps, and writes poetry. His natural environment provides the subject matter for much of his verse. "Poetry for me is like a keyhole," he says, "something I can drain myself through, really another world on the other side of the door." One of the more progressive of Canada's contemporary poets. One book in print.

Pierre Berton (1920-   ). Born in Whitehorse, Yukon. A distinguished editor, newspaper columnist, and well-known television figure. Has published three books on Canada's north, three collections of essays, a book for children, and a number of other works, including a recent and highly-acclaimed history of the Canadian Pacific Railway.

Earle Birney (1904-   ). A native of Calgary. Educated at the University of British Columbia and Toronto. Literary output over the years steady and impressive: six volumes of poetry and two novels. His verse is a fine blend of tradition and experimentation. Much of his early poetry influenced by his wilderness experience. "I grew up," he says, "in a country where the perils and accidents of climbing, or of just being loose in mountains at stormy times, were part of village news and tales." At his best, the best of Canadian poets who have treated the wilderness.

Fred Bodsworth (1918-   ). Born in Port Burwell, Ontario. Formerly a journalist. Now one of Canada's foremost naturalists. His numerous essays reflect the thought and study he has devoted to Canadian nature. Also has written four highly-regarded novels informed by years of observation of wild nature. His prose represents a nice union of the lyrical and laconic. An energetic and enthusiastic supporter of the current concern for wilderness preservation. Presently lives in Toronto and divides his time between writing and conducting world-wide naturalist tours.

Sheila Burnford (1918-   ). Born in Scotland and educated there, in England, and in Germany. Served as an ambulance driver during World War II. Moved to Canada in 1948 and has since written three books, the last of which is based on her visits to the remote reserves of the Cree and Ojibwa Indians. Prose is sensitive, evocative, and eloquent. Now lives in Thunder Bay, Ontario.

William Francis Butler (1838-1910). A British army officer who served in the Canadian Northwest. An almost compulsive adventurer and traveller, and a sensitive recorder of Canada's natural landscape. Makes his subject come alive by careful attention to detail and a vigorous prose style.

Morley Callaghan (1903-   ). Born and educated in Toronto. Worked as a reporter for the *Toronto Daily Star* where he met and was encouraged to write by Ernest Hemingway. Abandoned a promising law career to become a full-time writer. Since 1928 a steady and substantial literary output: nearly twenty volumes of short stories, novels, and plays. Deeply concerned in his work with the moral complexities of the human condition. Lives and writes in Toronto.

Wilfred Campbell (1858-1918). Born in Kitchener, Ontario. Took holy orders but resigned from the ministry after five years. A civil servant in Ottawa until his death. Composed eight volumes of poetry, the most impressive of which contain his imaginative descriptions of the world of nature. Also an editor, essayist, and publisher of five volumes of prose.

Emily Carr (1871-1945). Born in Victoria, British Columbia. A highly talented and individualistic painter and writer. Much of her subject matter in both media is drawn from her life in the B.C. forest among the West Coast Indians. Klee Wyck ("the laughing one") was the name given to her by Indian friends. Prose is chiefly auto-biographical: lively character sketches, insights into man's relationship with his natural environment, and comments on the artist's role in expressing the inherent values of wilderness.

René Chopin (1885-1953). Born in Québec. A musician, lawyer, and poet. Two volumes of verse in print. His poems reflect his interest in and sensitivity to the natural world. Characterized by complex imagery and exotic diction, his work demands close reading and careful interpretation.

Donald Creighton (1902-   ). Born in Toronto and educated at the University of Toronto and at Oxford University. Perhaps the most influential and distinguished of Canada's historians, he has been called a "bardic singer celebrating and creating a nation by giving it a past." Both scholar and artist, he has written nine volumes which illustrate an acute intelligence and a vivid, cogent prose style. Now teaches at the University of Toronto.

Peter Desbarats (1933-   ). Born in Montréal. Educated at Loyola College. A writer, editor, broadcaster, and sometime actor. Has published six books.

Phil DesJardins (1947-   ). Born in Québec. A teacher, editor, and poet. One book of verse reveals a serious and significant talent.

Alfred Des Rochers (1901-   ). Born in Saint-Elie-d'Orford, Québec. Has worked as a labourer and journalist. A translator, editor, and poet, he has published two volumes of verse. Speaks of Canadian nature with understanding and empathy. Lyric and philosophical in tone, his poems reflect the deadening effects on man of city life and the rejuvenating influence of wild nature. Poetry is traditional in terms of diction, rhythm, and structure.

Wayland Drew (1932-   ). Born in Oshawa. Educated at the University of Toronto. A former teacher and frequent canoe-tripper, he is a writer of fiction and essays of opinion. Contributes to various journals and also writes scripts and short stories for the Canadian Broadcasting Corporation. Deeply concerned with environmental integrity, he lives in a woodlot near Port Perry, Ontario.

Yorke Edwards (1924-   ). Born in Toronto. Educated in Forestry and Zoology at the Universities of Toronto and British Columbia.

Worked for twenty years in British Columbia with the Forestry Service and the Department of Recreation and Conservation. Has written many articles on wildlife, parks, and wilderness preservation. A director of the Federation of Ontario Naturalists. Has lived in Ottawa and worked for the Canadian Wildlife Society Service. Now makes his home in Victoria, B.C.

Blair Fraser (1909-1968). Born in Nova Scotia. Educated at Acadia University. An outstanding radio and television commentator, astute political analyst, and one of Canada's finest journalists. A world-wide traveller but sought refreshment and challenge by canoeing in the Canadian wilderness. To him the wilderness was "empty and lovely" – a place where he could "still enjoy the illusion of solitude." Died in a canoeing accident at Rollway Rapids on the Petawawa River, Ontario.

Oliver Goldsmith (1794-1861). Born in St. Andrews, New Brunswick. Worked in the commissariat department in Halifax for most of his life. Verse is conventionally eighteenth-century in meter and rhyme, but captures well the feelings and attitudes of Canada's early settlers struggling to make a new life in a new land.

Gilles Hénault (1920-). Born in Saint-Majorique, Québec. A journalist, art critic, and poet, he has published four books of poems. Expresses in an original and subjective way the primitive instincts of man and his response to nature. Works as curator of the Museum of Contemporary Art in Montréal.

Roderick Haig-Brown (1908-). Born in England. In 1926 he travelled to the Pacific coast where he worked in logging camps in the State of Washington before moving to British Columbia. There he worked as a logger, trapper, guide, and fisherman. His many books, both fiction and non-fiction, derive their vitality from his wilderness experience and extensive knowledge of nature. Recent writing reflects a deep concern for environmental problems. Lives on a farm at Campbell River on Vancouver Island.

Harold Horwood (1923-). Born in Newfoundland where his family have lived for over three hundred years. A journalist, illustrator, naturalist, and novelist, he has also been a member of the Newfoundland House of Assembly. Actively involved in the struggle for park preservation. Three books express an intimate and affectionate relationship with his native island. His latest work depicts "the love affair between a unique people and a unique country."

Bruce Hutchison (1901-). Born in Ontario and educated in British Columbia. A distinguished journalist and editor of several newspapers. Also a novelist, biographer, and historian, he has published many books. Writes with a passionate concern for Canada and a deep love for the Canadian landscape. Spends much time at his cabin beside a mountain lake on Vancouver Island.

Anna Jameson (1794-1860). Born in Dublin, lived most of her life in England, but travelled widely. Came to Toronto in 1836. Remained in Upper Canada for eight months, during which time she journeyed through the south-western part of the province and north to Sault Ste. Marie. Her account of these travels is clear, lively, and forthright.

David Keenleyside. No information available.

Dan Kennedy (1870-   ). Born somewhere on the prairies. Educated at St. Boniface College. Has lectured widely on his Assiniboine people and has written for the Canadian Broadcasting Corporation. Also has published one book. Now lives on the Carry-the-Kettle Reserve near Sintaluta, Saskatchewan.

William Kilbourn (1926-   ). Born in Toronto. Educated at Upper Canada College and at Toronto, Oxford, and Harvard Universities. Historian, teacher, and politician, he is much concerned with the quality of urban life. Taught at Harvard, McMaster, and York Universities. An accomplished prose stylist, he is the author of twelve books. An alderman in Toronto, he contributes to many journals, including *City Hall*. Stimulated by the wilderness in his youth, he retires periodically to "one of the last forested areas on Lake Simcoe."

Archibald Lampman (1861-1899). A native of Ontario who worked all his life as a clerk in an Ottawa post office. Disliked the mechanical nature of urban life and sought refuge and revitalization in the world of nature. His verse reflects the therapeutic effects of wild nature. Peculiarly "modern" in his conscious craftmanship: continually revised and polished his poetry to realize his intentions.

Patrick Lane (1939-   ). A native of Nelson, British Columbia. One of Canada's more advanced young poets: experimental and original in technique. Subject matter is drawn largely from his life in the mountain country of B.C. Four books in print: poems sometimes uneven but always interesting. "Now", he says, "moving to Hazelton, city in great north where I can dig into my old pure scene of god/ people mountains and my own love."

Cameron Langford (1928-1970). Born in Windsor, Ontario. Educated at North Toronto Collegiate. A radio announcer and advertising writer, he also contributed scripts to the Canadian Broadcasting Corporation. In 1952 an automobile accident deprived him of the use of seventy-five per cent of his body, including his hands, but he continued to write and paint despite his handicap. An enthusiastic camper in his youth, his love of nature remained keen after he was injured. Denied the direct experience of wilderness, he nonetheless wrote of it with great sensitivity and remarkable detail. Died just after completing the manuscript of his only book.

Irving Layton (1912-   ). Rumanian-born but lived in Montréal until recently. A prolific writer of verse, he has produced some dozen volumes of poetry as well as essays and short stories. Sometimes sensational and sentimental, sometimes perceptive and persuasive, he is always controversial. "Poetry", he says, "transports us out of our habitual selves and allows the angels to sweep new knowledge into the vacated space." Now teaches at York University in Toronto.

Father Paul Le Jeune (1591-1664). A Jesuit missionary. Came to Québec in 1632 as Superior of the Jesuit Missions in New France. Returned to France in 1649 but remained in active contact with the Canadian missions. Instituted the informative annual reports known as the Jesuit *Relations*. Writes with great clarity and nice logic.

Douglas Le Pan (1914-   ). Toronto-born and educated. Served as an artillery officer in the Second World War. Enjoyed a distinguished career in the Department of External Affairs before becoming Principal of University College in the University of Toronto. An essayist, novelist, and poet, but is best known for his poetry. At its best, his verse is mature and moving in imagery and idea, and reflects a careful and conscious craftsmanship.

Dorothy Livesay (1909-   ). Born in Winnipeg. Educated at the University of Toronto, the Sorbonne, and the University of British Columbia. Formerly a welfare worker and a teacher in Northern Rhodesia. Currently teaches at the University of Alberta. Spare diction, quiet rhythms, and precise imagery characterize some of the most impressive verse composed in Canada. Has published seven books.

Douglas Lochhead (1922-   ). Born in Guelph, Ontario. Educated at McGill University and the University of Toronto. Served in the Canadian infantry during World War II. Worked in advertising agencies and on newspapers before teaching at Cornell, Dalhousie, and York Universities. Currently librarian at Massey College and a teacher at the University of Toronto. A bird-watcher since the age of six, he has spent some forty summers in the bush of the Gatineau country. Seven books of poetry published.

Jack London (1876-1916). Born in San Francisco, ran away from home as a youth, and travelled widely. Joined the gold rush to the Klondike in 1897. This experience is reflected in his stories and novels of the northern wilderness. A voluminous literary output: over fifty volumes. Fought a drinking habit all his life. Finally committed suicide.

A. R. M. Lower (1899-   ). Born in Barrie, Ontario. Spent many of his student summers working in the bush. Widely regarded as one of the most important social historians of Canada. His writing is contentious, provocative, and influential. Much concerned with the formation and development of Canadian character and identity. Believes unity and nationhood will result only when various groups abandon their particular prejudices and cultivate the distinctive traditions of Canada as a whole.

Malcolm Lowry (1909-1957). English by birth but spent nearly a third of his life in Canada. A one-time jazz musician and composer, he was extremely unstable and an alcoholic. Produced most of his best work while living near Vancouver, perhaps because of the therapeutic effects of his wilderness environment. Has written three novels, a volume of short stories, and a collection of poems, all critically acclaimed.

L. A. MacKay (1901-   ). Born in Hensall, Ontario. A scholar, literary critic, dramatist, and poet. His best poetry employs traditional forms and images. Subtle, witty and allusive. Now teaches at the University of California.

Hugh MacLennan (1907-   ). A native of Glace Bay in Cape Breton Island. A Rhodes Scholar at Oxford University and a Ph.D. in Classics at Princeton University. Generally regarded as one of the few genuinely distinguished Canadian novelists. Also an estimable essayist and social critic. Some ten volumes of prose reveal an urbane intelligence and a finely-tuned awareness of the problems of Canadian identity. His writing is always informed by an incisive and intelligible search for the nature and meaning of Canadian experience. Vital, economical, and sophisticated prose style.

Sid Marty (1944-   ). English by birth but grew up in northern Alberta. A graduate student at Sir George Williams University and a Montréal folk singer of some note. Spends his summers as a park warden in Jasper and Yoho National Parks.

Gaston Miron (1928-   ). Born in Sainte-Agathe, Québec. One book of poetry reveals a promising contemporary poet of French

Canada. Consciously "modern" in technique: his work is elliptical, allusive, and sometimes convoluted.

W. L. Morton (1908-   ). Born in Manitoba and has taught at the University of Manitoba for most of his life. One of the most influential of Canada's historians. His writing demonstrates a keen insight into the social and political currents that have shaped the Canadian character. Lucid and penetrating in his arguments concerning Canadian identity. Also a noted editor and translator. Now teaches at Trent University.

Farley Mowat (1921-   ). Born in Belleville, Ontario. Has spent much time in wilderness areas, especially the Arctic and Newfoundland. A prolific and strongly opinionated writer, he has produced some dozen books which range from history to humour. Deeply concerned with the diminishing resources of wild nature. Now lives in Port Hope, Ontario.

John Newlove (1938-   ). Born in Regina, Saskatchewan but lived in British Columbia for some years. Once encamped and wrote in an abandoned warehouse in Vancouver. Now makes his home in Toronto where he works in a publishing house. Has published eight volumes of poetry. A "modern" poet: his verse is markedly original in rhythm and structure.

Alden Nowlan (1933-   ). Nova Scotian by birth, he is uniquely regional in his choice of subjects and themes. Experimental in his poetic techniques. Has produced six volumes of poetry. Currently writes a column for a newspaper in St. John and is a writer in residence at the University of New Brunswick.

Sigurd F. Olson (1899-   ). Born in Chicago. A writer, ecologist, and educator. President of The Wilderness Society and Consultant to the United States Secretary of the Interior. A leading voice among North American campaigners for wilderness preservation. A skilled canoeist, he has guided in Ontario's Quetico Park and made many trips into the Canadian wilderness. Of his six books, several deal with Canada's wild country, to which he is deeply attached. Lives in Ely, Minnesota, within easy paddling distance of the Canadian border.

Michael Ondaatje (1943-   ). Born in Ceylon but has lived in Canada since 1962. Educated at Bishop's University, the University of Toronto, and Queen's Uinversity. Presently teaches at York University in Toronto. A poet, critic, film-maker, and editor. One of the most gifted of the younger poets writing in Canada. Work is highly experimental: bizarre imagery and unconventional structures characterize his verse. He holds, he says, a "distrust of *all* critics and nearly all dogmatic aesthetics and all . . . schools of poetry." Four books published.

E. J. Pratt (1883-1964). A native of Newfoundland. Taught at the University of Toronto for some thirty-odd years. Published eighteen books of poetry. Widely acclaimed in terms of philosophic thought and technical innovation as one of the foremost of Canadian poets.

William O. Pruitt, Jr. (1922-   ). Born in Maryland but has spent much time in the Canadian North. A naturalist, biologist, writer, and university teacher, he is also a world authority on the ecology of snow. Has lectured at Memorial University in Newfoundland and at the University of Manitoba and has worked with the Canadian Wildlife Service. An ardent and active conservationist with a keen interest in wilderness preservation. Writes with a thorough scientific knowledge and a gift for popularization.

Al Purdy (1918-   ). Born and lives in rural Ontario but has travelled widely throughout Canada. Served in the R.C.A.F. during the war. One of Canada's most versatile men of letters: an editor, journalist, short-story writer, dramatist, critic, and poet. Has published an unbroken sequence of books since the mid-forties: nine volumes now in print. His earlier work conventional but uneven; his later work more experimental but more carefully crafted and critically praised.

Charles G. D. Roberts (1860-1943). Born in New Brunswick. Taught for ten years before devoting himself fully to writing. A massive literary output: fifty-odd volumes of prose, poetry, and translations. Best known for his excellent animal biographies, which are amalgams of natural history, fiction, and literary art.

Theodore Goodridge Roberts (1877-1953). Brother of Charles G. D. Roberts. Born in Fredericton and lived most of his life in the Maritimes. Was a correspondent in the Spanish-American War. Wrote some thirty adventure novels and historical romances. Produced less poetry but it is perhaps of higher quality than his prose. Captures the attitudes and ideas of Maritimers with precision and vision.

Gabrielle Roy (1909-   ). Born and educated in Manitoba where she taught school on the wilderness frontier. Later studied drama in London and Paris. Has worked for newspapers and periodicals and is the author of six highly-regarded novels, all of which have been translated from French into English. Several of her books have a wilderness setting. Much honoured, both in France and Canada, she is one of our outstanding literary figures. Now lives in Québec City.

Andy Russell (1915-   ). Born in the Rocky Mountain foothills of Alberta. A guide, hunter, naturalist, and wildlife photographer, he has also worked as a trapper and cowboy. Now runs a remote mountain ranch in Alberta. His writing is firmly rooted in intimate knowledge of the mountain wilderness, which he now sees as being threatened. Writes lucidly, simply, and persuasively of his colourful life in the wilds and of the values of the wilderness.

Franklin Russell (1922-   ). Born in New Zealand but came to Toronto in 1954. His four books of nature writing reveal a sensitive and patient observer of the rhythms of Canada's wild. A colourful and eloquent prose stylist, although he tends sometimes to be flamboyant in his descriptions.

Duncan Campbell Scott (1862-1947). Born in Ottawa. A Department of Indian Affairs position led to his gaining an intimate knowledge of wild country and its inhabitants which shows in his poems about Indians and loggers. His interest in art and music is reflected in the verbal colour of his descriptive verse. Also wrote travel sketches, short stories, essays, criticism, and biographies.

F. R. Scott (1899-   ). A native of Québec. A lawyer and teacher of constitutional law at McGill University until his retirement. Primarily a "public" poet, speaking in the language of the common man. Although chiefly a satirist and social critic, some of his verse demonstrates a fine feeling for the natural world.

Robert Service (1874-1958). Born in England but moved to Canada in 1894. Spent most of his life in British Columbia and in the North. "The Poet of the Yukon" is best known for his vigorous, rhythmic, and melodramatic narrative verse. Also wrote six novels.

A. J. M. Smith (1902-   ). One of the more perceptive and articulate of the Montréal poets. A critic as well as a practitioner of verse, he is a conscious and skilled craftsman. Has produced three volumes of poetry, as well as literary criticism and essays of opinion. Now lives and teaches in the United States.

Raymond Souster (1921-   ). Born and educated in Toronto. Served with the R.C.A.F. during the war. An editor, essayist, critic, and poet, he is also an enthusiastic and energetic supporter of younger poets of promise. His literary output over the years has been steady and sizeable: more than a dozen volumes of verse, along with a novel. Much of his subject matter deals with his native Toronto: its people, their problems, and their passions. His characteristic style is spare, laconic, and colloquial, and his best work represents some of the most carefully crafted of contemporary verse. Somewhat improbably works as a bank accountant in Toronto.

Wallace Stegner (1909-   ). Born in Iowa but spent his childhood in Saskatchewan near the Cypress Hills. A writer, teacher, and critic, he has produced a large body of highly-regarded fiction and non-fiction, including ten novels. Active in the cause of wilderness preservation, he writes with great sensitivity for the land and its natural communities. Now Director of the Creative Writing Center at Stanford University in California.

James R. Stevens (1940-   ). Born in Stratford, Ontario. Educated at Cornell University. Formerly a high school teacher and freelance writer. Now a counsellor at Confederation College in Thunder Bay. A collector and student of Indian folklore and legend. "You know," he says, "the north is really what this country is all about. It is simply the guts of the country. Anything I write in the future will be about the north." Three books in print.

R. D. Symons (1898-   ). Born in England. Grew up in Sussex where he "got much philosophy and knowledge," he says, "from consorting with cowmen, plowmen, shepherds, gamekeepers, and poachers!" Emigrated to Canada in 1914. Served in World War I. Ranched and homesteaded in Saskatchewan where he now lives. His sensitive and perceptive observations of the rhythms of the natural world are recorded in an unassuming, lucid prose style.

Ethel Wilson (1890-   ). Born in South Africa, raised in England, but has lived most of her life in Vancouver. An accomplished prose stylist, she is noted for her narrative and descriptive skills. Draws heavily upon the British Columbia wilderness for the physical context of the human conflicts in her work. Has also written six volumes of poetry.

J. Michael Yates (1938-   ). Born and raised in the United States but a Canadian by inclination and choice, he has lived in the Northwest Territories. "By and by," he says, "the wilderness came over me." An editor and poet, he has written four books, a book of "fictions," plus essays, criticism, and radio plays. Teaches creative writing at the University of British Columbia.

Ian Young (1945-   ). English-born but lives in Canada. Studied at the University of Toronto. A poet, essayist, and editor. One of the more promising of Canada's younger poets: poems are lucid, laconic, and carefully structured. Two volumes of verse in print.

Dale Zieroth (1946-   ). Born in Neepawa, Manitoba. Lived on and wrote of the prairies before moving to Toronto. Has worked as a teacher and labourer and was once wrestling champion of Canada. Has now left Toronto for the British Columbia wilderness where he lives in a cabin and writes. His experimental techniques in verse are sometimes highly successful but sometimes tend to be loose and undisciplined.

Acknowledgements

These pages constitute an extension of the copyright page. For permission to reprint copyright material, grateful acknowledgement is made to the following:

"Shrouded Trails" from *Many Trails* by R. D. Symons, by permission of Longman Canada Ltd.

Selection from *Western Windows* by Bruce Hutchison, by permission of Longman Canada Ltd.

"Arctic Spring" from *Across Two Worlds,* by David Keenleyside. Reprinted by permission of the author.

"The Once and Future Canadian" from *The Search for Identity* by Blair Fraser. Reprinted by permission of Doubleday and Company, Inc. Copyright © 1967 by Blair Fraser.

"Polar Landscapes" by René Chopin, translated by Francis Sparshott. Reprinted by permission of the author and translator.

"Fear of the Landscape" from T. O. NOW, copyright Ian Young, 1969. Reprinted by permission of House of Anansi.

"Farewell to Saganaga" from *The Singing Wilderness,* by Sigurd F. Olson. Copyright © 1956 by Sigurd F. Olson. Reprinted by permission of Alfred A. Knopf, Inc.

"What Is Grizzly Country?" from *Grizzly Country,* by Andy Russell. Copyright © 1967 by Andy Russell. Reprinted by permission of Alfred A. Knopf, Inc.

From *The Atonement of Ashley Morden,* by Fred Bodsworth. Reprinted by permission of Dodd, Mead and Company, Inc. Copyright © 1964 by C. Fred Bodsworth.

"The Forest Path to the Spring" from the book *Hear Us O Lord From Heaven Thy Dwelling Place* by Malcolm Lowry. Copyright, © 1961 by Margerie Bonner Lowry. Reprinted by permission of the publishers J. B. Lippincott Company.

"Divine Image" from *Collected Poems* by Irving Layton. Reprinted by permission of the author.

"Carrion Spring" from *Wolf Willow* by Wallace Stegner. Copyright © 1962 by Wallace Stegner. All rights reserved. Reprinted by permission of The Viking Press Inc.

From *Return to the River* by Roderick L. Haig-Brown, Wm. Collins Sons & Co. Canada Ltd. Toronto.

"Canadian Spring" from *The Fields of Noon,* by Sheila Burnford. Reprinted by permission of McCelland and Stewart Limited, the Canadian Publishers.

"The Boom" from *Animals of the North* by William O. Pruitt, Jr. Copyright © 1967 by William O. Pruitt, Jr. Reprinted by permission of Harper & Row Publishers, Inc.

"The Blue Heron" from *The Leather Bottle* by Theodore Goodridge Roberts, The Ryerson Press, by permission of McGraw-Hill Ryerson Limited.

"A Man," "the caribou are crossing," and "In many minds," by J. Michael Yates are reprinted from *The Great Bear Lake Meditations* by permission of Oberon Press.

"The Windigo Spirit," "The Windigo at Berens River," and "When the First Light Came" from *The Moons of the Cree* by James R. Stevens.

"Into the Swamp," by Douglas Lochhead from *Made in Canada* (Oberon Press, edited by Douglas Lochhead and Raymond Souster). Reprinted by permission of the author.

"Never Quite the Same," by Wayland Drew, from *The Wabeno Feast*. Reprinted by permission of the author.

"Surfaces," "Old Song" and "Laurentian Shield" from *Overtures* by F. R. Scott, reprinted by permission of the author. "Surfaces" by F. R. Scott, reprinted by permission of the author. "Hail to Thee," translated by F. R. Scott, reprinted by permission of the translator.

"Sleep" from *Klee Wyck* by Emily Carr. Copyright © 1951 by Clarke, Irwin & Company Limited. Used by permission.

From *The Watch That Ends the Night* by Hugh MacLennan, by permission of The Macmillan Company of Canada Limited.

From *They Shall Inherit The Earth* by Morley Callaghan, by permission of the author and The Macmillan Company of Canada Limited.

From W. L. Morton, *The Canadian Identity* (Madison: The University of Wisconsin Press; © 1967 by the Regents of the University of Wisconsin), pp. 4-5.

"The Bull Moose," by Alden Nowland. Reprinted by permission of the author.

"Snow Story," by L. A. Mackay from *Viper's Bugloss,* The Ryerson Press, reprinted by permission of McGraw-Hill Company of Canada Limited.

"In the Forest" from *Moving In Alone,* Contact Press, Toronto, 1965, by permission of the author.

"Canoe Trip" by Douglas Le Pan from *The Wounded Prince,* Chatto & Windus, reprinted by permission of the author and publisher.

"The Pond" from *The Foxes of Beachy Cove* by Harold Horwood. Reprinted by permission of Doubleday Canada Limited.

"The Spell of the Yukon" from *The Collected Poems of Robert Service* by Robert Service, The Ryerson Press, by permission of McGraw-Hill Ryerson Limited.

"The Beaver" from *What They Used To Tell About* by Peter Desbarats. Reprinted by permission of the author.

"Good Old Uncle Albert" from *Canada North* by Farley Mowat. Reprinted by permission of the author.

"Description Is a Bird" from *The Dainty Monsters* (Coach House Press, 1967, Toronto). Published with the permission of Michael Ondaatje and The Coach House Press.

From *The Winter of the Fisher* by Cameron Langford, by permission of Mrs. Langford and The Macmillan Company of Canada Limited.

"To Build A Fire" by Jack London, copyright 1972 Irving Shepard, reprinted by permission of the copyright owner.

From *The Cashier* and *The Hidden Mountain* by Gabrielle Roy, reprinted by permission of the author.

From *The Sparrow's Fall* by Fred Bodsworth. Copyright © 1967 by Fred Bodsworth. Reprinted by permission of Doubleday and Company, Inc.

"I Am the Dwindled Son," by Alfred Desrochers, translated by John Glassco, from *A L'Ombre de l'Orford,* Les Editions Fides. Reprinted by permission of the publisher.

"The Quest for the Peaceable Kingdom" by William Kilbourn from *Canada: A Guide to the Peaceable Kingdom,* edited by William Kilbourn, the Macmillan Company of Canada Limited. Reprinted by permission of the publisher.

From *The Innocent Traveller* by Ethel Wilson, the Macmillan Company of Canada Limited. Reprinted by permission of the publisher.

"Pioneer" from *Collected Poems: The Two Seasons* by Dorothy Livesay, the Ryerson Press. Reprinted by permission of McGraw-Hill Ryerson Limited.

"Do Seek Their Meat from God," from *Earth's Enigmas* by Charles G. D. Roberts. Reprinted by permission of McClelland and Stewart Limited, the Canadian Publishers.

"Trees at the Arctic Circle," from *North of Summer* by Alfred Purdy. Reprinted by permission of McClelland and Stewart Limited, the Canadian Publishers.

"Railroads" from *Recollections of an Assiniboine Chief* by Dan Kennedy. Reprinted by permission of McClelland and Stewart Limited, the Canadian Publishers.